To Roy

EUROS & VILLANS

ROB BISHOP

Very well — take the whole day.
But be here all the earlier
the next morning!

Love from
Rob x

First published in Great Britain in August 2018
by E&T Publishing

ISBN 978-1-5272-2463-6

E&T Publishing

Printed and bound by TJ International, Padstow, Cornwall

Contents

Foreword by Lee Child

Lee Child's Jack Reacher novels, which have sold more than 100m copies worldwide, regularly feature the names of Villa players and managers as characters.

Watching the Villa during my lifetime has been an up and down experience. There have been highs and lows, and I remember them all. Among them were legendary moments, like the first away game in the third tier, at Chesterfield in 1970, when an immense traveling army of claret-and-blue fans showed up in furious defiance of our temporary misfortune. I remember the visit from Santos of Brazil, with Pele and a 54,000 crowd on a cold February night in 1972, with only three floodlights working.

Most of all, I remember two types of games. The first were random and often meaningless, home and away, some wins, some draws, some defeats, marked out as special for me by the sheer fun of being with the people around me, most of whom I had never met before, and would never meet again, but for the couple of hours we were jammed together in the crowd, if the mood struck just right, there would be fast wit and blazing sarcasm, and laughs and jeers, and I couldn't imagine a better place to be.

In the 1980s my work schedule changed, and it made sense to have a season ticket for a couple of years, and I remember the slow-motion once-a-fortnight friendships that developed with the regulars sitting near me. One guy worked in the Jewellery Quarter and made me two sets of earrings at cost, from scrap material, one with chips of rubies, one with emeralds, that I gave my wife for Christmas. Major brownie points for me, for not much more than a Bovril and a meat pie.

But the best games were the European nights. The crisp, cold evenings, the high stakes, the sense of importance, the big stage. And the butterflies in the stomach, the slight sense of unease, the slight sense of fear – often we were playing huge, famous clubs, packed with stars. Now the Premier League gets who it wants, but back then our only foreign buys were Scottish or Irish, and it was the Italians and the Spanish who had the international superstars. I remember watching the warm-ups with a sense of dread. How were we going to beat these guys?

But beat them we did. Sometimes. Sometimes we beat them well. We had some amazing nights, with Villa Park an intense, boiling cauldron, with the players on the pitch responding with some sublime moments. Like against Inter Milan in October 1990 – five days before my birthday, and an early present. Kent Nielsen scored early, with the longest, hardest shot the Holte had seen in a hundred years. The place went insane. I have never known a moment like it. Then in the second half Sid Cowans dropped the most perfect lobbed pass the world had ever known, right onto David Platt's laces, and it was 2-0. The place went insane again. I will never forget the feeling.

And, of course, eight years earlier had come the biggest game of all, when we won the European Cup in Rotterdam. I was working for ITV, on the UK end of the transmission. I knew Tony Morley was going to beat their full back – but I didn't know he was going to beat him twice – and as the ball rolled along the six-yard line I knew we were going to score, and therefore probably win, and that split-second adrenalin rush is a feeling I will never forget either.

Mixed in through the years were some disappointments too, and in this book Rob Bishop captures it all, good and bad, immortal and forgettable. It's a record that should be read and remembered – so we're ready for when it happens again, which it will.

Lee Child
New York 2018

Introduction

Have you won the European Cup?

That question, sung to the tune of Yellow Submarine, has frequently been asked by the claret-and-blue faithful as a means of taunting supporters of teams who have never won the world's leading club competition.

Aston Villa are one of just five English clubs to have lifted the European Cup, now known as the UEFA Champions League. Only Liverpool, Manchester United, Nottingham Forest and Chelsea can make a similar boast. That was why, in 2001, I wrote The Road to Rotterdam, a book which traced Villa's triumphant 1981-82 campaign, culminating in a never-to-be-forgotten victory over Bayern Munich in the final.

Many people have since suggested that the book should be re-printed, which was the initial idea for this project. But it seemed a pity to concentrate on one European campaign when the club have been involved in so many. Villa, let's not forget, have also won two other European trophies – the UEFA Super Cup in 1983 and the Intertoto Cup in 2001 – as well as being involved in a host of nerve-tingling contests against continental opposition.

This book, then, comprises an abridged version of The Road to Rotterdam, plus chapters on each of Villa's 15 other continental campaigns. From Antwerp in 1975 to Vienna in 2010, Villa's European adventures are recalled in words and pictures, together with results, scorers and line-ups from all 89 of the club's European contests.

It is sure to provide Villa supporters with some wonderful memories.

Rob Bishop

Acknowledgements

I would like to thank Aston Villa Football Club for permission to reproduce images from the club's archives, the majority of them taken by former club photographers Terry Weir and Bernard Gallagher. Without the club's kind gesture, this project would have been unviable.

Other photos in this book are ©Mirrorpix, ©Neville Williams and ©Gerry Armes.

I'm also extremely grateful to UEFA for providing access to their official match forms from Villa's 89 European ties. The forms show the names of opposition clubs as they appear in their own language – the team we know as Slaven Belupo, for instance, carry the title Slaven Koprivnica in Croatia.

Players' names appear as they were presented on the forms, which might amuse Anthony Morley, Kenneth McNaught, James Rimmer, Andrew Townsend and Raymond Houghton. And for some reason, it was also felt necessary to include the middle names of John Mathew Deehan, Paul David Rideout, Dwight Eversley Yorke, Dean Nicholas Saunders and numerous others.

All the teams are listed in numerical order rather than the formation in which players lined up.

Thanks also to Thierry Vautrat of France's Sud Ouest newspaper and Stefano Armellini, chairman of the Latin Lions, for identifying Bordeaux and Internazionale players on some of the photos; to Liz and David Instone for formatting the pages; and to Dave Bridgewater for providing programmes from his vast collection of Villa memorabilia.

BIBLIOGRAPHY
Frank Holt and Rob Bishop: Aston Villa – The Complete Record
Richard Whitehead: Children of the Revolution
Steve Stride: Stride Inside The Villa
Graham Denton: Ron Saunders – The Odd Man Out
The Villa News & Record

Cover design – Dan Brawn
Copy-editor – Richard Whitehead

For Holte Ender Helen - and Villans all over the world

1975-76

In at the deep end

Six months earlier his shot from a penalty rebound had won the League Cup. But Ray Graydon wasn't celebrating when he scored another historically-important goal in September 1975. The winger's firmly struck shot, nine minutes from the end of the game against Royal Antwerp of Belgium, made him the first Villa player to score in European competition.

Sadly, it was no more than a consolation effort. Graydon's Wembley winner against Norwich City had provided a passage to Europe but the club's initial UEFA Cup adventure was over almost before it had begun. Four goals in the space of 16 minutes, including an 11-minute hat-trick from Austrian striker Karl Kodat, left them totally demoralised. It certainly wasn't the gentlest introduction to the continental game.

Perhaps the outcome shouldn't have come as a total shock to the system. Villa, back in English football's top flight after an absence of eight years, had struggled to readjust to life in the First Division during the opening weeks of the campaign, while Antwerp were riding high at the top of the Belgian league.

The business of playing abroad was nothing new to Villa, of course. Over the years, the club had ventured as far afield as America, Africa, Israel and the USSR, for pre-season and end-of-season friendly games. In a way, it seemed strange that their first competitive fixture on foreign soil should take them just across the channel. It was a case, though, of so near yet so far. Some supporters opted to fly to Belgium at a cost of £50, including an overnight stay (or £44 for those returning straight after the match). But the vast majority went for the cheaper option of a rail and ferry excursion, which was much cheaper at £22.50 but involved many hours of travel by train and boat, followed by a 30-minute walk from the station to the Deurne area of Antwerp. The train left Birmingham's New Street station at 5.30am on the day of the game, and returned just before midday the following morning.

Even though Birmingham to Antwerp was only 358 miles – much shorter than many of the long-haul journeys made by the club in previous years – there was still a culture shock in store.

Secretary Alan Bennett warned in the programme for the previous Saturday's game against Arsenal that toilet facilities at the Bosuilstadion were limited, advising travelling supporters: "Don't wait until you are in the stadium."

It wasn't much fun for the players, either. "We had to walk about 300 yards just to get from our coach to the stadium," recalls Charlie Aitken. "And when we got into the dressing room it was freezing cold. Ron Saunders tried to light a gas heater on the wall and BOOM! There was quite an explosion and Ron nearly got blown away."

Once the action was under way, it was the players' turn to be blown away. Everything seemed to be fine as Villa defended solidly for almost half an hour but then it all fell apart. In the 27th minute, Jos Heyligen picked himself up after being fouled by Leighton Phillips and curled a free-kick around the visitors' defensive wall and past keeper Jim Cumbes, who was off his line. Five minutes later, it was 2-0, Kodat's speculative 20-yard shot deflecting past Cumbes off Nicholl, and three minutes after that, Kodat pounced again, this time with the help of Louis Van Gaal, who went on to find managerial fame with Barcelona, Bayern Munich and Manchester United, as well as the Dutch national team. Van Gaal had moved from Ajax, in his home city of

First round, 1st leg
ROYAL ANTWERP 4 ASTON VILLA 1
17th September 1975, Bosuil Stadium, 15,817
1-0 HEYLINGEN (26) 2-0 KODAT (32) 3-0 KODAT (35) 4-0 KODAT (43) 4-1 GRAYDON (77)

ROYAL ANTWERP		ASTON VILLA	
1	Jean TRAPPENIERS	1	James CUMBES
2	Paul LIEBEN	2	John GIDMAN
3	Jos VELSER	3	Charles AITKEN
4	Robert GEENS	4	Ian ROSS (c)
5	Xavier CAERS (c)	5	Christopher NICHOLL
6	Jim DE SCHRIJVER	6	Leighton PHILLIPS
7	Louis VAN GAAL	7	Raymond GRAYDON
8	Jos HEYLINGEN	8	Robert McDONALD (HT)
9	Flemming LUND	9	Sam MORGAN
10	Karl KODAT (78)	10	Ian Chico HAMILTON
11	Jos DERAEVE	11	Frank CARRODUS
Subs:			
13	Gust WILLEMSEN (10)	13	John ROBSON (8)

The new era is fittingly marked as Ian Ross greets the match officials and swaps pennants with his Antwerp counterpart Xavier Caers just before Villa's first game in Europe

Amsterdam, as Antwerp's fourth foreign player, which meant he was only able to play in cup-ties. Villa must have wished he had stayed in Amsterdam as he orchestrated the home side's midfield. His part in Antwerp's third goal was to touch a cross from Flemming Lund into the path of Kodat, who did the rest with a powerful shot which left Cumbes helpless.

Two minutes before the interval, the lethal Kodat pounced again, this time following hesitancy in a shell-shocked Villa defence, and the tie was as good as over. Poor Cumbes, who was held accountable for the first and fourth goals, never played for the club again. "I was badly positioned for the free-kick," he conceded. "Then again, we had never seen free-kicks like that." In the following day's Birmingham Evening Mail, the paper's highly-respected football correspondent Dennis Shaw described Antwerp's blitz as "the most stunning and destructive I have seen in European football."

Even though Villa's considerably improved second half performance culminated in Graydon's goal, a fine angled shot into the far corner following an astute Frank Carrodus pass, the 4-1 defeat didn't bode well for Saunders' men. "It was a disaster but they were a bloody good team," said Graydon. "During the game, I remember thinking 'this is some standard.' We just played a much better side but I was pleased that we at least gave our supporters a bit of uplift for the long journey home. The goal gave me a great deal of satisfaction but it belonged more to Frank Carrodus. He did the spadework with his run

Not much consolation - but Ray Graydon creates a piece of Villa history by scoring the club's first goal in European competition

Close, but no close enough – Frank Carrodus sends a header over the bar, watched by Sammy Morgan (No9) and Antwerp's Louis Van Gaal (left)

from midfield, and his pass was inch-perfect. It took their full-back out of the game and left me with the easy bit. There wasn't anyone between me and the goal and you have to fancy your chances in that situation. It was great to hear the roar go up from our fans when it hit the net. I thought that at least we had given them something back for the wonderful support they gave us throughout the second half."

Graydon was convinced that if he had scored earlier, Villa might well have gone on to reduce the deficit further because, as he put it, the home side were "whacked" in the final 20 minutes or so. As it was, Sammy Morgan and Carrodus both went close in the closing stages, although those efforts failed to alter a grim scoreline which served as a reminder of just how much Villa had to learn about European competition.

Rather than flying straight home – a practice which became the norm on European ventures – the squad stayed overnight in Antwerp afterwards. Some players, though, were reluctant to head straight to bed, or even to the bar to drown their sorrows. Nicholl and room-mate Morgan went for a stroll along the River Scheldt, although the fresh air hardly lifted their mood. "There was a huge bridge and we were so distraught," said Nicholl. "It was like 'Shall we throw ourselves off?' It's usually hard to sleep after a match and we just went out walking. It was desperate – a nightmare."

Everyone around the club accepted that overcoming a three-goal deficit was going to be extremely difficult, although the manager certainly wasn't about to acknowledge that grim reality ahead of the second leg. On the Saturday before Antwerp arrived to defend their lead, Villa were at home to Birmingham City in the first Second City derby for a decade. Saunders wrote in his programme notes: "I am still confident that we are still in with a chance of pulling back the three-goal deficit at Villa Park next Wednesday." Villa's players did the business against Blues, goals from Chico Hamilton and Brian Little securing a 2-1 victory on the day John Burridge made his debut in goal. But the boss's optimism over the Antwerp game was unfounded.

Eighteen minutes in, the three-goal deficit became four as Kodat carried on where he had left off in Belgium two weeks earlier. The striker was unmarked as he latched on to Lund's pass and calmly fired past keeper Jake Findlay, who had replaced Cumbes for the previous two league games and was playing because new boy Burridge was ineligible. There was no further score so Villa at least avoided another drubbing but the club's first European night on home soil was hardly one to savour. John Moxley summed up the team's poor showing in The Daily Telegraph: "Aston Villa, full of effort but little else, failed totally to shake Antwerp."

A few harsh lessons had been learned from Villa's inaugural venture into European competition, as the club acknowledged in the following programme for League Cup tie against Manchester United, which also ended in defeat despite a goal from another new signing, Andy Gray. There was no match report, but two action pictures from the Antwerp game were accompanied by a brief message: "Although it was disappointing to be beaten in the first round, we are sure the club is now better prepared and more experienced to cater for future European engagements." Wise words, indeed.

First round, 2nd leg
ASTON VILLA 0 ROYAL ANTWERP 1
1st October, Villa Park, 31,514
0-1 KODAT (18)

ASTON VILLA		ROYAL ANTWERP	
1	John FINDLAY	1	Jean TRAPPENIERS
2	John GIDMAN	2	Paul LIEBEN
3	Charles AITKEN	3	Jos VELSER
4	Ian ROSS (c)	4	Robert GEENS
5	Christopher NICHOLL	5	Xavier CAERS (c)
6	Leighton PHILLIPS	6	Jim DE SCHRIJVER
7	Raymond GRAYDON	7	Louis VAL GAAL
8	Brian LITTLE	8	Jos HEYLINGEN
9	John ROBSON (54)	9	Flemming LUND
10	Ian Chico HAMILTON	10	Karl KODAT
11	Frank CARRODUS	11	Jos DERAEVE
Sub:			
13	Sam MORGAN (9)		

BEST IN THE WORLD

Villa's first UEFA Cup venture may have been something of a disaster football-wise, but in terms of supporters' behaviour it was a triumph. At a time when the reputation of British fans was rock-bottom on the continent, the claret-and-blue army were a credit to the club. Manager Ron Saunders thanked

Above: Suitably attired travelling supporters meet up with full-back John Gidman opposite the team's hotel in Belgium. Right: The hottest ticket in town. Facing page bottom: Phil Coldicott (left) and Steve Betteridge a few decades on

ROYAL ANTWERP FOOTBALL CLUB
STAMNUMMER 1 BIJ DE K.B.V.B.

UEFA-BEKER kompetitie
R. Antwerp F.C. — Aston Villa (Eng.)
17 SEPTEMBER 1975 TE 20 UUR — ANTWERP STADION

TRIBUNE II   BLOK N

F 250.—   0993

Taksen inbegrepen.
De Royal Antwerp F.C. is niet verantwoordelijk voor ongevallen gedurende
of ter gelegenheid van de wedstrijd waarvoor dit ticket is afgeleverd.
Door het aanvaarden van dit ticket ziet drager af van alle beroep tegen
Royal Antwerp F.C. of haar bestuurders.
Tonen op aanvraag.   Niet geldig zonder strook.
TICKET BERNAERTS, ANTWERPEN

them for their fantastic support, adding: "Not only did you do Aston Villa proud, you were shining examples to Europe that Villa supporters are the best in the world."

Villa also received a letter from Mr C Ripley, acting British Consul General in Antwerp, who could not have been more fulsome in his praise for the travelling contingent. "I have written a formal report to London," he wrote, "relating the visit to Antwerp of your supporters. It has given me particular pleasure to be able to report that all the hard preparatory work has paid off and that no incidents of hooliganism or vandalism have been reported to us by the Belgian police. In this day and age, when British football supporters (so-called) are in the headlines for their behaviour both during and after matches, may I congratulate Aston Villa and their supporters for their exemplary behaviour, despite the heartbreaking score-line at half-time. They were truly fine ambassadors for Britain in Belgium."

Mr Ripley's words were echoed in a letter written to the Daily Mirror by R Skelton of Dover: "With

Date 2/9/75   Receipt NS No 16472

Received from M.A. HOLT

Address
the sums stated below in respect of the items detailed, to be supplied if
available

ASTON VILLA

RAIL & SEA   22   50

p.p. ELLERMAN TRAVEL

TOTAL £ 22   50

CHQ.

Some of Frank Holt's vital documentation

so much violence among football fans, we were expecting the worst when our Sealink ferry brought nearly 700 Aston Villa fans home from the continent after a UEFA Cup match. But although their side had lost 4-1, their behaviour was impeccable. They were a credit to football and to Britain."

WHAT A BIRTHDAY...

Marcus Richmond had an eighth birthday to remember when he arrived in Antwerp with his father David. They decided to take a pre-match look at the stadium – and couldn't believe it when they bumped into Ron Saunders and his assistant Roy MacLaren, who were checking out the condition of the pitch. But that wasn't all. When Saunders realised it was the youngster's birthday, and how long he had gone without rest, he whisked them back to the team hotel.

Marcus slept for a couple of hours in the manager's room and then played table tennis with some of the players before accompanying them to the match. David said: "When Ron escorted Marcus off the team coach at the stadium, no-one could have wished for a better birthday."

FIRST GAME – AND LAST!

Villa's defeat in Antwerp was attended by a man who had never previously attended a live football match – and who hasn't been to one since! Steve Betteridge from Halesowen isn't a football fan but went along with his pals Phil Coldicott and Paul Farrington just for the chance of a trip abroad. He probably wishes he hadn't bothered, regardless of the result. The long journey, by train and ferry, was anything but a pleasure trip.

Coldicott, Halesowen Town's goalkeeper in the 1983 and 1985 FA Vase finals at Wembley, takes up the story: "The vision and smell from those train carriages lives with me still. They had wooden benches and a complete absence of usable toilets.

"The train discharged its passengers and left us to complete the journey to the stadium on foot. We wandered in a long processional line for some time before returning over a main road and returning the way we had come after a couple of

locals pointed vaguely to a distant landmark. We eventually found our way just in time for the match, but I have no recollection at all of eating or drinking. And the return journey mirrored the outbound trip – only with snoring bodies strewn on seats and aisles. Carnage!"

WE HAVE IT COVERED...

Villa's first home game in Europe was marked by an attractive postal cover, hand-stamped Birmingham Post Office '1 Oct 75'. Produced by Dawn Cover Productions in Cheshire, it was Villa's second appearance in the official Football League postal cover series, the first having been the League Cup final earlier in March that year.

The covers were priced at 40p, while the club shop also offered them at 25p for supporters wishing to stick their own stamps and post in a special box at Villa Park on the date of issue. It was a nice souvenir, even if the name of Villa's opponents was spelt incorrectly. The value hasn't rocketed but, 40 years later, the cover was offered on eBay for £8.99 – a fair increase on the original cost!

1977-78

Full of English promise...

Their naivety in foreign fields had been cruelly exposed two years earlier but Villa were undoubtedly in more confident mood when they set out on their second UEFA Cup adventure. By September 1977, Ron Saunders had taken his first steps towards building a squad which would ultimately be good enough to win both the League Championship and the European Cup.

After a tentative return to top flight football in 1975-76, when they finished 16th despite failing to record a single away win, the team had followed up with a campaign which saw them once again qualify for Europe in emphatic fashion. A finishing position of fourth would have done the trick anyway, but by then Villa were already assured of a UEFA Cup place after overcoming Everton in a marathon League Cup final which went to extra-time in a second replay at Old Trafford before Brian Little scored a dramatic late winner.

As Villa prepared for the first-round clash against Fenerbahce of Turkey, Little was one of only four players – along with John Gidman, Leighton Phillips and Frank Carrodus – who survived from the team comprehensively beaten by Royal Antwerp on the club's disastrous introduction to the European game. The squad had also been bolstered by a few signings, including Andy Gray, Dennis Mortimer Alex Cropley and John Burridge. "The side has changed drastically," said the manager. "Everyone connected with the club feels we are much better equipped to cope with the European challenge."

They were certainly well enough equipped to cope with the men from Istanbul. Fenerbahce had finished runners up in the Turkish League the previous season, but had no answer to Villa's strong running, hard tackling and precise passing. It took the home side just 12 minutes to make the breakthrough, Andy Gray having the distinction of coming up with the club's first European goal at Villa Park when he fired home left-footed at the Holte End. A fine John Deehan header soon after the half-hour increased the feeling

> **First round, 1st leg**
> **ASTON VILLA 4 FENERBAHCE 0**
> **14th September 1977, Villa Park, Att: 30,351**
> **1-0 GRAY (12) 2-0 DEEHAN (34) 3-0 DEEHAN (66) 4-0 LITTLE (80)**
>
> **ASTON VILLA**
> James RIMMER, John GIDMAN, John ROBSON, Leighton PHILLIPS (c), Kenneth McNAUGHT, Dennis MORTIMER, John Mathew DEEHAN, Brian LITTLE, Andrew GRAY, Alexander CROPLEY, Frank CARRODUS.
> **FENERBAHCE**
> Radmilo IVANCEVIC, Onur ALPKAYDOR (Zafer GONCULER 60), Yenal KACIRA, Cem PAMIROGLU, Alpaslan ERATLI (Aydin CELIK 25), Radomir ANTIC, Tuna GUNEYSU, Coskun DEMIRBAKAN, Onder MUSTAFAOGLU, Cemil TURAN (c), Sevki SENLEN.

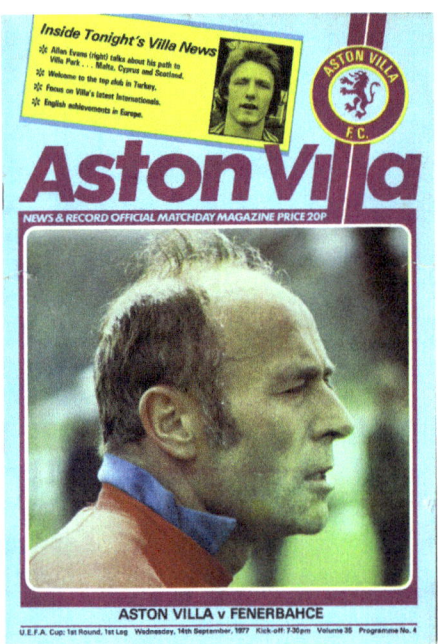

Inside Tonight's Villa News
* Allan Evans (right) talks about his path to Villa Park... Malta, Cyprus and Scotland.
* Welcome to the top club in Turkey.
* Focus on Villa's latest Internationals.
* English achievements in Europe.

Aston Villa
NEWS & RECORD OFFICIAL MATCHDAY MAGAZINE PRICE 20p

ASTON VILLA v FENERBAHCE
U.E.F.A. Cup: 1st Round, 1st Leg Wednesday, 14th September, 1977 Kick-off 7-30pm Volume 35 Programme No. 4

Getting ready for match night.......with a manager who stood no messing.

of comfort at the interval, and when Deehan popped up with another header mid-way through the second half, Villa were coasting – particularly when Little produced a superb solo run before calmly slotting home number four.

The visitors were so subdued that they didn't produce a single attempt at goal, despite the backing of support from all around the ground from Turks whose singing and flag-waving created a rousing atmosphere. A Birmingham Evening Mail headline "Turks Tamed" summed up perfectly what had taken place, reporter Dennis Shaw declaring that "Aston Villa were full of English promise", a nice variation on the popular advert for Fry's Turkish Delight, the chocolate bar which was, apparently, full of Eastern promise.

What Villa were promised in the second leg was plenty of hostility from a fervent Turkish crowd. And even though heavy rain in Istanbul kept the crowd down to well under half of the Sukru Saracoglu stadium's 50,000 capacity, the atmosphere was far from pleasant. It didn't help when, after arriving at the stadium, Villa discovered the kick-off had been delayed for half an hour and the mood worsened considerably when the action got under way. "There was a running track around the pitch, and they were throwing apples and oranges at us from the stands," said Alex Cropley. "The match ball over there was the heaviest I ever played with. Gordon Cowans controlled it on his chest and was wheezing afterwards!"

Cowans was so badly winded that he was substituted by Ivor Linton in the 65th minute. "Fenerbahce produced a ball which had clearly been used before, was completely mis-shaped and played all manner of tricks," he said. "It was absolutely throwing it down and the conditions were so heavy that the ball became like a medicine ball. At the time I only weighed around nine stone and one of their players hit the ball so hard against me that it knocked the stuffing out of me and I ended up going off. I didn't know what I was doing. When the final whistle went, their fans went mad. They lit fires on the terraces and bottles rained down on to the pitch. We had to shelter near the bench before the police took us to the safety of the dressing room."

First round, 1st leg
FENERBAHCE 0 ASTON VILLA 2
28th September 1977, Sukru Saracoglu, Att: 9,637
0-1 DEEHAN (7) 0-2 LITTLE (51)

FENERBAHCE
Gunor FUAT, Yenal KACIRA, Serkan ACAR (c), Onur ALPKAYDOR, Cem PAMIROGLU, Zafer GONCULER, Tuna GUNEYSU, Coskun DEMIRBAKAN, Kaya BAHRI, Onder MUSTAFAOGLU, Sevki SENLEN (KAMURAN 70).
ASTON VILLA
James RIMMER, John GIDMAN, Gordon SMITH, Leighton PHILLIPS (c), Kenneth McNAUGHT, Dennis MORTIMER, John Mathew DEEHAN (John GREGORY HT), Brian LITTLE, Gordon COWANS (Ivor LINTON 70), Alexander CROPLEY, Frank CARRODUS

Captain Leighton Phillips was convinced the match would not have played had it not been a European tie; such was the degree of waterlogging. But a postponement would have created all sorts of problems in terms of re-arranging the game, so the surface was declared fit and Villa effectively paddled their way to a 2-0 victory. Saunders called for an early goal to effectively put the tie out of Fenerbahce's reach and his players responded in stunning fashion, Deehan sweeping the ball home after a Cowans shot had been only partially saved by home keeper Gunor Fuat.

Five-up on aggregate, with one foot in the second round, Villa played the remainder of the game at their own pace, and Jimmy Rimmer's biggest concern was wiping the rain from his eyes. The keeper did, admittedly, face a 36th-minute penalty after Phillips had handled, but even then, the Turks squandered their opportunity, Yenal sending his spot-kick against the foot of a post. Five minutes after the interval, Little added number two with a shot which Fuat was unable to hold, and Villa created so much space that they might easily have repeated the four-goal romp they had produced in the first leg. Still, a 6-0 aggregate success was highly satisfying, the players celebrating with an in-flight meal of, appropriately, roast turkey before landing at Birmingham's Elmdon Airport at 4.00am the following day.

The second-round draw paired Villa with more opposition from Eastern Europe. This time they were to face Polish club Gornik Zabrze, and assistant manager Tony Barton was dispatched to Warsaw to watch their opponents against Legia. As in the first round, Saunders' men were at home in the first leg, and once again established a lead which would prove sufficient to ensure their progress. It wasn't quite as convincing as the four-goal thrashing of Fenerbahce but Villa, wearing an all-white kit, produced some superb football in a 2-0 victory.

High-flier – Ken McNaught climbs to head Villa's first goal at home to Gornik and help launch his career in the Midlands

Second round, 1st leg
ASTON VILLA 2 GORNIK ZABRZE 0
19th October 1977
Villa Park
Att: 34,138
1-0 McNAUGHT (11) 2-0 McNAUGHT (54)

ASTON VILLA
James RIMMER (John FINDLAY 89), John GIDMAN, Gordon SMITH, Leighton PHILLIPS (c), Kenneth McNAUGHT, Dennis MORTIMER, John Mathew DEEHAN, Brian LITTLE, Andrew GRAY, Alexander CROPLEY.
GORNIK ZABRZE
Waldemar CIMANDER, Bernard JARZINA, Jerzy GORGON, Zygmunt BINDEK, Henryk WIECZOREK, Zygfryd SZOLTYSIK (Janusc MARCINOWSKI 77), Ireneusz LAZUROWICZ (c), Jozef KURZEJA, Jerzy RADECKI (Marian WASILEWSKI 60), Adam POPOWICZ, Stanislaw GZIL.

19

Ken McNaught shares his delight with John Deehan and Andy Gray after the ball finds the net for his first goal - and his spectacular header (below) clinches a 2-0 home victory over Gornik

It was a seminal night for one player. Ken McNaught had joined the club that summer, having impressed for Everton in the previous season's League Cup final marathon, but by his own admission the Scottish central defender had struggled during the opening weeks of the campaign, not least because of his domestic circumstances. "My wife, Maureen, was still in Southport and Ron Saunders was pretty disciplined about what players could do," he explains. "I didn't get much chance to go back home on a regular basis. The boss even had us in training on Sundays, so most of my time was taken up with football.

"Maureen had had two miscarriages, so things were at an all-time low for us. To top it all, she was rushed into hospital with a broken arm on the night before the match against Gornik. It felt like things couldn't get any worse, and I couldn't get back to Southport because the game was the following night. The damage was done and her arm was in plaster. I was feeling a bit sorry for myself but things turned around for me that night. I scored both our goals and I was really pleased because they were both headers. Gornik had a big centre-half called Jerzy Gorgon, who played for Poland and they had dumped England out of the World Cup in 1973. Gorgon was the big name in their team but I managed to get above him for our first goal.

Then I scored with a diving header in the second half. To score twice in a European tie was special and I didn't look back."

The second leg took Villa to the grim Polish mining region of Silesia, where various grey buildings dominated the skyline – along with steel works and blast furnaces – and long queues at

> **Second round, 2nd leg**
> **GORNIK ZABRZE 1 ASTON VILLA 1**
> **2nd November 1977, Ernesta Phola, Att: 9,500**
> **1-0 MARCINKOWSKI (40) 1-1 GRAY (52)**
>
> **GORNIK ZABRZE**
> **Andrzej FISCHER, Bernard JARZINA, Jerzy GORGON, Ireneusz LAZUROWICZ (Jerzy RADECKI 69), Henryk WIECZOREK, Zygfryd SZOLTYSIK (c), Joachim HUTKA, Jozef KURZEJA, Stanislow GZIL, Adam POPOWICZ, Janusz MARCINKOWSKI (Marian WASILEWSKI 78).**
> **ASTON VILLA**
> **James RIMMER, John GIDMAN, Gordon SMITH, Leighton PHILLIPS (c), Kenneth McNAUGHT, Dennis MORTIMER, John Mathew DEEHAN (Gordon COWANS HT), Brian LITTLE, Andrew GRAY, Alexander CROPLEY, Frank CARRODUS.**

food stores were common. Three decades after the end of the Second World War, Polish people were still faced with austerity under a strict Communist regime, and their currency, the zloty, was practically worthless. Midfielder Frank Carrodus recalled: "We took a Polish-speaking chef over with us. He told us to take plenty of £1 notes because you could buy much more over there with pounds and dollars. The only thing was, there was nothing to buy except glass and vodka! I came back with some beautiful cut-glass vases that cost about £2.50."

The late-afternoon kick-off in Zabrze had the players anticipating an early return to Birmingham but that notion was thwarted by fog which left the charter flight grounded and Villa stuck overnight in Poland. Before that, they had to get themselves out of a sticky situation in the smog when Ireneusz

Villa Park deluge - rain cascades from Trinity Road stand during the first leg against Athletic Bilbao

Marcinowski scored five minutes before half-time to halve Villa's advantage from the home leg. Thankfully the danger lasted only until just after the break, when Andy Gray scored with a trademark header from a right-wing Carrodus cross. If you check out YouTube, you will find footage of the superb goal, which earned a 1-1 draw and a 3-1 aggregate success. But be prepared to strain your eyes – the fog, combined with the poor video quality, makes Gray's majestic moment fuzzy, to say the least. If the Scottish striker was happy with his goal, however, he was far from happy about the flight being delayed. "Andy and Gordon Smith were desperate to get back for a party at Snoopy's in Birmingham," said their fellow Scot Alex Cropley. "In the end, we didn't leave until the following morning."

After fog in Poland, Villa might not have been surprised by rain in Spain. In the event, it was on home soil that they had to endure a torrential downpour when Athletic Bilbao visited Villa Park for the first leg in the third round. Conditions were so bad that the Evening Mail described it as "the approximate equivalent of

NOT YET, LADS, BUT...

Not this time – Brian Little's shot is in the net but the effort was disallowed for a foul by Ken McNaught on keeper Iribar

playing with a shower turned full on." Some areas of the pitch became so waterlogged that the players effectively had to splash their way across the surface, and the home side undoubtedly adapted better to the conditions.

By the time the heavens opened, Villa were already in front, Bilbao's experienced keeper Jose Angel Iribar, who had played for Spain at Villa Park during the 1966 World Cup, carelessly punching Cropley's 33rd-minute corner into his own net. That unexpected gift came just after a spectacular Little volley had been disallowed by a marginal offside decision and it provided Villa with a platform from which to launch further attacks, although they had to wait until 12 minutes from the end before Deehan climbed in

> **Third round, 1st leg**
> **ASTON VILLA 2 ATHLETIC CLUB 0**
> **23rd November 1977, Villa Park, Att: 32,973**
> **1-0 IRIBAR CORTAJANERA og (34) 2-0 DEEHAN (78)**
>
> **ASTON VILLA**
> **James RIMMER, John GIDMAN, Gordon SMITH, Leighton PHILLIPS (c), Kenneth McNAUGHT, Dennis MORTIMER, John Mathew DEEHAN, Brian LITTLE, Andrew GRAY, Alexander CROPLEY, Frank CARRODUS.**
> **ATHLETIC CLUB**
> **Jose Angel IRIBAR CORTAJANERA (c), Agustin GUISASOLA, Andoni GOIKOETXEA, Fernando TIRAPU, Daniel ASTRAIN, Jose Ramon ALEXANCO VENTOSA, Daniel RUIZ BAZAN, Javier IRURETAGOYENA AMIANO, Carlos RUIZ HERRERO, Angel Maria VILLAR LLONA, Jose Ignacio CHURRUCA SISTIAGA.**

...NOW YOU *CAN* CELEBRATE!

Deehan delight – John Deehan climbs in front of Iribar and a defender to head home John Gidman's free-kick and double Villa's lead

front of Iribar and a defender to head home John Gidman's free-kick to secure a 2-0 scoreline. "As the pitch got worse, we dominated more," said Saunders. "Various people have said we won only because of goalkeeping mistakes but we were the better side on the night."

When Villa flew to Spain for the return clash, it was their second visit to the Basque region in the space of a few months. They had participated in a pre-season tournament at the San Mames stadium, along with Dynamo Kiev, Anderlecht and Bilbao, whose home advantage had enabled them to emerge as winners. That prompted Saunders to suggest that this tie was his team's toughest UEFA Cup test so far, although Villa's first-leg performance obviously gave them every confidence for the task they faced.

Having scored twice and kept a clean sheet, they went into the game knowing that even a 3-1 defeat would be sufficient to see them through to the quarter- finals on the away goals rule. In the event, they didn't have to rely on that safety net. Rather than trying to defend their lead, Villa went in search of more goals in a stadium where only Barcelona had beaten Athletic in the previous two years, and where steeply-rising stands packed with fervent fans provided an intimidating backdrop .

> **Third round, 2nd leg**
> **ATHLETIC CLUB 1 ASTON VILLA 1**
> **7th December 1977, San Mames, Att: 39,713**
> **0-1 MORTIMER (44) 1-1 RUIZ BAZAN (85)**
>
> **ATHLETIC CLUB**
> Jose Angel IRIBAR CORTAJANERA (c), Jose Maria LASA, Francisco Javier ESCALZA, Fernando TIRAPU, Daniel ASTRAIN, Jose Ramon ALEXANCO VENTOSA, Daniel RUIZ BAZAN, Javier IRURETAGOYENA AMIANO, Aitor AGUIRRE (Angel Maria VILLAR LLONA 49), Jose Ignacio CURRUCA SISTIAGA, Jose Maria AMORRORTU.
> **ASTON VILLA**
> James RIMMER, John GIDMAN, Gordon SMITH, Leighton PHILLIPS (c), Kenneth McNAUGHT, Dennis MORTIMER, Gordon COWANS, Brian LITTLE, Andrew GRAY, John GREGORY, Frank CARRODUS.

But there was no question of Saunders' men being intimidated by the team that had lost only on away goals to Juventus in the previous season's final. They carried the game to Bilbao, producing their best football of the season before being rewarded a minute before half-time. Gidman floated in a cross from the right-hand corner of the penalty area and midfielder Dennis Mortimer beat Iribar with a clever downward header which bounced just inside the post as the keeper dived in vain. Bilbao now had to score four, and all they could manage was an 85th-minute equaliser from Dani. As they left the pitch, Villa were given a warm reception by a sporting home crowd, who recognised that their English visitors had overcome their favourites with a magnificent display.

But it was about to get even tougher. The draw for the last eight paired Villa with another Spanish club, and this time it was Barcelona. The home leg of the quarter-final was the first great European night at Villa Park as nearly 50,000 turned up for the clash against one of the world's most famous clubs and a glimpse of Dutch master Johan Cruyff, who was making his farewell appearance in this country. The fans were not disappointed, and not just because Cruyff produced a performance worthy of any stage and was duly given a standing ovation when he was substituted towards the end. They were even more delighted to see Villa storm back from two-down to score twice in the final five minutes and force a 2-2 draw.

The occasion was also special for one Villa player. It was the night Allan Evans made his debut in

The programme for Villa's second-leg trip to northern Spain

A Barca ballet – Brian Little leaps to put pressure on Barcelona's defence in the quarter-final first leg

claret and blue. And even though the Scottish centre-back went on to play 475 games, winning the League Championship, European Cup and European Super Cup along the way, this is the game which stands out most vividly in his memory – both in the dug-out and on the pitch. Signed from Dunfermline six months

Quarter-final, 1st leg
ASTON VILLA 2 BARCELONA 2
1st March 1978, Villa Park, Att: 49,619
0-1 CRUYFF (20) 0-2 ZUVIRIA (80) 1-2 McNAUGHT (87) 2-2 DEEHAN (89)

ASTON VILLA
James RIMMER, David EVANS (Allan EVANS 60), Gordon SMITH, Leighton PHILLIPS (c), Kenneth McNAUGHT, Dennis MORTIMER, John GREGORY, Brian LITTLE, John Mathew DEEHAN, Gordon COWANS, Frank CARRODUS.
BARCELONA
Pedro Maria ARTOLA, Jose Antonio RAMOS HUETE, Miguel BERNARDO BIANQUETI, Antonio OLMO RODRIGUEZ, Jesus Antonio DE LA CRUZ, Enrique ALVAREZ COSTAS (Juan Jose ENRIQUEZ GOMEZ 65), Rafael ZUVIRIA, Carlos REXACH CEDRA, Hendrik Johan CRUYFF (c) (Jose MACIZO 82), Juan Manuel ASENSI RIPOLL, Francisco FORTES.

earlier as a striker, Evans had been restricted to Central League games but had just scored six against Sheffield United reserves and was drafted into the first-team squad because manager Saunders had a few injury problems, with Andy Gray, John Gidman and Gordon Cowans among the absentees.

Evans started on the bench but admits: "Even that was a privilege. I witnessed some superb football from Braca, particularly from Cruyff. He ran the show in the first half and fired them into the lead with a low 25-yard shot which gave Jimmy Rimmer no chance." The newcomer's big moment arrived in the 61st minute when he went on to replace another debut boy, David Evans , although not in the right-back role his namesake had occupied. Saunders reshuffled the line-up so the Scot could play up front, with instructions to run around and cause problems. When Rafael Zuviria headed Barca's second goal 12 minutes from the end, though, Villa looked dead and buried.

Dutch master – Johan Cruyff goes off to a standing ovation following his magnificent display. His departure sparked a Villa comeback

But when Cruyff went off, it seemed to give Villa fresh heart. Ken McNaught reduced the deficit with a diving header from Gordon's Smith's free kick, and three minutes from the end the home side were level. "As the ball came into the penalty area, I challenged their keeper and he spilled it to John Deehan, who put it in the net from a few yards," said Evans. "To be honest, I was expecting a free-kick to be given for my challenge but the ref allowed the goal to stand. The atmosphere that night was electric."

Understandably, Villa were underdogs for the second leg in Spain, and an uphill task assumed mountainous proportions when Gidman reacted angrily to being elbowed by Jesus De La Cruz before half-an-hour had elapsed at the imposing Camp Nou stadium. Gidman retaliated by lashing out with his foot – and turned to face the inevitable red card. Yet even with 10 men, the visitors battled gamely in front of 80,000 partisan Catalonian supporters and even had the audacity to stun the locals into silence when Little opened the scoring nine minutes after the interval, jabbing the ball into the net after a McNaught header had been cleared.

Copa de la U.E.F.A.
F.C.BARCELONA-ASTON VILLA

Campionat Nacional de Lliga 1977-78
F.C.BARCELONA-U.D.SALAMANCA

For a while, against overwhelming odds, a famous victory seemed possible, particularly with keeper Jimmy Rimmer making save after brilliant save. But Miguel Bernardo Bianqueti equalised on 67 minutes, Juan Manuel Asensi added a second 10 minutes later – and Villa's European adventure was over.

In the following day's Evening Mail, Dennis Shaw left no-one in any doubt about where the blame lay. The paper's chief football writer described Gidman's dismissal as "an act of gross indiscipline by an experienced campaigner who should have known better." Despite that costly moment of madness, though, Shaw had every admiration for the way Villa had performed in one of football's greatest arenas.

Quarter-final, 2nd leg
BARCELONA 2 ASTON VILLA 1
15th March 1978, Camp Nou, Att: 90,000
0-1 LITTLE (57) 1-1 BERNARDO BIANQUETI (67) 2-1 ARENSI RIPOLL (77)

BARCELONA
Pedro Maria ARTOLA, Jose Antonio RAMOS HUETE (Manuel CLARES 65), Miguel BERNARDO BIANQUETI, Antonio OLMO RODRIGUEZ, Jesus Antonio DE LA CRUZ, Juan Jose ENRIQUEZ GOMEZ, Francisco FORTES (Johan NEESKENS 65), Carlos REXACH CERDA, Hendrik Johan CRUYFF (c), Juan Manuel ASENSI RIPOLL, Rafael ZUVIRIA.
ASTON VILLA
James RIMMER, John GIDMAN, Gordon SMITH, Leighton PHILLIPS (c), Kenneth McNAUGHT, Dennis MORTIMER, John GREGORY, Brian LITTLE, John Mathew DEEHAN, Gordon COWANS, Frank CARRODUS.

"They must settle for the not inconsiderable consolation," he wrote, "that they left behind a hard-won reputation as a new Euro-force in this breathtaking home of so much fame. As one who sat at Doncaster on a wet Friday in Division Three, I can confirm that narrow and honourable defeat at the Nou Camp has considerably more appeal."

LITTLE'S GOAL MEANS A LOT

Brian Little's goal in Barcelona may not have been enough to prevent defeat but it is one the striker still savours. "To score against a team of that quality in such a famous stadium was a very special moment," he said. By a strange quirk, his breakthrough effort, which John Deehan watches fly over the line in the photo above, came just over ten minutes into the second half. Barca equalised ten minutes later and the winner came a further ten minutes aftere that - from their no 10 Juan Manuel Asensi Ripoll.

FROM IPSWICH TO ISTANBUL

Villa's players, officials and fans were shattered when they touched down at Elmdon at 4.00am after the tie against Fenerbahce in Istanbul. But even as they waited for their cases, one hardy supporter was looking ahead to a meeting in Yorkshire that afternoon. "There won't be much rest for me," Barry Owen told the Villa News & Record. "I've got a business appointment in Skipton at 3.00pm." It transpired that despite living in Lancashire, Barry never missed a Villa match, whether at Ipswich or Istanbul, having first watched them in 1954. He was accompanied in Turkey by his 11-year-old son, Barry Jnr.

POP GOES TO POLAND

Villa's oldest supporter at the away leg against Gornik was Jack Griffin, who turned 83 the day after returning from Poland. It was a long trip for the man known by younger fans as "Pop" because he made the journey by road with the Villa Travel Club. "It was rather tiring," he said. "But it didn't worry me. I had a touch of sickness at the match – to do with the food, I think – but I was all right when I got home. I had a drink, caught the bus back to Acock's Green and was in bed by 11.30pm." Jack had watched Villa since 1902, and had fond memories of their FA Cup-winning teams of 1913 and 1957.

1981-82, first round

Over the moon

Footballers often talk about being "over the moon." When Villa's players made their first European Cup trip in 1981, they thought they had landed on it. As their chartered Boeing 727 descended towards the extraordinary landscape of Iceland before landing at the US Air Force base in Keflavik on a Monday afternoon in late September, there were gasps of astonishment all around the cabin. As far as the eye could see, the bleak terrain offered little more than black dust and volcanic rock, conjuring up images of a lunar landscape. "When we arrived, it was like landing on the moon," recalled striker Gary Shaw. "The place was covered in rocks and dust. I'd never seen anything like it."

That wasn't the only shock to the senses suffered by Shaw and his team-mates when they took on Valur, of Reykjavik, in the second leg of a first-round tie. A training session had to be curtailed because of the awful stench drifting across from an adjacent fish factory – and the match was played in freezing temperatures and a 40-mile-an-hour wind. "I've never been so cold on a football pitch," says Shaw. "Most of us wore long sleeves and a few of us had T-shirts underneath, which was something we never normally did. The wind was strong, too. One of my goals was a left-foot volley which I must admit was wind-assisted as it flew past their keeper and into the top corner. The guy had no chance."

Shaw, who had missed Villa's 5-0 first-leg romp through injury, netted twice as Ron Saunders' men won 2-0 to complete an emphatic aggregate success. Despite the smell, the cold and the wind, Villa produced a professional display in football's most northerly outpost. Shaw scored the first following

Cool climate, warm greeting. Dennis Mortimer meets his Valur counterpart Saevar Johnsson before the second leg in Reykjavik

Gary Shaw gets in front of his marker to meet Dennis Mortimer's free-kick to put Villa ahead in Iceland

Dennis Mortimer's 24th-minute free-kick before doubling the lead with the 20-yard volley which owed a lot to the elements as it swirled and dipped into the net. And two might have become three, only for the striker to be denied a hat-trick by a goal-line clearance.

If the victory margin was comfortable, though, the experience was anything but – particularly for the substitutes. Tony Morley, who had scored Villa's first-ever European Cup goal in the home leg, was on the bench for the return and while he had no argument with the manager's decision to rest him, he didn't enjoy it one bit. "There wasn't a dug-out, so we were out in the open," he said. "I've never been so cold in my life. My feet were like blocks of ice. I was sitting next to Ivor Linton and the gel in his hair started to freeze!"

It was an icy blast that Villa's players would never forget but little could they have imagined they would face another on their return to Birmingham – from their manager. Villa may have overcome their first European Cup hurdle with relative comfort but Saunders was unimpressed, to say the least, when word reached him that some players had been drinking in a nightclub on the evening they arrived in Reykjavik. Their joviality, to be fair, had quickly subsided when secretary Steve Stride and the club's medical officer Dr David Targett walked through the door. "We thought the

First round, 2nd leg
VALUR 0 ASTON VILLA 2
30th September 1981, Laugardalsvollur, Att: 4,291
0-1 SHAW (26) 0-2 SHAW (70)

VALUR
Sigurdur HARALADSSON, Ottar SVEINSSON, Thorgimur THRAINSSON, Matthias HALLGRIMSSON, Dyri GUDMUNDSSON, Saevar JOHNSSON (c), Magni Blondal PETURSSON, Jon Gunnar BERGS, Valur VALSSON, Hilmar SIGHVATSSON (Thorvaldur THORVALDSSON 81), Njall EIDSSON.
ASTON VILLA
James RIMMER, Kenneth SWAIN, Colin GIBSON, Allan EVANS, Brendan ORMSBY, Dennis MORTIMER (c), Desmond BREMNER, Gary SHAW, Peter WITHE, Gordon COWANS, Andrew BLAIR.

Gordon Cowans retrieves the the ball after Gary Shaw's wind-assisted shot ends up in the net for the second goal away to Valur

match was going to be a cakewalk, so there didn't seem much harm in going out for a drink," says Gary Shaw. "We were all having a good time when in walked David Targett and Stridey. To be honest, I think they kept it to themselves but the boss found out somehow and when we got back home, he called us in for a meeting. He seemed to know certain players had been there, although I'm not sure he knew I was one of them. In the end we all owned up. I can't recall being fined; Ron just wanted to make his point and let us know we couldn't get away with things like that."

Tony Morley and Gordon Cowans were also among the group who broke the curfew and both recall that the hugely popular "Doc" Targett joined in the festivities. "At one point, we were doing the pogo dancing that punks were into at the time," said Morley. "The first inkling of Doc Targett being in the place was when he appeared on the dance floor and started doing it with us. He was that sort of guy and the lads thought the world of him." Cowans added: "We were on the dance floor and suddenly Doc Targett was bouncing around between us. The chairman and the other directors were there, too, so we made a swift exit. The directors didn't seem to mind but the manager was furious when he found out. He sat us in the dressing room and asked who had gone out. Eventually, we all owned up and he let us know in no uncertain terms that he wasn't happy."

Saunders had also been unhappy on the day before the match, as Allan Evans vividly recalls. "Our directors were invited on a sight-seeing flight in a small plane and our physio Jim Williams wanted to go," said the Scottish central defender. "Ron said it was okay as long as he was back in time for our training session. When Jim didn't turn up, Ron decided to play a trick on him so we strapped up the legs of Mark Jones, one of our young reserves, to make it look as if he had suffered a fracture. Jim was waiting for us outside the hotel when we got back and his face was a picture when he saw Mark. We had poured some brandy over the lad and when Jim smelled it he was horrified. He asked if Mark had been drinking and Saunders snapped back: 'Of course he has been drinking. It was the only way we could kill the pain!' I don't think Jim ever missed another training session..."

Villa's biggest problem in the first leg was also off the pitch rather than on it. The match at Villa Park clashed with an autumn fair at the National Exhibition Centre and every hotel in Birmingham and its immediate boundaries was fully booked. It threatened to be a major embarrassment for the club ahead of their first European Cup tie, and secretary Stride spent hours trying to find suitable accommodation for Valur's travelling party. The nearest he could find was the Post House at Stoke-on-Trent, and thankfully the Icelandic directors accepted without complaint the inconvenience of being based 50 miles north of Birmingham. That was possibly because Stride told a white lie by suggesting the journey from the Potteries to Villa Park would take around half an hour. As if to test the theory, he really put his foot down when returning from Valur's hotel the night before the match and was stopped by the police when his speed on the M6 touched 90mph!

The game itself was played at a much slower pace, Villa coasting to an emphatic victory which rendered the second leg a formality. They were ahead after just six minutes, Morley firing home hard and low from the edge of the penalty area following a short free-kick from skipper Dennis Mortimer, and by half-time the tie was as good as over. Peter Withe headed in Des Bremner's 37th-minute cross to double the lead and five minutes later Terry Donovan pounced to make it 3-0 after Withe had headed down a Kenny Swain free-kick.

All Jimmy Rimmer was required to do before the interval was to deal with a couple of long-range shots from the visitors, and the keeper wasn't troubled at all in the second half as Villa added two more. Withe powered his way through to make it 4-0 in the 68th minute before Donovan, a 23-year-old reserve striker standing in for the injured Shaw, outjumped the Valur defence to claim his second goal. It should really have been more, with Donovan and Withe both guilty of some glaring misses, as Villa's No 9

We have lift-off – Tony Morley makes a piece of club history as he scores Villa's first European Cup goal to open the scoring against Valur

readily acknowledged. "It was one of the few occasions when Terry had an opportunity to come into the side," said Withe. "He was a strong player and we complemented each other well in that match. He took his goals well, although we both came off the pitch feeling we should have scored hat-tricks."

Donovan agrees. "It was great to score two on such an important occasion. But it should have been at least three. Peter and I both missed easy chances. To have been able to say I'd scored a hat-trick in the European Cup would have been incredible, but I still look back on it as the highlight of my career. Valur were no great shakes but no-one can take away the fact I scored twice in Europe's top competition. Gary was fit for the return match in Iceland, so I was on the bench. All I remember from that trip was how cold it was!"

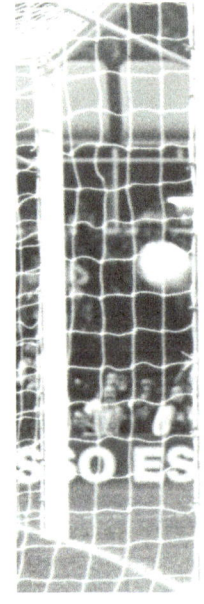

Get in! Peter Withe is a picture of delight as he scores Villa's second against Valur. Little could he have envisaged what would happen eight months later…

SORRY, LOVE - CALL OFF THE WEDDING

Villa's first involvement in the European Cup caused a spot of inconvenience for full-back Gary Williams – he was forced to postpone his wedding! Williams and fiancée Liz were due to be married on Sunday 27th September but when the UEFA draws were made, they realised he would have to fly to Iceland for the second leg against Valur within 24 hours of the ceremony.

As it turned out, they could have stuck to that date because Williams was injured and didn't travel but he admits: "I was glad we put the wedding back. I wanted the other players to be there, and that would have been difficult if we had stuck to the original date." Gary and Liz were married two weeks later at St Paul's Church, Hamstead. The Villa squad reported back for training next day minus one man - the newly-weds were given the luxury of a honeymoon. All two days of it!

First round, 1st leg
ASTON VILLA 5 VALUR 0
16th September 1981, Villa Park, Att: 20,481
1-0 MORLEY (7) 2-0 WITHE (37) 3-0 DONOVAN (40) 4-0 WITHE (68) 5-0 DONOVAN (70)

ASTON VILLA
James RIMMER, Kenneth SWAIN, Colin GIBSON, Allan EVANS, Brendan ORMSBY, Dennis MORTIMER (c), Desmond BREMNER, Terrence DONOVAN, Peter WITHE, Gordon COWANS, Anthony MORLEY.
VALUR
Sigurdur HARALDSSON, Ottar SVEINSSON, Thorgimur THRAINSSON, Thorvaldur THORVALDSSON (Grimur SAEMUNDSEN 74), Dyri GUDMUNDSSON, Saevar JONSSON, Njall EIDSSON. Hilmar SIGHVATSSON, Thorsteinn SIGURDSSON (Matthias HALLGRIMSSON HT), Gudmundur THORBJORNSSON (c), Valur VALSSON

Cold War classic

Villa have had their backs to their wall on numerous occasions down the years, but never more so than when they visited East Germany in October 1981. The first leg of their second-round tie against Dynamo Berlin took place just a few yards from the Berlin Wall. The Jahn-Sportpark stadium was overlooked by the barrier which divided east and west from 1961 to 1989, during which time up to 200 people were estimated to have been shot while attempting to escape from the Communist-controlled Eastern Bloc.

It was a miserable existence for anyone living on the "wrong" side of the city, and Villa's players had a sample of what it must have been like when they were drawn against the East German champions at the second stage of their campaign. "It was grim and depressing," said Tony Morley. "When we were training we could hear the guard dogs barking in the distance." Grim and depressing it might have been, and the fact that the match was played on a cold damp night hardly helped to lift Villa's mood. Yet the team's performance against a side who had won their domestic title for the previous three seasons was arguably their best of the competition. It was also a personal triumph for Morley.

Just five minutes had elapsed when the winger rounded off a classic counter attack to open the scoring. Accepting a pass from Allan Evans just inside the Dynamo half, Gary Shaw made a smart turn before releasing the ball into Dennis Mortimer's path. The skipper played it wide to Des Bremner, who chipped a teasing cross into the goalmouth, where Shaw missed out in an aerial challenge. Fortunately, the ball dropped just inside the penalty area for Morley to deliver an unstoppable volley

Breaking down the wall – Tony Morley opens the scoring against Dynamo with an unstoppable right-foot volley

past 6ft 7in keeper Bodo Rudwaleit and into the bottom corner.

They held their lead until six minutes after the interval when the man they most feared, East German international Hans-Jurgen Riedeger, equalised with a downward header. And the situation looked certain to deteriorate still further when Ivor Linton, on as a substitute for the injured Gary Williams, was penalised for his challenge on Wolf-Rudiger Netz. It looked a perfectly fair sliding tackle but Austrian referee Franz Wohrer saw it differently and immediately pointed to the penalty spot.

What followed was one of the key moments of Villa's European Cup campaign. Although Artur Ullrich sent Jimmy Rimmer the wrong way, his spot-kick hit the left-hand post. A goal still looked inevitable as the ball hit the keeper's foot and rolled back into Ullrich's path. But the midfielder was unable to get any power

Europapokal der Landesmeister
Achtelfinale   Hinspiel
BFC DYNAMO –
                      ASTON VILLA

PROGRAMM

Mittwoch, 21. Oktober 1981, 20.00 Uhr
Friedrich-Ludwig-Jahn-Sportpark · 0,50 M

behind his follow-up shot, which hit Rimmer's trailing left leg and looped over the bar. That was a huge relief to Linton, who admitted he can't recall much about the game beyond giving the penalty away. "People tell me it was a harsh decision but I can't say because I've never seen the incident," he said. "It happened so quickly that I didn't really have time to think about it before the penalty was taken. Thankfully Jimmy saved it, but if you start to think deeply about it, Villa might have lost if the guy had scored. We would probably have been out of the European Cup."

That was also the moment Tony Morley was convinced Villa would go on to win the competition. "I'm a great believer in fate," he said. "When Jimmy kept out the rebound I felt we had one hand on the cup, even though it was only the second round." Five minutes later, the winger brought his gut feeling a step closer to reality when he scored what was arguably the best goal of that season's competition. That was certainly Peter Withe's view, anyway. "Tony had scored the goal of the season in our championship-winning campaign," said the striker. "But his second goal in Berlin was even better." Withe made an unorthodox contribution to the goal, heading away a left-wing corner to relieve the pressure on Villa's under-siege defence. Morley, who had also dropped back to a defensive position, simultaneously started a run from the penalty spot, and as the ball bounced over Gary Shaw, the winger took it in his stride, skipped clear of a lunging tackle and embarked on

Second round, 1st leg
BERLINER DYNAMO 1 ASTON VILLA 2
21st October 1981, Steffenstrasse, Att: 20,100
0-1 MORLEY (5) 1-1 RIEDIGER (50) 1-2 MORLEY (85)

BERLINER DYNAMO
Bodo RUDWALEIT, Michael NOACK, Norbert TRIELOFF, Ralf STRASSER, Rainer ERNST, Rainer TROPPA, Frank TERLETZKI (c), Arthur ULLRICH, Hans-Jurgen RIEDIGER (Roland JUNGLING 78), Bernd SCHULZ, Wolf-Rudiger NETZ.
ASTON VILLA
James RIMMER, Gary WILLIAMS (Ivor LINTON 70), Colin GIBSON, Allan EVANS, Brendan ORMSBY. Dennis MORTIMER (c), Desmond BREMNER, Gary SHAW, Peter WITHE, Gordon COWANS, Anthony MORLEY.

Match-winner Tony Morley is embraced by Peter Withe and Gordon Cowans after his wondrous individual strike, with Colin Gibson racing to join in the celebrations.

the loneliest run of his life. But even with various desperate opponents bearing down on him, he maintained both his speed and composure before firing low past Rudwaleit from just inside the penalty area.

It was as clinical a piece of finishing as you could wish to see, and it gave Villa a crucial 2-1 victory, yet Morley's reaction was to run towards the bench and stick two fingers up to Ron Saunders. It transpired that the player and the manager had exchanged words in training the previous day. "I had been trying a few things and Ron said: 'You'll never score two goals in a match because you're too flash.' So after my second I ran past the dugout and stuck two fingers up to him. I was just trying to tell him I'd scored twice! He

We know the score – the Dynamo scoreboard lights up the grim Berlin night sky and reveals that Tony Morley's brace has clinched a first-leg advantage

didn't say a word to me after the game but a week later he called me in and told me: 'Those were the two best goals I've ever seen. And by the way, I'm fining you a week's wages!' At least he gave the money to charity."

Victory behind the Iron Curtain was a massive achievement, particularly against such formidable opponents. Full-back Colin Gibson said: "Dynamo were no mugs but we gave a great team performance that night. It was almost unreal to have the guards watching from the Berlin Wall. Going from West to East Germany didn't seem like just like going into a different country; it felt as though we were going into a different world altogether."

Two weeks later, in the return leg at Villa Park, the dramatic events of the closing stages in Berlin assumed even greater significance. After 14 minutes, Villa were opened up down the right wing and Dynamo skipper Frank Terletzki drove low past Rimmer to bring the tie level on aggregate. Suddenly, nerves were jangling in the knowledge that a second goal from the visitors would mean the end of the European adventure. As it turned out, the threat of another Dynamo breakthrough was evident only during a nail-biting final 15 minutes after a succession of Villa efforts which were denied either by the giant Rudwaleit or by other means. Some amazing goal-line clearances had Withe and Gordon Cowans shaking their heads in disbelief, especially, as the ball refused to go in and put Villa's minds more at ease.

Then, late on and with nothing to lose and everything to gain, Dynamo pressed forward with plenty of intent. "We are fully

> **Second round, 2nd leg**
> **ASTON VILLA 0 BERLINER DYNAMO 1**
> **4th November 1981, Villa Park, Att: 28,175**
> **0-1 TERLETZKI**
>
> **ASTON VILLA**
> **James RIMMER, Kenneth SWAIN, Colin GIBSON, Allan EVANS, Gary WILLIAMS, Dennis MORTIMER (c), Desmond BREMNER, Gary SHAW, Peter WITHE, Gordon COWANS, Anthony MORLEY.**
> **BERLINER DYNAMO**
> **Bodo RUDWALEIT, Dirk SCHLEGEL, Norbert TRIELOFF, Christian BACKS, Rainer ERNST, Rainer TROPPA. Frank TERLETSKI (c). Arthur ULLRICH, Hans-Jurgen RIEDIGER, Bernd SCHULZ (Ralf STRASSER 62), Wolf-Rudiger NETZ.**

Determined Dynamo – Peter Withe gets in a header at Villa Park but it was the Germans who emerged 1-0 winners in the second leg

aware that we were living dangerously at the end," admitted Gary Shaw. "Jimmy made a great save and Berlin hit the upright as well. If either of those two efforts had gone in, it would have been curtains for us there and then."

TICKETS, PLEASE!

Steve Stride, pictured right, received plenty of requests for tickets during his time as Villa secretary, but arguably none were more unusual than the one that went his way for the away game against Dynamo.

On the day before the second leg, three British corporals stationed in West Berlin turned up at the team's hotel, saying they were desperate to attend the game.

The trio had to hang around nearly six hours while Stride negotiated with Dynamo officials and awaited a reply, but their long wait was rewarded with the tickets they were seeking.

Mesmerising Morley – having run almost the length of the pitch, Tony Morley sends a low shot past keeper Bodo Radwaleit for Villa's late winner in Berlin; much to the delight of three patient British officers!

1981-82, third round

Pink champagne in Ukraine

The draw for the European Cup quarter-finals was made in Zurich on 11th December and Villa learned that they faced another trip behind the Iron Curtain, this time to face Soviet champions Dynamo Kiev. But it was more than two months later before they discovered where the away leg would be played. It was very much a game of wait and see. Villa readily accepted that the game would not be in Kiev, where freezing temperatures in February and March invariably rendered the pitch unplayable. While the host club could do nothing about the weather, though, their laissez-faire attitude to finding an alternative stadium was hardly conducive to east-west relationships. When a deputation of Dynamo officials attended Villa's match against Liverpool at the end of January, they even suggested it might be the day before the game before the venue was established.

That was clearly out of the question, if only because the Russian Embassy would not grant the necessary visas until they were informed of the venue. Villa's patience finally snapped when secretary Steve Stride was informed that the game may take place in Kiev after all – but that Tashkent on the Chinese border and Sevastopol on the Black Sea were two other possibles. At that juncture, the club lodged an official complaint with UEFA, who ordered on 19th February that Dynamo must find a venue within four days. The deadline was met – the first leg was to be played at Simferopol, the capital of Crimea, 300 miles south of Kiev.

Preparations for the 2,000-mile journey into the

OUR HOTEL ?

Not exactly travel-brochure luxury – the run-down hotel where Villa's players and officals were based during their stay in Simferopol

unknown could finally get under way, and, given the Soviet Union's dubious reputation for hygiene at the time, Villa decided to take their own food. When their Aeroflot 160-seater plane took off from Birmingham on the first day of March, the players and officials were accompanied by 150 steaks, 12 dozen eggs and 112lbs of potatoes, plus bread, cereals, tea and coffee. But even that culinary caution was initially rendered a futile exercise. The signs were ominous almost as soon as the plane had landed at the third attempt after coming down through dense cloud. Many of the visiting party were still feeling queasy when they were further sickened by an announcement that their accommodation had been switched. They had received written assurances that they would be staying in luxurious accommodation at the Black Sea resort of Yalta, but it turned out that Dynamo were staying there. Instead, Villa's players and officials were taken to the Hotel Moscow in Simferopol, an establishment with sparse furnishing, tiny baths and rock-hard beds more suited to an army barracks than a hotel. "The toilets left a lot to be desired, too," said skipper Dennis Mortimer. "The seats weren't attached to the WC and we joked that we would have to carry them around with us in case someone nicked them!" But really, it was no laughing matter, and Peter Withe was alarmed when water from the taps in the wash basin ran in shades of green and yellow.

Simferopol proved to be just as depressing as East Berlin. Everywhere was dimly lit, and there was the constant imposing presence of KGB officers. When the players took a stroll around the shops, they were astounded by the scarcity of goods on display. "We went to a huge department store but it was like a jumble sale," said Gary Williams. "There were piles of clothes on what looked like wallpaper pasting

Mixing with the locals – Gary Shaw is all smiles in Simferopol as Villa prepare for a training session

boards, and shoes were scattered all over the floor. I also remember people queuing for everything. The poverty we saw made you appreciate what you had back home."

The training facilities in that uninviting corner of the USSR also left a lot to be desired and Villa's preparations were further disrupted when central defender Allan Evans was ruled out with a shoulder injury sustained in a challenge with Coventry City striker Garry Thompson the previous Saturday. Evans' absence meant a reshuffle. Ken McNaught, who had missed the first two rounds through injury, was partnered at the back by midfielder Des Bremner, while Andy Blair was drafted into the midfield and entrusted with the task of man-marking former European Footballer of the Year Oleg Blokhin. "I felt I did a good job on Blokhin," said Blair. "He hit the post early on but apart from that, I kept him reasonably quiet. I kept talking to him to put him off his game. He didn't speak English but I think he understood most of what I was saying. Most of it was accompanied by the word 'off'! It was a great experience to pit my wits against one of the best players in Europe."

The game, played against a backdrop of an appreciative but largely unenthusiastic crowd, was far from a classic, although Villa were more than happy with a goalless draw. Blair's persistence, plus some resolute defending by McNaught and Bremner, ensured that Blokhin did not have

Quarter-final, 1st leg
DYNAMO KYIV 0 ASTON VILLA 0
3rd March 1982, Lokomotiv Stadium, Simferopol |Att: 19,978

DYNAMO KYIV
Viktor CHANOV, Vladimir BESSONOV (c) (Alexandre KHAPSALIS 19), Serguei BALTACHA, Sergei ZHURAVLIEV, Anatoly DEMIANENKO, Vladimir LOZINSKY, Leonid BURIAK, Andriy BAL, Viktor KHLUS, Vladimir VEREMEEV (Vadim EVTUSHENKO 66), Oleg BLOKHIN.
ASTON VILLA
James RIMMER, Kenneth SWAIN, Gary WILLIAMS, Desmond BREMNER, Kenneth McNAUGHT, Dennis MORTIMER (c), Andrew BLAIR, Gary SHAW, Peter WITHE, Gordon COWANS, Anthony MORLEY.

Near miss – as close as Villa went in the first leg against Kiev. Gary Shaw looks a certain scorer but his shot went just wide

Club photographer Terry Weir captures the scoreboard in the closing minutes in Simferopol, where the 5.00pm kick-off for live TV coverage made life easier for the travelling press (picture below)

another clear-cut chance after his early shot against the woodwork. It was an excellent result for a Villa team now under the charge of Tony Barton, who had stepped up from his assistant manager role following Ron Saunders' shock resignation three weeks earlier. Barton's boys might even have snatched a win, had it not been for Kiev keeper Victor Chanov's brilliant save from Tony Morley and a miss by Gary Shaw.

With a highly satisfactory result under their belts, the players were able to relax for the first time since landing on Soviet soil. The Villa party had decided to fly home the following day so they were able to attend a post-match function organised by Dynamo and the Ukraine football association. There was a price to pay, though, for the revelry which followed two-and-a-half days of frugal existence – and Gary Williams woke up the following morning with more than just a thick head. "Everyone was drinking pink champagne," said the Wolverhampton-born full-back. "I had too much and had to be carried back to my room. When I woke up I was covered from head to toe in toothpaste, and glitter had been sprinkled

Just write! Members of the English press file their reports from Simferopol after the goalless first leg against Dynamo Kiev – although the man from the Birmingham Mail seems to have gone missing

41

on it! I still had glitter on my face when we got to the airport, and for about a week afterwards it was still coming off in the shower."

The frivolity was quickly forgotten. When Dynamo arrived in Birmingham for the second leg, the Cold War resumed, and once again the match venue was at the heart of the controversy. A severe English winter had left the Villa Park pitch in a dreadful state and parts of the playing surface had resembled a squelchy bog of turf and sand during the previous Saturday's game against Wolves. Having surrendered home advantage in the first leg, Kiev were in no mood for this one to go ahead in such poor conditions, and at one point there was a danger that the game would either have to be postponed or switched to another ground. Fortunately, the heavy rain subsided, allowing groundsman Tony Eden and his staff to work around the clock to ensure the go-ahead. For all that, the conditions were far from perfect and the pitch was brown rather than green. It was nevertheless one of Villa Park's truly great European nights.

Striker David Geddis wasn't in the squad and watched from the stand. "The crowd were more intense than in any other home tie," he said. "You sensed that people were starting to believe we could win the European Cup."

Just four minutes and 15 seconds had elapsed when Gary Shaw opened the scoring with a low angled left-foot shot which squeezed between keeper Victor Chanov and the near post – and

Tight angle – Gary Shaw's low left-foot shot squeezes in to provide a morale-boosting early lead at Villa Park. Inset: The programme cover from Villa Park showing the pre-match formalities from the away leg

Heading for the semi-finals – Ken McNaught is all determination as he meets Gordon Cowans' right-wing corner with a firm header to secure a 2-0 victory over the Russians. The central defender's predictable reaction is captured below as Peter Withe and Allan Evans join in the celebration

three minutes before half-time Villa's passport to the semi-finals was as good as rubber-stamped. 'Sid' Cowans delivered a corner from the right and McNaught climbed in a crowded goalmouth to score with a downward header which left the visitors down and almost out.

A famous Villa win was unfortunately was marred by a painful injury to Dennis Mortimer a couple of minutes from the end. And that was only the start of his problems. "I caught one of their players and went down," he said. "Normally you put your arms out to protect your fall but for some reason my arm had got twisted. Instead of my fingers going down first, it was the back of my hand. The momentum snapped my arm, and I thought I'd broken it. I was in agony.

"Doc Targett strapped my arm and put it in a sling. He decided I should go to hospital and we went in his car but by then the crowd were leaving the ground and the traffic was horrendous. It took nearly an hour and a half to get there and I was in so much pain, it seemed like a lifetime. It would have been quicker to walk. Luckily, the arm wasn't broken - it was damage to the ligaments. I missed the next few games but at least I was back for the semi-final."

COWANS AND THE COCKROACH

Villa's painstaking travel plans unravelled from the moment they set eyes on their hotel in Simferopol. Unfortunately, they arrived late and found there was insufficient time to unload the skips carrying their provisions, so the kitchen staff were asked to rustle up a snack of chicken soup and bread.

Pain game. Dennis Mortimer is led away by club doctor David Targett after suffering an arm injury in the closing minutes

It wasn't the most appetising of meals, particularly for Gordon Cowans. When the midfielder broke open his bread roll, a dead cockroach fell out! "It was a big, horrible thing which looked like it had been there for an eternity," he said. "I lost my appetite at that point. The dining room was desperate anyway. It was basic beyond belief and most of us decided to wait until the next morning, when we could have our own food."

The first of Villa's steaks were served on the Tuesday, although it quickly became clear the chef had imposed some form of rationing. "When they arrived on the table, we couldn't believe it," said Ken McNaught. "They had been cut into three pieces, so someone had to tell him we were actually allowed a whole one each! The guy must have thought we were really greedy but it showed how food was in such short supply over there. When we left, there were a few steaks left over so we gave them to the chef. He was over the moon because it meant he could feed his family for the next three months."

Quarter-final, 2nd leg
ASTON VILLA 2 DYNAMO KYIV 0
17th March 1982, Villa Park, Att: 38,274
1-0 SHAW (6) 2-0 McNAUGHT (41)

ASTON VILLA
James RIMMER, Kenneth SWAIN, Gary WILLIAMS, Allan EVANS, Kenneth McNAUGHT, Dennis MORTIMER (c) (Andy BLAIR 88), Desmond BREMNER, Gary SHAW, Peter WITHE, Gordon COWANS, Anthony MORLEY.
DYNAMO KYIV
Victor CHANOV, Aleksandr BOIKO, Serguei BALTACHA (Aleksandr SOROKALET 76), Sergei ZHURAVLIEV, Anatoly DEMIANENKO, Andriy BAL, Vladimir LOZINSKY, Vadim EVTUSHENKO, Viktor KHLUS, Vladimir VEREMEEV (Alexandre KHAPSALIS 40), Oleg BLOKHIN (c).

1981-82, semi-final

The battle of Brussels

Their march to the semi-finals had been conducted with almost military precision, so it was ironic that Villa's carefully-planned strategy should suddenly be unhinged by a member of Her Majesty's Armed Forces. The players had become accustomed to crowds heavily populated with soldiers during their trips to East Berlin and the Soviet Union. But little could they have imagined that their hopes of European Cup glory would be jeopardised by a moment of madness involving an off-duty British serviceman.

A night of violence in Brussels reached its climax during the second leg of Villa's last-four tie against Anderlecht. As the Belgian champions launched a first-half attack which ended with a shot over Jimmy Rimmer's bar, the mayhem which had engulfed the Emile Verse stadium exploded into total confusion. A spectator wearing a claret polo shirt suddenly appeared in the goalmouth, lying down in the six-yard box before he was dragged away by half-a-dozen police officers. It later emerged that the intruder was a member of the Sherwood Foresters and had taken time off from his military duties in West Germany to attend the big match. His excuse for running on to the playing area was that he was trying to get away from the fighting which was raging on the terraces behind the goal at that end. That, though, was scant consolation to Villa officials when their opponents subsequently cited his unusual intervention as a basis for demanding that the game should be re-staged.

The incident resulted in a six-minute hold-up and there was subsequently a much longer wait while the UEFA disciplinary committee debated

Marking Morley – Having scored the winner in the first leg, Tony Morley was understandably subjected to some close marking in Brussels

Semi-final, 2nd leg
ANDERLECHT 0 ASTON VILLA 0
21st April 1982, Emile Verse stadium, Att: 21,253

ANDERLECHT
Jacques MUNARON, Luka PERUZOVIC, Hugo BROOS, Juan Jose LOZANO BOHORQUEZ, Michel DE GROOTE, Frank VERCAUTEREN, Walter DE GREEF, Wilhemus HOFKENS (Micun JOVANIC 59), Willy GEURTS (Per FRIMANN 78), Ludo COECK (c), Kenneth BRYLLE LARSEN.
ASTON VILLA
James RIMMER, Kenneth SWAIN, Gary WILLIAMS, Allan EVANS, Kenneth McNAUGHT, Dennis MORTIMER (c), Desmond BREMNER, Gary SHAW, Peter WITHE, Gordon COWANS, Anthony MORLEY.

whether Villa's 1-0 aggregate victory should be allowed to stand or the goalless second leg be played again. It was an anxious time for the club, although the trouble was no great surprise to secretary Steve Stride, who admitted feeling much trepidation ever since he made his customary pre-match visit to check out Anderlecht's facilities and the security arrangements.

Gary Shaw goes unorthodox at the Emile Verse Stadium

The Belgian club's precautions against crowd problems, he had discovered, were virtually non-existent, a piece of red tape providing the only segregation between rival supporters. As a barrier, it was hopelessly inadequate and the running battles that took place between Belgian and English fans resulted in 88 arrests plus hospital treatment for 18 injured people, including three policemen.

"It was a hostile atmosphere," said left-back Gary Williams. "Their supporters were chucking beer cans and other objects at the bus as we arrived at the stadium, which was pretty intimidating. We wondered what we were going into." Ken McNaught vividly recalls the sight of riot police with shields shining in the reflection of the floodlights, while Kenny Swain was aware of policemen running up and down the touchline with their dogs. Allan Evans even attempted an appeal for Villa's fans to calm down. "It was wrong because I should have been fully concentrating on what I was doing," he said. "But at every goal-kick, my gaze was drawn to the terraces. English fans already had a terrible reputation and I was pretty worried about the consequences. When the guy ran on the pitch, particularly, who knows what might have happened?"

To Villa's considerable

No bother here – Villa fans in good spirits in Brussels, with no sign of the trouble which would mar the clash with Anderlecht

credit, they were totally professional both before and after the unscheduled hold-up, carefully protecting the single-goal lead they had established at Villa Park two weeks earlier. They should, in fact, have extended their aggregate advantage. Shaw was unlucky when he controlled Kenny Swain's chest-high cross with his left foot before unleashing a stinging right-foot drive which Anderlecht keeper Jacky Munaron tipped over for a corner.

And Withe was even more frustrated when he fired home an unstoppable shot from just outside the penalty area, only for his glee to become a growl when a linesman raised his flag for offside. "I thought it was a great goal," he said. "Gordon Cowans had knocked the ball forward and Gary Shaw flicked it on. I lashed it in, giving the keeper no chance. When I realised the flag was up, I went mad at the linesman."

By the time the first leg was played, Tony Barton had shed his caretaker role to become manager, with coach Roy Maclaren appointed as his assistant. The internal promotions were a just reward for some impressive results which had seen Villa climb the First Division table as well as overcoming Dynamo Kiev in the quarter-finals of the European Cup. The duo were aware, though, that a club who had been Belgian champions 17 times and were experienced campaigners in European competition presented the most searching examination yet of their managerial ability.

Despite Anderlecht's reputation, their Yugoslav coach Tomislav Ivic was unpopular because of the negative approach that had made them mean and miserly, with the main intention to stifle opponents. "Ivic's game" had already gained notoriety in Belgium, based on a well-organised offside trap combined with mass attacking or, more frequently, mass defending. They had scored 14 goals in reaching the last four, just to prove they also had plenty of firepower, but were in no mood for adventure at Villa Park,

after Jimmy Rimmer pushed away Frank Vercauteren's shot in a counter-attack early on. The outcome was a dour, sterile contest which prompted a scathing attack on the Belgians' boss by Leon Hickman in the Birmingham Evening Mail the night after. "Clearly a negative thinker" he wrote, "he has found footballers of undoubted skill and turned them into a collective farm where

Tony Morley tries his luck at Villa Park with a fine left-foot shot that seriously threatened the Belgians' goal.

Simply sublime – Tony Morley strokes home a low left-foot shot to put Villa ahead at Villa Park

everyone does exactly as he is told and free expression is allowed only if it is ordered. Football Communism, perhaps."

Having sampled the real thing during their trips to Eastern Europe, Villa were dismayed to have football's equivalent of Communism thrust upon them in their own back yard. But if the match was instantly forgettable, Tony Morley's 28th-minute winner was a classic. Williams, Gordon Cowans and Gary Shaw linked fluently down the left before Cowans delivered an incisive pass which epitomised his illustrious career. It was perfectly weighted to complement Morley's darting run, and the winger barely halted his stride as he controlled the ball with his right foot, advanced to the edge of the penalty area and stroked a sublime left-footer beyond Munaron and in off the far post. Morley's fourth European Cup goal was a blueprint for any team striving to break down a blanket defence. It also made amends for his howler earlier in the match, and pacified a critic in the crowd. "I had a good chance in the first 10 minutes, a one-on-one with the keeper," he said. "But I miscued my shot and it hit the corner flag.

As I walked back up the touchline, a supporter had a real go at me. So when I scored I ran over and gave the guy a bit of verbal. He didn't seem bothered – I think he was just delighted we were in the lead."

It proved to be the goal which assured Villa's passage to the final, and the players were understandably ecstatic when the final whistle sounded in the second leg in Brussels. After the ecstasy on the night, however, Villa then endured the agony of having to wait for UEFA's response to Anderlecht's appeal. For

Semi-final, 1st leg
ASTON VILLA 1 ANDERLECHT 0
7th April 1982, Villa Park, Att: 38,539
1-0 MORLEY (28)

ASTON VILLA
James RIMMER, Kenneth SWAIN, Gary WILLIAMS, Allan EVANS, Kenneth McNAUGHT, Dennis MORTIMER (c), Desmond BREMNER, Gary SHAW, Peter WITHE, Gordon COWANS, Anthony MORLEY.
ANDERLECHT
Jacques MUNARON, Luka PERUZOVIC, Hugo BROOS, Juan Jose LOZANO BOHORQUEZ, Michel DE GROOTE, Frank VERCAUTEREN, Walter DE GREEF, Michel RENQUIN (Micun JOVANIC HT), Petur PETURSSON (Willy GEURTS 59), Ludo COECK (c), Albert CLUYTENS.

eight days after they had stoically drawn at the Emile Verse stadium, the players were left wondering whether their endeavours would be rewarded by a rightful place in the final or if they would have to travel back to Belgium.

With that concern on their minds, Villa sent a deputation to meet sports minister Neil Macfarlane to formulate a report which criticised Anderlecht's handling of the match. The Villa party, which included FA chairman Bert Millichip, secretary Ted Croker and former Minister for Sport Denis Howell, argued that the Belgians had ignored UEFA guidelines for crowd control by sending supporters to wrong areas of the ground and failing to enforce effective segregation. On Thursday, 29th April, Howell – the MP for Small Heath and a lifelong Villa supporter – accompanied Steve Stride to Zurich to present the club's case and await UEFA's decision, knowing that Anderlecht were claiming they had been about to score when the off-duty soldier ran on the pitch.

"I feared the worst because I couldn't recall the state of play when the match was stopped," said Stride. "From the moment we entered the room for the hearing in Zurich, I felt we were up against it. English clubs always seemed to be more heavily punished than other European clubs for the misbehaviour of supporters and I had the distinct impression the knives were out for us. Then Denis, bless, him, came up with the question which ensured the game would not have to be re-staged. Anderlecht claimed they were denied a goal by the fan running on the pitch but Denis was a former first-class referee

Good Evans – Allan Evans sends a far-post header just too high in the second leg, with Peter Withe well positioned to capitalise on any rebound

and knew exactly what our approach should be. He simply asked where the game had been re-started and the answer was that it had resumed just inside our half. The Belgians could hardly argue they were going to break through our defence from there."

Villa were fined 50,000 Swiss francs and ordered to play their next European home game behind closed doors, but that hardly mattered. Their place in the final was assured; it was time to start preparing for the biggest match in the club's history.

Flag day – Morley can't hide his delight as he salutes Villa's travelling supporters after the game

'BETTER THAN THE FINAL'

Several of Villa's Class of '82 have since admitted that winning the semi-final against Anderlecht gave them a bigger thrill than actually lifting the trophy a few weeks later. "I was more excited that night than I was when we won the final," said Allan Evans. "When supporters ask me for my best memory of the competition, I always say it was that Anderlecht tie because it was such an achievement for us to have reached the European Cup final. Just getting there gave me goose bumps."

Midfielder Des Bremner had no hesitation in agreeing. "Everyone says there's nothing worse in football than losing a semi-final," he said. "Having come this far, we were determined it wouldn't happen to us. We just played our normal game and it was brilliant to think it had got us to the final." Winger Tony Morley said: "When the final whistle blew in Belgium, I remember kicking the ball into the crowd and went straight over to our supporters to celebrate. To see the looks on Tony Barton's and Roy Maclaren's faces was wonderful." And Kenny Swain added: "We felt we had climbed our Everest when we came through that tough semi-final. Now everyone was wondering if we could repeat it..."

It must be...it is! Peter Withe!

Brian Moore's succinct description will remain forever etched on the memory of everyone of a claret-and-blue persuasion. Those who watched the match on ITV were probably too engrossed in what was happening to take a great deal of notice of the commentary at the time, but those three brief sentences have become synonymous with the greatest moment in Villa's history. And if the goal was nowhere near the best Peter Withe scored for the club, he couldn't have cared less. With arguably the most awkward contact of his career, he had scored the most significant goal of his career. Withe's 67th-minute strike was enough to secure victory over Bayern Munich at the De Kuip Stadium in Rotterdam – and Villa were champions of Europe. So who better than the man himself to recall exactly how it happened?

"Tony Morley turned a defender one way and then the other," said Withe. "Klaus Augenthaler was marking me, but he sensed the danger and moved across to cover, which left me unmarked as I reached the six-yard box. Tony drove the ball hard across the goalmouth but it seemed to happen in slow motion. I said to myself: 'Concentrate!' The ball hit a divot as it reached me and it half hit my shin and half hit

my ankle before flying against the post and in. I'm convinced that if I'd hit it properly the keeper would have saved it, but he didn't expect that. I was too close to the goal to run to our supporters, so I ran into the net to celebrate. Gary Shaw was the first to reach me and then Gordon Cowans jumped

You beauty! Peter Withe's face says it all as his shot beats keeper Manfred Muller

on my neck and dragged me to the ground. I must have resisted a bit because he kept saying: 'Get down, you bastard!'"

Cowans' forceful utterance was very much a term of endearment which was echoed by every one of Villa's players. All the same, Withe's unconventional goal has been the butt of some affectionate mickey-taking down the years. Cowans, a keen golfer, has always described the crucial strike as a "shank", insisting: "Withey did his best to miss it but somehow it went in!" Given Withe's penchant for scoring with his left foot, it came as a surprise that the most important goal of his impressive collection of over 200 should be struck with his right. "Withey didn't score too many with his right," said Des Bremner. "Watching that one, you could see why! But it doesn't matter how they go in. It was marvellous that Peter scored at the end where our supporters were massed."

The haphazard nature of the winner arguably reflected Villa's approach to the final in Rotterdam. Although it was the biggest game of their lives, they were genuinely relaxed about the whole thing. Before the game, there was an almost carefree air about the players as they waved to their wives and girlfriends in the crowd before a few of them produced cameras and started taking photos on the pitch. The laid-back approach didn't go unnoticed by Brian Clough, who had managed Nottingham Forest to European glory in 1979 and 1980 and was commentating alongside Moore for ITV's live coverage. "I can't believe this team have come to a European Cup final," Clough observed. "We've had players on the pitch, taking photographs of each other!"

Rotterdam line-up – Back row: Peter Withe, Andy Blair, Nigel Spink, Pat Heard, Gary Shaw, Ken McNaught, Allan Evans, Dennis Mortimer, Jimmy Rimmer. Front: David Geddis, Colin Gibson, Gordon Cowans, Gary Williams, Tony Morley, Des Bremner, Kenny Swain

Tony Morley was more relaxed than most. "I didn't even get changed until 20 minutes before kick-off," he said. "Some lads I knew wanted tickets so I met them outside the stadium. The Germans were warming up and I wasn't even in the ground! The guys I had the tickets for were a bit concerned, and asked if I was playing. I told them it would only take me 10 minutes to get changed. I never liked being ready a long time before a game."

Villa had arrived in

This, or that? Referee Georges Konrath seems to be weighing something up with Dennis Mortimer before kick-off in the European Cup final. Bayern skipper Paul Breitner is clearly unmoved by the conversation

Rotterdam two days before the final, their training sessions attracting around 200 locals, who made it clear they were backing Tony Barton's boys to beat the Germans. No-one, though, was under any illusions about the size of the task. Bayern had won the trophy three times during the 1970s and boasted a team packed with world-class players, like classy sweeper Klaus Augenthaler, lethal marksman Dieter Hoeness, inspirational skipper Paul Breitner and European player of the year Karl-Heinz Rummenigge. Yet there was a quiet belief in the Villa camp that their name was on the cup, and skipper Dennis Mortimer was certainly full of confidence. "In the week leading up to the final, I started thinking about how Liverpool and Nottingham Forest had won the previous five finals between them," he said. "It occurred to me: 'Why not us?' I'd seen Phil Thompson lift the trophy and he was in the year below me at school, Brookfield Secondary in Kirkby. I started to imagine what it would be like for that school to have two former pupils lifting the European Cup."

Just nine minutes into the final, Villa's self-belief was tested to the limit. No-one had paid much attention the previous day when Jimmy Rimmer ricked his neck in training, and even when pain-killing injections were given before kick-off, it barely raised a comment. But with the match settling down, Gary Williams suddenly became aware that all was not well. "I was the first to realise something was wrong," said Williams. "Jimmy shouted at me 'I need to come off'. I couldn't believe what I was hearing." Although they had known about the injury, Barton and his assistant Roy MacLaren were also taken aback. The manager later revealed: "We didn't take a calculated gamble in playing him because a decision of fitness can only be taken by the player. Jimmy said he was okay and I was perfectly satisfied because he had gone through an intensive work-out that morning, without any sign of discomfort."

53

The pain game – A distraught Jimmy Rimmer is led off by Tony Barton and assistant boss Roy MacLaren

Rimmer's injury meant that Barton had to send on 23-year-old Nigel Spink, who had played only one first-team game and whose domestic football during the 1981-82 campaign had amounted to 36 reserve games. But now the No 2 keeper was being thrust into the biggest game in Villa's history – with words of encouragement from his fellow substitutes ringing in his ears. "Even when Nigel had to go on, he didn't seem too worried," said Pat Heard, who was also on the bench. We just joked with him and I said: 'Go on, Spinksy, you'll be all right – don't let one in! Somehow I knew he would be okay. I'd played in the reserves with him and I knew exactly what he could do."

Despite the enormity of the occasion, the boy from Chelmsford did everything that was asked of him, and more. His only previous senior game had been against Nottingham Forest two-and-a-half years earlier but his performance at the stadium known as The Tub made him an instant claret-and-blue hero. "When I went on, it came totally out of the blue," he said. "I didn't have a clue that Jimmy had a problem. I didn't think for one minute that he wouldn't play the whole of the final so I was very relaxed in the build-up. I'd been out on the pitch an hour before kick-off to warm up. I wanted to get as much of the atmosphere as possible. That warm-up probably did me good when I had to go on."

It was half an hour before Spink was seriously tested, diving to his right to hold Bernhard Durnberger's low drive, but he made numerous crucial saves in a second half Bayern dominated. And even when he was beaten by an Augenthaler header, Kenny Swain was perfectly positioned to clear off the line. But if Spink's heroics were a major factor in Villa's triumph, an early

That's mine – Spink climbs to hold a cross as Bayern press for an equaliser

Resolute defence – Ken McNaught and keeper Nigel Spink quell a Bayern attack as Dieter Hoeness slides in

tactical switch also contributed significantly to quelling the German spearhead.

"Allan Evans and I used to take sides," Ken McNaught explained. "If the opposition only played with one striker, he would mark the guy and I would pick up the pieces. But we were very flexible. After a few minutes, we realised that Hoeness was outjumping Allan and Rummenigge was outstripping me. So we decided to go for man-to-man marking and it worked."

For all their resilience, Villa endured some anxious moments as the match drew agonisingly slowly towards its conclusion, and three minutes from time they were caught out by long through ball from Kurt Niedermayer, which was headed on by Gunther Guttler for Hoeness to drill a low shot past Spink. Thankfully, a linesman's flag was raised to indicate that Hoeness was offside when the ball was headed forward. "We got away with a lot that night," admitted Evans. "I swapped shirts with Rummenigge and as I went up the steps to collect my medal I saw the German players sitting

ASTON VILLA 1 BAYERN MUNCHEN 0
26th May 1982, Stadion Feijenoord, Rotterdam, 39,776
1-0 WITHE (67)

ASTON VILLA		**BAYERN MUNCHEN**	
1	James RIMMER (9)	1	Manfred MULLER
2	Kenneth SWAIN	3	Wolfgang DREMMLER
3	Gary WILLIAMS	3	Udo HORSMANN
4	Allan EVANS	4	Hans WEINER
5	Kenneth McNAUGHT	5	Klaus AUGENTHALER
6	Dennis MORTIMER (c)	6	Wolfgang KRAUS (78)
7	Desmond BREMNER	7	Bernd DURNBERGER
8	Gary SHAW	8	Paul BREITNER
9	Peter WITHE	9	Dieter HOENESS
10	Gordon COWANS	10	Reinhold MATHY (51)
11	Anthony MORLEY	11	Karl-Heinz RUMMENIGGE (c)
Subs:			
16	Nigel SPINK (1)	13	Kurt NIEDERMAYER (6)
		16	Gunter GUTTLER (10)

A beaming Dennis Mortimer proudly holds aloft the European Cup, while Kenny Swain clenches his fist in triumph behind him. Like several team-mates, Swain had secured a Bayern shirt, but it's fitting that the skipper should have been wearing the kit in which Villa became champions of Europe

around the centre circle, looking dejected. I couldn't understand why Rummenigge felt so bad - he had my shirt!"

Victory was sweet for every member of the side, but particularly so for the man with the honour of being presented with the cup. "All I could think about in the last few minutes was getting my hands on that trophy," said Dennis Mortimer. "When the final whistle went, it was joy, joy, joy. I couldn't wait to get up those stairs to collect the cup but all the lads were behind the goal, celebrating with our supporters. One of the UEFA delegates asked if I could gather the players together. I thought: 'You must be joking!' "Once I was holding the cup, I didn't want to l let it go. I kept it in my hands as long as possible to make sure there were lots of photographs of me with it! To have won such a prestigious tournament was absolutely wonderful. Every time I watch the final on TV even now, I always find it a very special moment when the trophy is presented. I think, yes, I've been there, done that. It still gives me a magical feeling."

A PAIN IN THE NECK

Jimmy Rimmer described his decision to come off after just nine minutes of the final as "the hardest thing I ever had to do as a footballer." "I'd been aware since the previous Friday that there might be a problem," he said. "Bob Latchford had backed into me during our final league match against Swansea and I'd fallen awkwardly on my neck. The injury was kept a secret and I know Tony Barton was anxious for me to play in the final because Nigel had next to no first-team experience. I had some treatment over the weekend but I woke up in the early hours on the day of the final and I just couldn't move my neck.

"I should have realised then that I wasn't going to make it but I was determined not to let anyone down. After a couple of pain-killing injections I felt okay, and I was confident I could get through it. But I knew after only two or three minutes that I wasn't going to be able to play the whole game. Rummenigge hit a shot from long range and although it went wide I realised that if he'd been on target I wouldn't have got there. The next few minutes were mental agony. I realised it was useless trying to continue so I shouted to Gary to let the manager know. That was the hardest thing I ever had to do as a footballer. I can't even begin to describe how devastated I was. I'd played in every other game and this should have been the crowning point of my career, but it was all over after nine minutes."

Even so, Rimmer became only the second player, after Italian Saul Malatrasi, to collect European Cup winner's medals with two different clubs. He had been Manchester United's unused sub in the 1968 Wembley triumph over Benfica.

HIJACKING THE BEER...

Goal hero Peter Withe and central defender Ken McNaught literally had nothing left in the tank after the final. The duo made that discovery when they were randomly chosen, along with Bayern's Klaus Augenthaler and Bernd Durnberger, to undergo post-match drugs tests.

"We were taken to a two-berth caravan under the stand and they gave us phials to provide urine samples," said Withe. "But no-one could manage anything for a while because we had all sweated so much out on the pitch. We had a look out of the caravan window and someone happened to be walking past with a crate of beer. We asked where he was taking it and he said it was for the Villa dressing room – so we hijacked it! We knocked back about four beers each before it had the desired effect."

The golden moment that sent beer consumption in Rotterdam soaring.....

Hold it high – Gary Shaw and Tony Morley lift the trophy while clad in shirts swapped with opponents

Augenthaler also recalls the waiting game over the delivery of urine samples after the match. "The two Villa players came in, downed a crate of beer extremely fast and were gone from the room in about 20 minutes," he says. "But we were there for ever."

THE TOILET TROPHY

It's one thing being champions of Europe. But what do you do with 11kg of silver after you've won it? That was the dilemma for Villa's players as they travelled by coach from Rotterdam for the club's post-match banquet at the Apollo Hotel in Amsterdam. Initially, they were content to pass around the 74cm-tall trophy, but then a problem arose. Where could they put it without it falling over? Empty seats and the floor of the coach failed to provide a solution – so it was despatched to the loo!

"No-one wanted to take on the responsibility of looking after it and keeping it upright," recalled Pat Heard, one of Villa's five substitutes in the final. "Then someone came up with the bright idea of putting it in the toilet. It may sound surprising but that's where it stayed until we reached our destination in Amsterdam."

BAYERN'S UNLUCKY 13

The 1982 European Cup final proved to be unlucky 13 for Bayern. The German club had previously contested 12 finals throughout the course of their history – and had won every one. Less than a month before Rotterdam, they had beaten Nuremberg 4-2 in the German Cup final, and the team managed by Hungarian coach Pal Csernai were hot favourites to beat Villa.

But defeat by Tony Barton's men proved too much for Csernai. Instead of travelling back to Munich for a civic lunch the following day, he headed straight home from the airport. His absence didn't go down well with the Bayern players, and an angry Paul Breitner said: "Someone who should be here isn't. If we lose, we lose together. A bit more decency would have been in order."

It was the beginning of the end for the Hungarian's reign with Bayern. He departed the following year after his team had finished a disappointing fourth in the Bundesliga, no fewer than eight points behind Hamburger SV.

VILLAINS, NOT VILLANS!

Best-selling author Lee Child regularly uses Villa names for his Jack Reacher thrillers, with three members of the European Cup-winning team – Swain, Shaw and Withe – all having featured in his novels. But for his 21st Reacher book, Night School, Lee made a radical tactical change – he included

Shaw thing – Gary Shaw, partly obscured by Allan Evans, climbs in front of Udo Horsmann to send a header towards the Bayern goal. The striker has been celebrated in Lee Child book but not as a baddie!

four names from the 1982 Bayern team. "I don't like using Villa names for the bad guys," he said. "So I've used four from the Bayern Munich side from the 1982 European Cup final – Durnberger, Augenthaler, Muller, and Dremmler." The characters couldn't have been more appropriate. The book is a prequel, set in 1996 in Hamburg.

HOW THE FINAL UNFOLDED

3 min A long throw by Evans is partially cleared, and the central defender darts into the Bayern penalty area for a header which just clears the bar.

7 Withe climbs highest to meet a Cowans free-kick and send a 10-yard header just too high. .

9 Rimmer indicates he is unable to continue, and is replaced in goal by Spink.

12 A piece of Morley trickery is followed by a testing left-wing cross which Muller is unable to hold. The Bayern keeper gathers the ball at the second attempt as Shaw looks to capitalise on the mistake.

Stylish Sid – Gordon Cowans maintains his balance as he holds off a challenge in Rotterdam

14 Morley unleashes a 25-yard right-footer which takes a deflection and is well held by Muller.

19 Withe accepts a Cowans pass and turns away from his marker to shoot wide.

22 Shaw's superb cross from the left is menacing but is just beyond Withe's reach.

27 Bremner drives off target from around 30 yards following a fine Villa move involving Williams, Withe and Mortimer.

29 Spink's first test as Durnberger cuts inside from the left and fires a powerful low drive which the substitute keeper clutches while diving to his right.

30 A Morley corner is flicked on by Withe, but Shaw's weak close-range header is comfortably held by Muller.

31 Bayern suddenly step up the pace. Rummenigge's blistering drive is pushed away by Spink, with Evans getting in the way of Mathy's shot from the rebound.

32 Rummenigge has everyone gasping as he meets Breitner's cross from the right with an acrobatic overhead kick which flashes only inches wide of Spink's left-hand post.

37 Augenthaler, moving forward for the first time, launches a move which sees Rummenigge's flick release Breitner through the middle. The Munich captain is crowded out before McNaught's attempted clearance ricochets off Hoeness and goes just wide.

39 Williams is handed the only yellow card of the final, being cautioned by referee Konrath for an over-zealous challenge on Kraus.

43 Despite being shadowed by Evans, Rummenigge gets in a shot on the turn which flashes wide. On the stroke of half-time the striker goes close again with another low drive.

Half-time: Villa 0 Bayern 0

53 McNaught heads clear from Breitner's delicately-floated free-kick, and the Bayern skipper

follows up with a volley which goes well over from just outside the penalty area.

56 Rummenigge races on to a long through ball but McNaught comes to the rescue with a well-timed sliding tackle to get the ball back to Spink.

57 Villa are in disarray as Augenthaler charges through the right channel. Bremner's sliding tackle fails to halt the German, while Evans slips to the ground. But the chance goes begging when Bayern's sweeper fires wide of the far post, infuriating three team-mates who are waiting in front of goal.

60 Augenthaler makes a superb pass to Rummenigge, who plays it inside to Durenberger. The midfielder pushes the ball forward to Breitner before moving on to the return pass to unleash a hard drive which Spink holds diving to his right.

63 Spink is beaten for the first time as Augenthaler produces a well-placed header which catches the keeper off balance. But Swain is perfectly positioned to head off the line.

64 Spink scoops away a dangerous low cross from Dremmler, just as Hoeness, sliding in at the far post, looks certain to score.

65 Having absorbed 20 minutes of German pressure, Villa produce their first effort of the second half, Morley moving on to Mortimer's short pass and turning away from his marker to shoot over.

Goal coming up – Tony Morley turns past full-back Hans Weiner before providing the cross which produced the only goal in Rotterdam

67 Almost unbelievably, Villa are in the lead! The move starts in their own goalmouth, where Evans cuts out a Breitner centre intended for Rummenigge. Bremner tidies up by touching the ball back to Spink, who throws it out to Williams on the left. The full-back passes inside to Cowans, who pushes it forward to Withe, just inside the opposition half. Easing away from a challenge by Hoeness, the striker touches it back to Mortimer, who continues the patient build-up with an accurate forward pass to Shaw. Drifting to the left-hand touchline, Shaw produces a superb piece of skill which completely unbalances the Bayern defence. His clever run leaves Dremmler on the ground before he plays a piercing through ball into Morley's slipstream. The winger arrogantly leaves Weiner prostrate after turning him inside-out and his low cross is converted by Withe at the far post.

69 Twice in 60 seconds, substitute Guttler shoots wide as Bayern go in search of a quick equaliser.

71 Muller punches clear under pressure from Withe after Shaw neatly heads on a Morley centre.

72 Collecting Swain's pass on the right, Cowans smartly sweeps inside to hit a powerful left-foot shot which Muller does well to hold just inside the right-hand post.

73 Creating space for himself in a crowded goalmouth, Hoeness stoops to meet Rummenigge's left-wing corner with a header which goes wide.

86 Withe goes tumbling under Dremmler's challenge as they contest a deep cross from Bremner, but the striker's appeals for a penalty go unheeded by the ref.

Cool on camera as well - Nigel Spink survived a late scare before being able to tell Gary Newbon and ITV viewers back home all about Villa's epic triumph

87 Villa's hearts are in their mouths as they are caught out by a penetrating pass from substitute Niedermayer which Guttler nods forward for Hoeness to send a low dive past Spink and into the net. Thankfully, a linesman's flag indicates that Hoeness had been offside when the ball was headed forward.

90 After almost a minute of stoppage time, the whistle - Villa stand proud as European champions.

Full-time: Villa 1 Bayern 0

Memorable mural – Especially for users of the Holte End concourse

EVENING MAIL SPECIAL — MAIL 25TH ANNIVERSARY EDITION   THURSDAY, MAY 27, 1982   **11**

ASTON VILLA F.C. **EUROPEAN CUP FINAL** F.C. BAYERN MÜNCHEN E.V.

VILLA–EUROPEAN CHAMPIONS '82

A HOMECOMING JUST MADE FOR HEROES

Plane sailing! Above: Dennis Mortimer emerges from Villa's KLM flight from Amsterdam with a precious piece of cargo. Below: Happy scenes at the civic reception – while Villa's other players focus on the thousands of fans beneath them, skipper Mortimer turns on the balcony of Birmingham Council House to show club photographer Terry Weir the club's prized possession

1982-83

The sound of silence

There have been some unforgettable European occasions at Villa Park; nights when the place has reverberated to the sound of thousands of supporters singing and chanting in unison. When Villa began their defence of the European Cup, though, the match was played in the afternoon rather than the evening – and the famous stadium was all-but deserted.

Crowd trouble at the previous season's semi-final against Anderlecht in Brussels had resulted in UEFA punishing the club by insisting that their next European home tie be played behind closed doors. On the afternoon of Wednesday 15th September 1982, the only people able to attend the first-round, first-leg tie against Besiktas of Turkey – apart from the players, coaching staff and officials – were

EMPTY SEATS, MY LORD

Pressing forward – Gary Williams makes a cross against the backdrop of a Trinity Road stand populated only by reporters in the press box and invited guests in the directors' box

reporters, photographers and a few policemen who patrolled the terraces with dogs. The official attendance was recorded as just 167; it was a surreal experience, to say the least. "I'm sure the crowd figure was made up!" said Steve Stride , the club's former secretary. "UEFA had stipulated there should be no more than 200 people inside the ground, and the spectators also included police, stewards and security staff."

Although no members of the public could gain admission, some diehards just couldn't stay away. One group gathered on the grass banks outside Aston Hall, where they were afforded a restricted view of about an eighth of the pitch through the gap between the Trinity Road stand and the Holte End. A few members of Villa's staff were more fortunate, being allowed time off from their administrative duties to watch the game.

"It was a weird experience, very eerie," said Pam Bridgewater, who was working in the club's Development Association office at the time. "We sat in the directors' box – but only because we weren't allowed to sit or stand anywhere else in the ground. Quite a lot of guests of the Besiktas directors were also in the directors' box so at least we created a bit of an atmosphere in that area! Some of the club's part-time staff were brought in to make sure everything ran smoothly in the offices while we were outside. At half-time, we popped back inside to make sure they were managing okay. But we ended up feeling guilty because we were able to watch the game and they weren't."

Despite the absence of a proper crowd, the club still produced a limited number of programmes, which have become collectors' items. In his notes, manager Tony Barton wrote: "We welcome the Istanbul club to Villa Park and hope that we have an enjoyable game despite the problem of having to play behind closed doors. Obviously this is a matter of regret, both from the point of view of disappointing our regular supporters and of the team losing the normal advantage of enthusiastic support

First round, 1st leg
ASTON VILLA 3 BESIKTAS 1
15th September 1982.
Villa Park
Att: 167
1-0 WITHE (4) 2-0 MORLEY (9) 3-0 MORTIMER (29) 3-1 EKSI (74)

ASTON VILLA
James RIMMER, Gary WILLIAMS, Patrick HEARD, Desmond BREMNER, Kenneth McNAUGHT, Dennis MORTIMER (c), Andrew BLAIR, Gary SHAW, Peter WITHE, Gordon COWANS, Anthony MORLEY.
BESIKTAS
Rasim KARA (c), Samet AYBABA, Kadir AKBULUT, Ulvi GUVENIROGLU, Mehmet EKSI, Haluk SERENLI, Necdet ERGUN, Riza CALIMBAY, Ali Kemal DENIZCI, Bora OZTURK (Cakar HALUK HT), Fikret DEMIRER (Ziya DOGAN 70).

from the home crowd. It will not be easy for the players to adapt to the strange atmosphere in an almost deserted stadium, but I am sure that, as good professionals, our lads will adjust to the circumstances."

His prediction was spot on. Chief scout Malcolm Beard had undertaken a scouting mission to check out Besiktas during the run-up to the game, and his report proved to be invaluable. After just seven minutes, Peter Withe carried on where he had left off in Rotterdam in May. And unlike his winner against Bayern Munich, there was no mishit this time as he drilled a left-foot volley past Besiktas keeper Rasim Kara.

Three minutes later Tony Morley's well-placed shot – also with his left foot – put Villa two-up, and by the half-hour mark it was three, Dennis Mortimer firing home with his right from just inside the penalty area. All three goals were scored at the Holte End, although they were greeted by silence rather than tumultuous applause. Villa had found their own motivation without the backing of the fervent fans who had followed them through their triumphant Euro campaign the previous season.

Strangely, however, Barton's boys were unable to press home their advantage after the interval

When left is right…Tony Morley's well-placed shot puts Villa two-up against the Turks

Above: Morty on the mark – Skipper Dennis Mortimer fires home Villa's third goal against the Turks. Below: Calm before the storm - BRMB Radio's George Gavin waits to interview Peter Withe at training on the day before the second leg in the much warmer temperatures of Istanbul

against a team described by Leon Hickman of the Birmingham Evening Mail as "about the standard of Cambridge United". And when Mehemet Eksi reduced the deficit with a deflected 25-yarder that Jimmy Rimmer failed to hold, a pleasant stroll in the sun was suddenly transformed into an anxious finale. The visitors went close to scoring again in the closing minutes, and even at 3-1 down, they felt confident of achieving a 2-0 home win which would be enough to see them through to the second round – particularly as they would have the backing of a crowd as hostile as Villa's players and officials had ever encountered.

The second leg was also an afternoon game, kicking off at 4.30pm local time, but the contrast with the atmosphere at an empty Villa Park could not have been more extreme. Indeed, secretary Stride recalls the Inonu Stadium in Istanbul as the most intimidating ground he visited during his 35 years with the club.

"It was pretty frightening," he said. "The atmosphere was as hostile as anything I've experienced. Before the match, I went out with the players to look at the playing surface. The dressing rooms were under the

Allan Evans gets forward to fire a shot at goal during the second leg against Besiktas

pitch and you had to walk down a long corridor before climbing the steps into daylight. As we emerged, it was as if the whole place was about to collapse on our heads – the home fans went through what amounted to a war-cry from all corners of the ground. They chanted 'Besik-tas-yah!' over and over again, and all the time it kept getting faster and louder."

The stadium was full two hours before kick-off, so when Villa emerged again for the kick-off they were stepping into what *Evening Mail* reporter Martin Swain described as "a screaming cauldron of Turkish fervour." But Villa's players had learned a lot from their debut European Cup campaign and it soon became evident that Besiktas did not have the talent to match the gusto of their supporters. On a bumpy surface more akin to a parks pitch, Villa took control from the outset, Mortimer scraping a post with an angled drive inside four minutes. And although the visitors were ultimately unable to add to their two-goal advantage from the first leg, it became evident long before the end of an untidy 0-0 draw that nothing

First round, 2nd leg
BESIKTAS 0 ASTON VILLA 0
29th September 1982
Inonu Stadyumu, Istanbul
Att: 28,654

BESIKTAS
Adem IBRAHIMOGLU, Samet AYBABA, Kadir AKBULUT, Ulvi GUVENIROGLU, Mehmet EKSI (c), Haluk SERENLI, Necdet ERGUN, Ziya DOGAN, Ali Kemal DENIZCI, Fikret DEMIRER (Bora OZTURK 67), Cakar HALUK (Riza CALIMBAY 34).
ASTON VILLA
James RIMMER, Mark JONES, Gary WILLIAMS, Allan EVANS, Kenneth McNAUGHT, Dennis MORTIMER (c), Desmond BREMNER, Gary SHAW, Peter WITHE, Gordon COWANS, Anthony MORLEY.

was going to threaten their passage to round two.

The second-round draw paired Barton's men with Dinamo Bucharest, and after arriving in Romania ahead of the first leg, Villa's officials were taken for a look at their opponents' vast complex, which catered for a range of sports, including hockey, basketball and gymnastics, as well as football. To round off the tour, they were shown a huge gymnasium where dozens of youngsters were practising various routines, and were introduced to one of the coaches. She was Nadia Comaneci, the gymnast whose gold-medal achievements and sparkling personality had charmed TV viewers worldwide at the 1976 Olympic Games in Montreal.

But if Nadia greeted the Villa party with a beaming smile, the same could hardly be said for the grim-faced gentlemen in charge of Dinamo's football affairs. "They were constantly accompanied by stern-looking

A souvenir for Dan – A young Romanian, posing with soldiers, shows off Villa's European Champions pennant

individuals but we were never introduced," said Steve Stride. "I had the feeling these 'silent shadows' were security officers. Even when we were offered glasses of vodka, which we were expected to knock back in one, their faces never cracked. We couldn't quite understand why there was no sign of the security

Floodlit football, Bucharest style - The names of Villa's players shine brightly against a dark sky

people when Dinamo's directors arrived at our hotel at lunchtime on the day of the game. But we all piled into a limousine and I couldn't help noticing that that the limo picked up speed as we got closer to the centre of Bucharest.

"It was pretty hair-raising, particularly when we saw people leaping out of our way. But suddenly, we screeched to a halt and were ushered into a large hall. As we went inside, the limo roared away – it turned out the driver was giving the security officers the slip so they could show us a good time. For the next three hours or more, we all ate, drank, exchanged stories and sang songs. At one point, after a few straight vodkas, our hosts were even dancing on the tables!" It was a different story when the Dinamo people returned that evening to take their guests to the massive Stadionul 23 August. The security officers were back and Stride was greeted by a curt handshake from one of the officials who had earlier embraced him like a lifelong friend. "They had clearly been ordered not to socialise with us," said Stride. "Throughout the match, we all just sat there stone-faced."

It was certainly a surreal situation, the two sets of officials displaying absolutely no emotion while

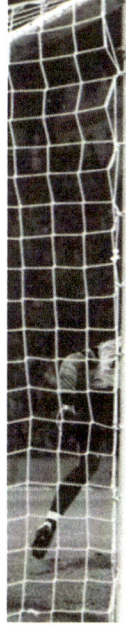

all around them fervent fans created an amazing atmosphere. And who knows what the outcome might have been had a 10th-minute shot from Cornel Talner hit the net rather than the top of the bar? That narrow escape, though, proved to be the catalyst for Villa to take control, the visitors responding with a swift counter-attack involving Colin Gibson and Tony Morley, whose accurate cross picked out Peter Withe at the far post. Rather than go for goal, Withe unselfishly headed the ball down for Gary Shaw to swivel and fire home right-footed from close range.

Left: Central defender Ken McNaught puts the Dinamo defence under pressure at the 23 August Stadium. Below: Thanks pal – Gary Shaw (partly obscured) fires Villa into the lead after Peter Withe (left) had unselfishly headed across the goalmouth

From that moment, the outcome was never in doubt. Morley repeatedly sprinted past Dinamo right-back Ion Marin to set up a succession of openings, one of which saw Dennis Mortimer unleash a drive which beat keeper Dimitru Moraru and hit the post, while Withe and Shaw both let chances slip from their grasp during a spell of second-half dominance.

Second round, 1st leg
DINAMO BUCURESTI 0 ASTON VILLA 2
20th October 1982
23 August Stadium
Att: 37,682
0-1 MORLEY (17) 0-2 SHAW (83)

DINAMO BUCURESTI
Dumitru MORARU, Ion MARIN, Teofil STREDIE, Ionel AUGUSTIN, Alexandru NICOLAE, Corneliu Constantin DINU (c), Cornel TALNAR, Gheorghe MULTESCU, Florea VAETUS (Pompiliu IORDACHE 75), Alexandru CUSTOV, Costel ORACA (Marin DRAGNEA HT).

ASTON VILLA
James RIMMER, Mark JONES, Colin GIBSON, Allan EVANS, Kenneth McNAUGHT, Dennis MORTIMER (c), Desmond BREMNER, Gary SHAW, Peter WITHE, Gordon COWANS, Anthony MORLEY.

Just when it looked as though Villa would have to settle for a single-goal victory, however, Morley once again reached the bye-line before swinging over a centre for the perfectly positioned Shaw to head in number two. The striker felt this was his best performance for quite a while, adding: "To score two away goals in a European game has to be very satisfying. Normally, there isn't much joy for strikers

Job done. Shaw clinches a 2-0 win with a fine header from Tony Morley's cross

Villa Park scene setters - Gary Shaw opens the scoring with a diving header (left) then heads home his second despite being clattered by Dinamo keeper Dumitru Moraru

because there is limited freedom when you are up against the man-to-man marking of continental teams."

If the club's directors had been bemused by the reception they were given in Romania, it was Dinamo's players who were inconvenienced before the second leg. Tucked up in bed on the night before the game, they were forced to leave their rooms when fire alarm bells started ringing at the Holiday Inn. The visiting party were convinced it was a prank by a Villa fan to disrupt their night's sleep, but the hotel's general manager Steve Carver assured them it was a genuine alarm and that the players had been evacuated for their own safety.

It wasn't the best preparation for the Turks, although Villa were just as impressive on home soil as they had been in Bucharest – with Shaw again in lethal form as they stormed into the quarter-finals with a 4-2 victory which took the aggregate score to an emphatic 6-2. Shaw's crisp, instinctive hat-trick took his personal haul for the tie to five, and the visitors were simply unable to cope. Just six minutes had been played when he opened the scoring with a diving header from Morley's cross, and although Gheorghe Multescu equalised after half an hour, it was merely a blip. Ten minutes after the interval, Shaw restored the lead when

Second round, 2nd leg
ASTON VILLA 4 DINAMO BUCURESTI 2
3rd November 1982, Villa Park, Att: 22,244
1-0 SHAW (6) 1-1 MULTESCU (31) 2-1 SHAW (53) 3-1 SHAW (67) 3-2 IORDACHE (72) 4-2 WALTERS (88)

ASTON VILLA
James RIMMER, Gary WILLIAMS, Colin GIBSON, Allan EVANS, Kenneth McNAUGHT, Dennis MORTIMER (c), Desmond BREMNER, Gary SHAW (Mark WALTERS 71), Peter WITHE, Gordon COWANS, Tony MORLEY.
DINAMO BUCURESTI
Dumitru MORARU, Ion MARIN, Teofil STREDIE, Marin DRAGNEA, Alexandru NICOLAE, Corneliu Constantin DINU (c), Cornel TALNAR, Gheorghe MULTESCU (Florea VAETUS 76), Pompiliu IORDACHE, Alexandru CUSTOV, Costel ORACA (Ionel AUGUSTIN HT).

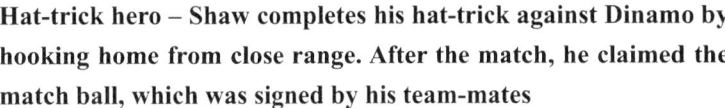

Hat-trick hero – Shaw completes his hat-trick against Dinamo by hooking home from close range. After the match, he claimed the match ball, which was signed by his team-mates

he headed in a Des Bremner cross despite being fouled by both Cornel Dinu and keeper Moraru, and on 69 minutes the hungry marksman completed his hat-trick by hooking home a shot from close range. Pompiliu Lordache reduced the deficit but it was no more than a consolation effort before sub Mark Walters – who had replaced the injured goal hero Shaw – made it 4-2.

Villa were through to the last eight for the second year running and in the space of just 14 months, they had become seasoned European Cup campaigners. In the quarter-final, they would face Italian giants Juventus, but in the meantime they had other business against foreign opposition. In December, they made the long journey to Tokyo, where they lost 2-0 to the South American champions, Penarol of Uruguay, in the World Club Championship, and the following month they won the European Super Cup, beating Barcelona 3-1 on aggregate.

The pulsating 3-0 second leg victory over Barca undoubtedly warmed the hearts of the Villa faithful that winter, but there was a spring chill in the air when Juventus arrived in the West Midlands for the first leg of the quarter-final at the beginning of March. Barton's men were caught cold when Paolo Rossi put the Italians ahead with a bullet header inside the near post after Villa were opened up down the left. It was the first time they had trailed in a European Cup-tie, and to say it sent a shiver down their spines would be an understatement. Their opponents, after all, were arguably the most star-studded team in the world, boasting French ace Michel

> **Quarter-final, 1st leg**
> **ASTON VILLA 1 JUVENTUS 2**
> **2nd March 1983, Villa Park, Att: 45,531**
> **0-1 ROSSI (1) 1-1 COWANS (51) 1-2 BONIEK (83)**
>
> **ASTON VILLA**
> Nigel SPINK, Gary WILLIAMS (Eamonn DEACY 40), Colin GIBSON, Desmond BREMNER, Kenneth McNAUGHT, Dennis MORTIMER (c), Andrew BLAIR, Gary SHAW, Peter WITHE, Gordon COWANS, Anthony MORLEY.
> **JUVENTUS**
> Dino ZOFF (c), Claudio GENTILE, Antonio CABRINI, Massimo BONINI, Sergio BRIO, Gaetano SCIREA, Roberto BETTEGA, Marco TARDELLI, Paolo ROSSI, Michel PLATINI, Zbigniew BONIEK.

Platini, the brilliant Pole Zbigniew Boniek and six members of the Italian team that had won the World Cup the previous summer – Rossi, Dino Zoff, Claudio Gentile, Marco Tardelli, Antonio Cabrini and Geatano Scirea.

For the opening 10 minutes or so, Villa's players simply froze, seemingly spellbound by the sheer quality of their opponents, who were described by John Wragg of the Daily Express as "a World Cup team thinly disguised as a club side." Even the otherwise impressive Colin Gibson was in such a state of bewilderment that he contrived to send a header against his own bar. Not that Villa were helped by referee Walter Eschweiler. In the 14th minute, Ken McNaught was convinced he had equalised when he headed home a Gordon Cowans corner, only for the German official to rule that an offence had been committed in the goalmouth – although the foul was a mystery that even repeated TV action replays could not uncover. And when Gary Shaw was brought down in the penalty area by Massimo Bonini, the Evening Mail's Leon Hickman observed that "the ref was so far

First post – Gary Shaw makes sure Juve defenders can't relax as they await a corner from the left

away that he would have needed binoculars to have been sure of a penalty offence."

But ten minutes after half-time, Barton's boys were level, Cowans playing the ball wide to Gibson and then darting into the penalty area to launch himself at the full-back's floated cross and send an unstoppable

Pure grit – Gordon Cowans launches himself to meet Colin Gibson's cross and head the equaliser against the Italian giants

header past keeper Dino Zoff. Sadly, there was no denying the class of the Serie A outfit under the guidance of renowned coach Giovanni Trapattoni. Platini set up Rossi for an 82nd-minute right-foot drive which Nigel Spink parried on to his left-hand post, but a couple of minutes later Platini's superb through ball enabled Boniek to drill home Juve's winner. In the end, Villa were undone by a Frenchman and a Pole.

Even so, the game is recalled fondly by Spink. "Whenever I see highlights from that one, it still makes the hairs stand up on the back of my neck," he said. "The atmosphere that night was incredible. It was as good as anything I experienced as a player, possibly because it was such a massive game against a team with jaw-dropping talent. We were the holders, but with the likes of Platini, Rossi, Bettega and Gentile, there was no doubt that Juve were the favourites. Even after Rossi scored inside a minute, Villa Park was really rocking, and the place erupted when Gordon Cowans equalised. It could have gone either way after that but we knew we were losing our grip on the trophy when Boniek scored that late winner."

That grip was well and truly relinquished in a one-sided second leg at a rain-lashed Stadio Comunale

Mark Walters takes evasive action from a desperate Juventus challenge in Turin

in Turin, where Juve gave Villa a football lesson and went one better than the first leg with a comfortable 3-1 scoreline. It would have been a daunting task in any circumstances, but Villa certainly weren't helped by errors by two normally dependable players. Spink, the hero in Rotterdam nine months earlier, was a villain in Turin as he allowed a harmless Platini shot through his legs with just 15 minutes on the clock. And after Marco Tardelli had headed Juve's second, McNaught's hesitancy allowed Platini to nip in and make it 3-0. The demolition job was complete, although Villa at least managed a consolation goal nine minutes from time when Withe headed in Gibson's cross from the left.

The Evening Mail headline declared that Villa had suffered some "Turin torture", reporter Ian Willars writing that "England's proud standing as the club kings of Europe took a severe battering." For six successive years, English clubs had ruled supreme by being crowned European champions, Villa's glorious 1982 triumph following three wins for

Quarter-final, 2nd leg
JUVENTUS 3 ASTON VILLA 1
16th March 1983
Stadio Olimpico, Turin
Att: 65,941
1-0 PLATINI (14) 2-0 TARDELLI (27) 3-0 PLATINI (68) 3-1 WITHE (81)

JUVENTUS
Dino ZOFF (c), Claudio GENTILE, Antonio CABRINI, Massimo BORINI, Sergio BRIO (Giuseppe FURINO 62), Gaetano SCIREA, Roberto BETTEGA, Marco TARDELLI, Paolo ROSSI, Michel PLATINI, Zbigniew BONIEK.
ASTON VILLA
Nigel SPINK, Gary WILLIAMS, Colin GIBSON, Allan EVANS, Kenneth McNAUGHT, Dennis MORTIMER (c), Desmond BREMNER, Gary SHAW, Peter WITHE, Gordon COWANS, Mark WALTERS.

GOALSCORER WITHE DOWN AND OUT IN TURIN

Liverpool and, a lot more improbably, two for Nottingham Forest. But on the night Barton's team were tormented in Turin, Liverpool also made their exit, losing to Polish club Widzew Lodz. Juventus defeated Widzew in the semis but even their silky skills came up short as SV Hamburg won the final in Athens.

MEANS OF COMMUNICATION

Among the 167 people recorded as the official attendance at the behind-closed-doors game against Besiktas was Villa fan Peter Stokes, who was working as a communications engineer supplying telephone and radio links for the press all over Europe. And Peter, pictured below in the Trinity Road stand on that surreal afternoon, believes he is the only supporter to have been in both the highest and lowest crowds ever recorded for Villa first-team home games.

As a boy, he attended the FA Cup quarter-final against Derby County, when a record 76,588 packed into Villa Park. "Along with many small boys, I remember being passed over the heads of the men on the open terrace at the Witton End," he said. "We were passed down to the very front to peer through the iron railings to watch the game at ground level. I had a much better view of the game against Besiktas!"

DON'T FORGET THE DOLL!

Harry Lawrence brought a Turkish delight home from Villa's first-round away game against Besiktas, but it certainly wasn't edible. The lifelong supporter, who had first watched Villa before the Second World War, revealed that he had the blessing of his wife Carol to

follow the team wherever they played in Europe – on one condition. "She tells me to go," he said. "It's okay as long as I bring back a doll from each country to show where I've been!"

Although he was born near Villa Park, Harry had moved to the south in 1947 and in the early 1980s was chairman of the London branch of the Villa supporters club. Four years before the Turkey trip, he struck up a friendship with Gordon Cowans, with whom he is pictured above at 35,000 feet, having met the midfielder at an England match in Copenhagen.

GETTING SHIRTY....

Football supporters love replica shirts, particularly ones which are worn only occasionally by their favourite team. But when Villa were forced to amend their design for European matches in 1982-83, the alternative shirt never went on general sale. The difference was that the club badge, normally positioned in the centre of the shirt, was moved to the left, with the emblem of shirt manufacturers Le Coq Sportif on the right.

"Our normal strip has the emblem on both sleeves," said secretary Steve Stride. "But when we play in Europe, only so many square centimetres of advertising are allowed."

1982-83

We are the super kings

Villa had already followed in the footsteps of Manchester United, Liverpool and Nottingham Forest by becoming the fourth English club to win the European Cup. Now their aim was to emulate the latter two by adding the UEFA Super Cup to their trophy cabinet. Liverpool had thrashed Hamburg 7-1 over two legs in 1977, while Forest had edged out Barcelona 2-1 on aggregate two years later. On both occasions, it was a triumph for the First Division champions over the cup-holders from Germany and Spain respectively. Could Villa make it a hat-trick?

Like Forest in 1979, Tony Barton's men came up against the might of Barcelona, the 1982 Super Cup showdown actually being played in January 1983, at a time when Villa still had their sights on a second consecutive European Cup triumph. The first leg took them back to the Camp Nou, scene of their UEFA Cup exit nearly five years earlier, although not surprisingly the Villa line-up was vastly different to their previous visit to Catalonia. Only Ken McNaught, Dennis Mortimer and Gordon Cowans remained from the team beaten 2-1 by Barca in March 1978. If the personnel had changed considerably, though, the outcome was very similar – another narrow defeat as Marcos Alonso's 25-yard drive took a wicked deflection to leave Nigel Spink helpless and give the Spaniards a 1-0 win. In truth, the margin could have been wider, with the visitors subsequently having to survive several nerve-jangling moments.

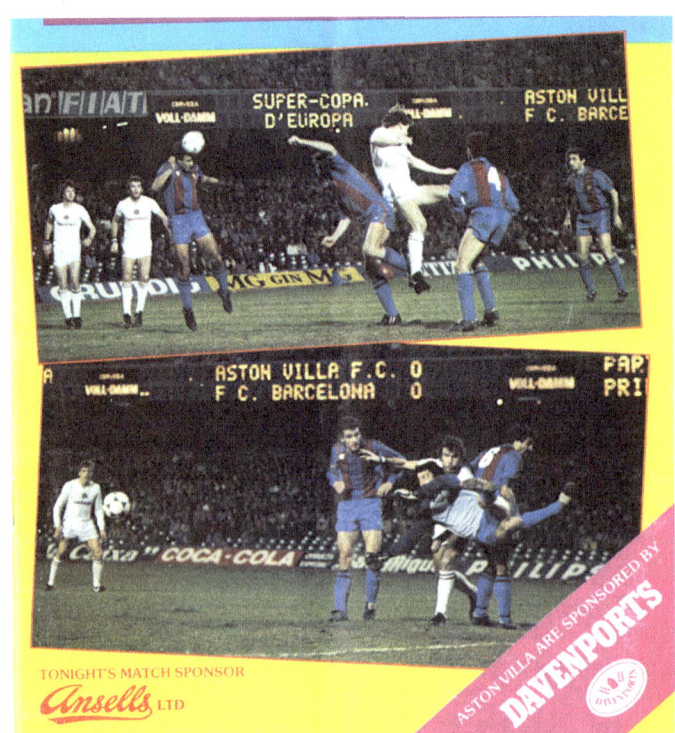

Images from Villa's testing night at the Camp Nou - as shown on the front of programme for the return leg.

The Spanish press and public regarded it as Barca's best performance of the 1982-83 campaign, and Tony Barton readily acknowledged it had somewhat been a backs-to-the-wall effort by his

Sharing the armband around

Above: In front of what is clearly a below-capacity crowd, Barcelona skipper Jose Sanchez goes through the familiar routine as he exchanges pennants at the Nou Camp with Dennis Mortimer – but Ken McNaught was his side's acting captain (right) at Villa Park for the second leg.

European Super Cup, 1st leg
BARCELONA 1 ASTON VILLA 0
19th January 1983, Camp Nou, 35,000
1-0 ALONSO PENA (52)

BARCELONA		ASTON VILLA	
1	Francisco URRUTICOECHEA GONZALEZ	1	Nigel SPINK
2	Jose Vicente SANCHEZ FELIP (c)	2	Mark JONES (73)
3	Miguel BERNARDO BIANQUETI	3	Allan EVANS
4	Julio Albert MORENO CASAS	4	Kenneth McNAUGHT
5	Miguel Angel PERICO ALONSO (76)	5	Gary WILLIAMS
6	Jose Ramon ALEXANCO VENTOSA	6	Desmond BREMNER
7	Marcos ALONSO PENA	7	Dennis MORTIMER (c)
8	Bernd SCHUSTER	8	Gordon COWANS
9	Enrique CASTRO GONZALEZ (70)	9	Gary SHAW
10	Victor MUNOZ MANRIQUE	10	Peter WITHE
11	Francisco Jose CARRASCO HIDALGO	11	Anthony MORLEY
Subs:			
12	Urbano ORTEGA CUADOS (5)	12	Colin GIBSON (2)
13	Angel ALONSO HERRERA (9)		

players, but at least Villa went into the return match with a fighting chance. Fighting was an apt description of what unfolded at Villa Park in the second leg. There hadn't been a single booking at the Camp Nou but as Barcelona desperately attempted to cling to their slender advantage, the return clash turned into a bruising, brawling contest. Belgian referee Alexis Ponnet clamped down with 10 bookings – including seven for Barcelona – while three players were sent off.

Allan Evans and Julio Alberto were both dismissed after committing second bookable offences, while Alonso – scorer of the goal which had given Barca their advantage at the Camp Nou – was given

a straight red after an off-the-ball foul on substitute Mark Walters in extra-time. Barca coach Udo Lattek commented bitterly afterwards that this wasn't a football match and the Evening Mail's Ian Johnson concurred. "As a boxing correspondent, it was more like being at the ringside," wrote Johnson, who accused Barca of "blatant cheating, time-wasting and blood-chilling tackling."

"All hell let loose…" Players from both sides are involved in angry exchanges on a stormy night at Villa Park

While the yellow and red card statistics made

The relief is all too evident as Gary Shaw and his team-mates celebrate after the striker swept home the goal which sent the Super Cup clash to extra-time

grim reading, however, the scoreline was a sheer delight – 3-0 to Villa after extra-time, giving them a 3-1 aggregate success which had seemed highly unlikely approaching the final 10 minutes of normal time. Until the 79th minute, the visitors' cynical strongarm tactics had enabled them to keep their first-leg lead intact. But when Andy Blair floated a teasing ball into the penalty area, Des Bremner side-footed it across the face of goal and Gary Shaw pounced to fire Villa ahead on the night and level on aggregate. Peter Withe also played a part in the goal, albeit one that would surely have been punished by at least a yellow card had it been spotted. The striker elbowed Migueli as Shaw lined up his shot, leaving the

European Super Cup, 2nd leg
ASTON VILLA 3 BARCELONA 0 (aet)
26th January 1983, Villa Park, 31,570
1-0 SHAW (80) 2-0 COWANS pen (100) 3-0 McNAUGHT (104)

ASTON VILLA		BARCELONA	
1	Nigel SPINK	1	Francisco Javier URRUTICOECHEA GONZALEZ
2	Gary WILLIAMS	2	Jose Vicente SANCHEZ FELIP (c)
3	Allan EVANS	3	Migel BERNARDO BIANQUETI
4	Kenneth McNAUGHT (c)	4	Julio Alberto MORENO CASAS
5	Colin GIBSON	5	Urbano ORTEGA CUADROS
6	Andrew BLAIR	6	Jose Ramon ALEXANCO VENTOSA
7	Desmond BREMNER	7	Marcos ALONSO PENA (120)
8	Gary SHAW (113)	8	Bernd SCHUSTER
9	Peter WITHE	9	Miguel Angel PERICO ALONSO
10	Gordon COWANS	10	Victor MUNOZ MARIQUE
11	Anthony MORLEY (75)	11	Francisco Jose CARRASCO HIDALGO
Subs:			
12	Paul BIRCH (9)	12	Enrique CASTRO GONZALEZ (11)
13	Mark WALTERS (11)	13	Jose Manuel MARTINEZ TORAL (12, 55 min)

On the spot – Gordon Cowans blasts home the rebound after his extra-time penalty was saved by Barca keeper Francisco Urruitcoechea

defender on the floor and needing stitches in a split lip.

Then came the flashpoint for which this famous night is best remembered. Nine minutes into extra-time, Walters was tripped by Jose Sanchez, and Ponnet pointed to the penalty spot. Gordon Cowans admits that his memory of most of his 527 Villa games is vague, but he has never forgotten what occurred next. "The Barcelona players spent so much time arguing with the referee about his decision that when I stepped up to the ball, I hit the worst penalty of my career," he recalled "I normally put them in the bottom corner but this time I hit it only a yard to the keeper's left and he managed to parry it. Fortunately the ball came straight back to me and I smashed it into the net. I followed it over the line and hit it against the net for a second time in sheer delight – only for the keeper to kick my legs from under me! All hell let loose in the goalmouth, with players squaring up to each other before the ref managed to calm things down. It was one of the most physical games I ever played in."

Super Mac – Ken McNaught is mobbed by team-mates after launching himself to meet a Cowans free-kick for the diving header which put Villa beyond Barca's reach

Ken McNaught, captain in the absence of the injured Dennis Mortimer, sealed victory a few minutes later with a fine diving header after Cowans had whipped in a free-kick from the left. It was then a matter of seeing out the second period of extra-time. At one stage, Villa were saluted by shouts of "Ole!" as they kept possession and had the Spanish giants chasing shadows, only for Allan Evans to misplace a pass and then send Urbano Ortego sprawling as he attempted to atone for his error. It was a reckless challenge which earned the Scottish centre-back a second yellow card, followed by an inevitable red.

The offence would ultimately prove costly for Villa, with Evans suspended for the next UEFA match – the first leg of the European Cup quarter-final against Juventus. But that was the last thing on the minds of the claret-and-blue faithful as McNaught was presented with the trophy, which was a plaque rather than a cup, and the players celebrated on the pitch. Aston Villa were the Super kings of Europe.

Villa's players proudly parade the UEFA Super Cup – or maybe Super Shield would be a better description. Back row: Gary Williams, Colin Gibson, Peter Withe, Nigel Spink, Gary Shaw. Front: Andy Blair, Des Bremner, Mark Walters, Ken McNaught, Gordon Cowans, Tony Morley. Top: The super shield – McNaught holds the trophy aloft

1983-84

Cold comfort from the KGB

Villa launched their 1983-84 UEFA Cup campaign in the Portuguese wine region of Vinho Verde, which literally translates as green wine. As you might imagine, the wine isn't that colour – but Tony Barton's men might have been described as green on this occasion. The outcome of their opening match wasn't nearly as catastrophic as the club's 4-1 mauling in Antwerp eight years earlier, but a single-goal setback at the hands of Vitoria Guimaraes wasn't exactly what the manager and his players had in mind when they arrived in Portugal.

With just eight minutes remaining, Villa looked set to return home with a satisfying goalless draw. But one calamitous moment undermined their hard work of the previous 82 minutes. When Steve McMahon innocuously challenged Vitoria's most dangerous player Francisco Saura – more commonly known as Paquito – French referee Joel Quiniou pointed to the penalty spot. Villa's players were convinced Paquito had taken a dive but the official wasn't going to change his mind, leaving full-back Gregorio Penteado to send his kick past Nigel Spink. In that moment, the whole context of the evening changed, as skipper Dennis Mortimer readily acknowledged. "It's down to inexperience," he said after the game. "European football is all about patience. When we stayed on the ball and played simple short passes, we looked as if we could do something. But we let ourselves down by losing the discipline to do that."

The costly late lapse would have been of no great consequence had Villa taken their chances. But Peter Withe saw an early volley well saved by keeper Silvino Almeida and Allan Evans was guilty of squandering two chances. That was a big relief to the capacity crowd, plus hundreds of other Vitoria supporters who had a free view from the tall trees round the ground and nearby apartments. A dozen or so others were perched on a crane being used for the construction of a new stand. They had to be careful not to get too excited when Vitoria scored.

First round, 1st leg
VITORIA 1 ASTON VILLA 0
14th September 1983, Estadio Afonso Henriques, 12,000

1-0 PENTEADO FREIXO (82 pen)
VITORIA
Silvano ALMEIDA LOURO, Gregorio PENTEADO FREIXO, Amandio RAMIRO BARREIRAS, Alfredo FERREIRA SILVA MURCA, Alfredo MAGAHAES SILVA RODRIGUES, Nivaldo GOMES DA SILVA (c), Antonio Joacquim BARRINHA (84), Francisco SAURA, Eldon Armond BRAVO, Jose Severino DA SILVA (57), Joaquim Fernando MURCA. Subs: Flavio Jose DAS NEVES (7), Orlando Antonio FONSECA COSTA (10).
ASTON VILLA
Nigel SPINK, Gary WILLIAMS, Colin GIBSON, Allan EVANS (c), Brendan ORMSBY, Dennis MORTIMER, Alan CURBISHLEY, Paul David RIDEOUT (Anthony MORLEY 81), Peter WITHE, Stephen McMAHON, Andrew BLAIR (Mark WALTERS 71).

Driving force – Villa's players and officials pose with directors of the Austin Rover dealership in Portugal

If the result was a big disappointment, at least it was a pleasant trip for supporters who travelled with the official party to northern Portugal's main wine-growing region. Apart from the flight, hotel and match ticket, their package also included a tour of the Sandeman wine cellars near Oporto. Villa's players and officials, meanwhile, brought the main thoroughfare in Oporto to a standstill when they arrived for a visit to club sponsor Austin Rover's main dealership in the area.

Poor Gary Shaw and Des Bremner went nowhere, the striker and the midfielder both staying behind at Bodymoor Heath to continue their recovery from injuries. It was the first time Shaw had missed a Villa European trip since he broke into the first team, and he admitted: "It seemed very strange and quiet at the training ground, especially as the youth team were away at the same time. I listened to the match on the radio and from what I could gather the team were playing comfortably until that dubious penalty."

He couldn't have known it at the time, but Shaw would never play another European game for Villa. Although deemed fit enough to be among the substitutes for the second leg, he remained on the bench and was also ruled out of both legs of the second-round tie against Spartak Moscow.

Ahead of the return game against Guimaraes, Shaw was Villa's leading Euro scorer with nine goals, and was the only player from the club to have scored a hat-trick in a European tie. As he watched from the bench at Villa Park, he saw his long-time striking partner Peter Withe edging to within one goal of his total with a treble of his own which sent the Portuguese visitors packing. Less than two minutes had been played when Withe headed the opening goal from Tony Morley's prefect cross to bring the tie level on aggregate. Yet Villa were

Withe super finishing like this.....

Peter Withe leans in for a fine header that was fumbled over the line by keeper Silvano Almeida for his and his side's second goal. Below: Four-midable – full-back Colin Gibson slots home the fourth following an unlikely excursion.

sluggish for long periods of the first half and it was only after the break that they asserted their authority.

Withe's 49th-minute header was fumbled over the line by Silvano, and five minutes later Brendan Ormsby glanced home a Mortimer corner to effectively book his team's passage to the second round. And after that the Villa faithful savoured what amounted to a claret-and-blue carnival. Colin Gibson, regarded by many at that time as the best attacking full-back in the country, skipped past two defenders to slide home number four before Withe powered home a shot which completed his treble and an

emphatic 5-0 victory. Despite their shortcomings in Portugal, it seemed Villa were not so green after all.

Next up was another long trek to the Eastern Bloc, this time to Moscow and the very heart of Communism. There was culture galore before the first leg against Spartak, but also a feeling that visitors – even footballers – were not to be trusted. "Excursions were arranged for members of the official party," recalled secretary Steve Stride. "We went to the Kremlin, Lenin's Tomb and Red Square. But you were always left with the impression of being shown only what they wanted you to see."

There was quite a panic when Villa president Trevor Gill went missing during the tour of Red Square. Heading back to the hotel, the coach accompanied by police motorcyclists at both the front and

> First round, 2nd leg
> ASTON VILLA 5 VITORIA 0
> 28th September 1983, Villa Park, Att: 23,732
>
> 1-0 WITHE (2) 2-0 WITHE (48) 3-0 ORMSBY (58) 4-0 GIBSON (76) 5-0 WITHE (90)
> ASTON VILLA
> Nigel SPINK, Gary WILLIAMS, Colin GIBSON, Allan EVANS (c), Brendan ORMSBY, Dennis MORTIMER, Alan CURBISHLEY, Mark WALTERS, Peter WITHE, Stephen McMAHON, Anthony MORLEY.
> VITORIA
> Silvano ALMEIDA LOURO, Gregorio PENTEADO FREIXO (c), Amandio RAMIRO BARREIRAS, Alfredo FERREIRA SILVA MURCA , Alfredo MAGAHAES SILVA RODRIGUES, Nivaldo GOMES DA SILVA, Flavio Jose DAS NEVES, Francisco SAURA, Eldon Armond BRAVO, Joaquim Fernando MURCA, Orlando Antonio FONSECA COSTA (Julio Carlos DA COSTA AUGUSTO 57)

Relaxing in Russia – Peter Withe tries on a hat he borrowed from a local in Moscow, although his short sleeves suggest he wasn't too cold

the rear, it suddenly occurred to Stride that the president wasn't on board. He informed the Spartak officials, and the reaction could not have been more dramatic. "Before I knew it, there were sirens wailing and lights flashing as we performed a U-turn on a busy dual carriageway," said Stride. "It was hair-raising to say the least. The Spartak people were clearly concerned what might happen if Trevor was left on his own for long but thankfully he was still standing there. He had a worried look on his face but it soon turned to a broad smile as he saw the coach approaching."

The Villa contingent were also offered a visit to the Bolshoi Ballet or a tour of the British Embassy. Stride opted for the latter, primarily because it offered the opportunity to phone home, calls to the UK having proved pretty much impossible from the hotel. As he was shown around the embassy, Steve chatted with the staff then asked if he could call England. The response was total silence but he was led into a room and

A good man for fostering east-west relations....captain for the night Allan Evans exchanges pennants with Spartak skipper and keeper Rinat Dasavev

pointed towards a desk with a red telephone. As he started dialling, he looked up and saw a notice which warned, in large bold letters: BE CAREFUL, THIS CONVERSATION IS BEING LISTENED TO.

"I certainly didn't have any Soviet secrets," he said. "But it was an eerie feeling knowing that every word I uttered was being monitored by the KGB." Stride also suspected for a while that his opposite number in the Spartak set-up may be on the payroll of the Russian secret service, because he was subdued and seemed reluctant to make any sort of conversation.

On the day of the game, the Spartak secretary arrived at Villa's hotel while the team were having lunch and said he needed a word in private. "He led me away to another room and I wondered what I had done wrong," said Stride. "I still didn't have a clue when he reached inside his coat pocket but he broke into a smile for the first time since we had met – and handed me a tin of caviar!"

It was a tasty appetiser to a game which attracted a crowd of 50,400 to the Dynamo Stadium, Spartak having switched the match from their own smaller home. The main course proved to be a compelling contest in which honours were even at 2-2, with the visitors suffering just a touch of indigestion after they were denied victory by a debatable stoppage-time penalty. When Vladimir Sochnov toppled over as a result of a Brendan Ormsby challenge, it looked innocuous, to say the least. If the incident had come in the modern game the Russian might even have been booked for diving but without even consulting his linesman – whose flag stayed down – referee Roger Shoefers awarded a penalty which Yuri Gavriov side-footed calmly past Nigel Spink as the keeper dived the wrong way.

Second round, 1st leg
SPARTAK MOSKVA 2 ASTON VILLA 2
19th October 1983, Dynamo Stadium, Att: 50,400

0-1 GIBSON (47) 1-1 GAVRILOV (51) 1-2 WALTERS (67) 2-2 GAVRILOV (89 pen)
SPARTAK MOSKVA
Rinat DASAEV (c), Vladimir SOCHNOV, Boris POZDNIAKOV, Sergei BAZULEV, Aleksandr BUBNOV, Evgeni KUZNETSOV (Yuri REZNIK 72), Sergei RODIONOV, Gennadi MOROZOV, Yuri GAVRILOV, Fyodor CHERENKOV, Sergei ARGUDIAEV (Valeri GLADILIN 64).
ASTON VILLA
Nigel SPINK, Gary WILLIAMS, Colin GIBSON, Allan EVANS (c), Brendan ORMSBY, Dennis MORTIMER, Desmond BREMNER, Mark WALTERS, Peter WITHE, Stephen McMAHON, Anthony MORLEY.

That was Gavriov's second goal, his first having been converted at close-range in the 52nd minute as Villa's defence faltered for the only time in the match. By contrast, both Villa goals were crackers. Two minutes after half-time Colin Gibson made a forceful run down the left before firing past keeper Rinat Dasaev and inside the near post, while Mark Walters restored the lead with a simply brilliant goal, a precise left-footer which was delivered with power and accuracy from the right-hand edge of the penalty area.

Allan Evans climbs for a header against in Moscow, while Peter Withe has to settle for a watching brief

Lost in translation – the scoreboard in Moscow, showing Villa 2-1 ahead in the first leg against Spartak

As the main headline in the Villa News & Record observed amid a play on words, it was a case of "All Square in Moscow". With a couple of away goals as a touch of insurance, though, Barton's boys went into the return match two weeks later with high hopes of progressing to the third round. But once again they suffered an agonising late blow – one from which there was to be no way back. Writing in the Evening Mail, Leon Hickman described it as "an inhumanly cruel twist of fortune", adding: "The second tie ended seconds before the final whistle, just as the first had, with a goal that must have been brought along as a travelling talisman from the Dynamo Stadium."

The outlook had been so promising when Peter Withe powered home a second-minute header to claim his ninth goal in European competition but in truth, there could be no complaints about the final outcome. Some of Spartak's one-touch passing was a sheer delight and they outplayed Villa for long periods. Fyodor Cherenkov brought the score level just after half-time, and the Russians contrived to squander opportunity after opportunity before Cherenkov's curling shot deflected past Spink off Dennis Mortimer to give them a 2-1 victory on the night and a precious passage to the third round.

The Russians had been so adventurous and entertaining that they were applauded off by home supporters choking back the disappointment of seeing their team eliminated just when an away-goals success was imminent. Villa's squad that night included eight players who had been involved against Bayern Munich in Rotterdam 18 months earlier but for most of them it was their last taste of European action.

> **Second round, 2nd leg**
> **ASTON VILLA 1 SPARTAK MOSKVA 2**
> **2nd November 1983, Villa Park, Att: 29,511**
>
> **1-0 WITHE (2) 1-1 CHERENKOV (46) 1-2 CHERENKOV (90)**
> **ASTON VILLA**
> Nigel SPINK, Mark JONES, Colin GIBSON, Allan EVANS (c), Brendan ORMSBY, Dennis MORTIMER, Desmond BREMNER, Mark WALTERS, Peter WITHE, Stephen McMAHON, Anthony MORLEY.
> **SPARTAK MOSKVA**
> Rinat DASAEV (c), Vladimir SOCHNOV, Boris POZDNIAKOV, Sergei BAZULEV, Aleksandr BUBNOV, Evgeni KUZNETSOV, Valeri GLADILIN, Gennadi MOROZOV, Yuri GAVRILOV, Fyodor CHERENKOV, Sergei RODIONOV.

MOSCOW EXPRESSWAY!

Villa had more than 2,500 fans cheering them on in Moscow – from a building in the shadow of the Aston Expressway. Although only 22 supporters went on the official trip to Russia, interest in the tie was such that the club arranged a satellite beaming of the game to the old Aston Villa Leisure Centre.

Fans were able to follow the action on a giant screen in what amounted to an indoor Holte End, and they were treated to more than just a football match in an extravaganza masterminded by commercial manager Tony Stephens. Gordon Cowans and Gary Shaw, who were both recovering from injury, joined Brian Little – by then the club's youth team coach – on a panel chaired by Beacon Radio sports editor Pat Foley. Little also linked up with Radio WM's Paul Franks during the interval to provide comments on the first half – and there was even a special programme printed for the event.

PRESS 4 FANS 2

Villa's foreign trips in the early 1980s occasionally featured matches involving the reporters who accompanied the team to foreign fields. In March 1983, before the away leg against Juventus, a British Press team beat their Italian counterparts in dreadful conditions in Turin. The weather was much better in Portugal in September when the press boys organised another game, this time against Villa fans who had travelled on the official club flight.

The press team were captained by former non-League defender Pat Foley and won the eight-a-side game 4-2 with two goals from BRMB's George Gavin plus one each from Dave Wigley of Radio WM and Villa secretary Steve Stride. Paul Harvey and Dave Bridgewater netted for the VIP Supporters.

A VETERAN ABROAD

Veteran Villa supporter William Johnson had travelled the world as he approached his 80th birthday. But the Spartak tie enabled him to make his first visit to Moscow. Bill, who had followed the club's fortunes for 60 years, was among the small group of fans on the official trip. "The attraction of Moscow and the friendship I found on other trips with Villa made up mind," he said. "I wasn't let down. We had a wonderful reception and I'm pleased I've been there."

Are you watching, Bill? Tony Morley slips past Gennady Morozov at the Dynamo Stadium. Perimeter advertising was a new feature in Russia at the time

1990-91

Probably your best goal ever?

It had been five long years since English clubs had blazed a trail across the Continent, but in September 1990 Villa had the honour of being one of the first teams to return to European competition. The ban imposed in the wake of the Heysel disaster had been lifted, although UEFA deemed that it was still too soon for Liverpool to be re-admitted after their part in the incidents which led to the deaths of 39 Juventus fans before the 1985 European Cup final in Brussels.

So when English clubs were allowed back, it was in the form of FA Cup winners Manchester United in the Cup Winners' Cup, and Villa – runners-up to Liverpool in the 1989-90 title race – in the UEFA Cup. Graham Taylor had masterminded Villa's excellent First Division campaign but had departed to become England coach and been replaced by the first foreign manager in the club's history, although not the one that had been predicted in the local press. According to a front-page story in the Birmingham Evening Mail that summer, Franz Beckenbauer was the man Doug Ellis had in mind as Taylor's successor. As the Mail's Villa reporter at the time, I wrote that story after receiving a tip-off from a reliable source, and although it never came to fruition, the chairman revealed in his autobiography Deadly eight years later that the German legend had, indeed, been his initial target.

When the club's first foreign manager was unveiled in 1990, though, it wasn't Beckenbauer, but someone very few people in this country were even aware of. Ellis opened the late-summer press conference with the words: "Does anyone know this man?" He was greeted by silence. The new boss was Dr Jozef Venglos, who had recently guided unfancied Czechoslovakia to the World Cup quarter-finals. And sadly, despite the fact he was well versed in European football, it was an appointment that simply didn't work out. At the end of the season, after Villa had narrowly avoided relegation, Dr Jo graciously acknowledged that he wasn't suited to the English game and departed by mutual consent.

One thing had become evident long before then. Villa's

A big night for all concerned, including (pictured here on the programme cover) Joe Venglos and his assistant, John Ward

new manager was not at all popular in Ostrava, home of Villa's first-round UEFA Cup opponents. Only one Banik player, skipper Viliam Hyravy, had been selected for the Czech squad at Italia 90 – and even he had seen no action throughout the finals. "People wondered how we should finish runners-up in the league two years running and yet not have a single player playing in the World Cup," said Banik's general manager Jan Pavliska during the build-up to the first leg at Villa Park. "He [Venglos] is not popular here because of that. But by

Take Platt – David Platt's aerial attempt to claim his second goal of the night is thwarted at Banik keeper Pavel Srnicek punches clear. Srnicek signed for Newcastle United the following year

appointing him, Villa have someone who is tremendously experienced and knows Czech football very well. You might say they are 1-0 up already."

In reality, it was Banik who went 1-0 up. After Villa's return to the European stage had been marked by the release of 10,000 claret and blue balloons, accompanied by commentary of the 1982 final in Rotterdam, the welcome-back party threatened to fall flat when the visitors grabbed a 31st-minute lead through Radomir Chylek. Not only were Villa behind, they had also conceded a goal which would count double in the event of the aggregate scores being level. Thankfully, the situation was rectified before home players and supporters had time to worry unduly about it. Within a minute, Gordon Cowans curled in a free-kick from the right and when Banik defenders made a mess of their attempted clearance David

Platt drove home left-footed from close range. It was the first goal scored by an English club in a European tie for more than five years.

Thirteen minutes after the interval, Platt played a short pass back into the path of Chris Price, who burst into the danger zone before Derek Mountfield virtually took the

First round, 1st leg
ASTON VILLA 3 BANIK OSTRAVA 1
19th September 1990, Villa Park, Att: 27,317

0-1 CHYLEK (31) 1-1 PLATT (32) 2-1 MOUNTFIELD (57) 3-1 OLNEY (79)
ASTON VILLA
Nigel SPINK, Chris PRICE, Stuart GRAY (c), Paul McGRATH, Derek MOUNTFIELD, Kent NIELSEN, Tony DALEY, David PLATT, Kevin GAGE (Ian ORMONDROYD HT), Gordon COWANS, Anthony CASCARINO (Ian OLNEY 57).
BANIK OSTRAVA
Pavel SRNICEK, Zbynek OLLENDER, Pavel KUBANEK, Karel KULA, Petr SKARABELA, Roman SIALINI, Radomir CHYLEK, Ivo STAS (c), Dusan HORVATH, Radim NECAS, Jan PALINEK.

Up in arms – Defender Derek Mountfield savours the moment after firing Villa ahead against Banik

ball off his toe. Not that the right-back was complaining as Mountfield's powerful right-foot drive left keeper Jan Palinek helpless. And on 79 minutes, Villa completed a triumphant UEFA Cup return when Cowans delivered another teasing free-kick, this time from the left, and substitute Ian Olney climbed in front of Palinek to score with a fine header.

All three goals were well taken, although Mountfield's effort carried extra significance. He had been a member of Everton's title-winning team in 1984-85 (when they also won the European Cup Winners' Cup), only to be denied the opportunity of a second Euro adventure as a result of the UEFA ban. "To win the league and then play in the European Cup was everyone's ambition and we had really fancied ourselves to go and do well in it," said the central defender. "To have it taken away from you like that was really hard to swallow and soul-destroying, so it felt good to be back in European competition a few years on. People seemed to

Nice to see you again - Stuart Gray goes through the pre-match formalities in Ostrava with his counterpart, Ivo Stas

Czech-mates – Villa line up ahead of the second leg against Banik. Back row: Derek Mountfield, Nigel Spink, Kent Nielsen, Ian Ormondroyd, Mark Blake, Ian Olney, Lee Butler, Paul McGrath, Andy Comyn, Dwight Yorke. Front: Paul Birch, Tony Daley, Chris Price, Stuart Gray, David Platt, Gordon Cowans

think I was an experienced player regarding Europe but before Villa qualified I'd only played one season."

Those late goals from Mountfield and Olney meant Villa travelled to Czechoslovakia for the return match with a two-goal cushion but knowing that they walked a fine line because a 2-0 defeat would see them eliminated on the away-goals rule. Such a scenario wasn't beyond the realms of possibility when Banik went ahead three minutes before half-time at the Bazaly Stadium, a Radim Necas free-kick taking a deflection past Nigel Spink.

But by the hour mark, any such fears had been well and truly dispelled. Mountfield, clearly determined to make up for lost time in Europe, drilled home a 52nd-minute equaliser after a Cowans corner from the right was headed on by Kent Nielsen at the near post. And nine minutes later a Cowans

Gordon Cowans and Derek Mountfield can't disguise their delight after Villa won 2-1 in Czechoslovakia to complete a 5-2 aggregate victory

First round, 2nd leg
BANIK OSTRAVA 1 ASTON VILLA 2
3rd October 1990, Bazaly Stadium, Att: 13,544
1-0 NECAS (42) 1-1 MOUNTFIELD (52) 1-2 STAS og (59)

BANIK OSTRAVA
Ivo SCHMUCKER, Pavel KUBANEK, Dusan HORVATH, Karel KULA, Petr SKARABELA, Roman SIALINI, Radomir CHYLEK (Radek BASTA 74), Ivo STAS (c), Zbynek OLLENDER, Radim NECAS, Dusan VRTO.
ASTON VILLA
Nigel SPINK, Chris PRICE, Stuart GRAY (c), Paul McGRATH, Derek MOUNTFIELD, Kent NIELSEN, Tony DALEY, David PLATT, Ian OLNEY, Gordon COWANS, Ian ORMONDROYD.

free-kick skimmed off the head of home skipper Ivo Stas and beyond the reach of keeper Ivo Schmucker. With a comfortable 5-2 aggregate victory in the bank, Villa faced a much more formidable hurdle in the second round after being drawn against Italian giants Inter Milan.

One glance at the Inter squad was enough to reveal the size of the task. Their trio of imports were Lothar Matthaus, Jurgen Klinsmann and Andreas Brehme, all members of West Germany's World Cup-winning team just a few months earlier, plus Walter Zenga, Giuseppe Bergomi, Riccardo Ferri, Nicola Berti and Aldo Serena, who were part of the Italy team that had knocked out Venglos's Czech side at the quarter-final stage before unexpectedly losing in the last four. Villa's England international David Platt, who had faced West Germany in the World Cup semi-finals and Italy in the third-place play-off, was under no illusions about the task facing his team. "Inter haven't got a weakness," he said. "They have the Italian keeper, three internationals in the back four, then people like Matthaus and Klinsmann."

The draw also meant a trip to the imposing Guiseppe Meazza Stadium – popularly known as the San Siro – which had been given a major makeover before the World Cup and now resembled a giant spaceship that had landed on the edge of Milan. First, though, the Italians travelled to Birmingham, even though the first leg should have been played in Italy. The dates were switched because Inter's ground-sharers Milan were playing at home in the European Cup on the night on the night Villa were scheduled to visit the San Siro.

We will never know how the tie would have unfolded had the two legs been played as they had originally been scheduled. What we do know is that many claret-and-blue aficionados regard the first leg as one of the greatest Villa Park occasions they have experienced. Best-selling thriller writer Lee Child was on the Holte End that night to witness a famous 2-0 Villa victory; so was Marc Baylis, the actor who played Coronation Street murderer Rob Donovan in 2014. Both immediately brought the game to mind when asked by the club's official TV channel, AVTV, to recall their most memorable Villa games. That's hardly surprising because it truly was a vintage performance. As Andy Colquhoun observed in the Birmingham Post: "For all the money Inter's coach Giovanni Trapattoni has lavished on his side, it was Villa's more

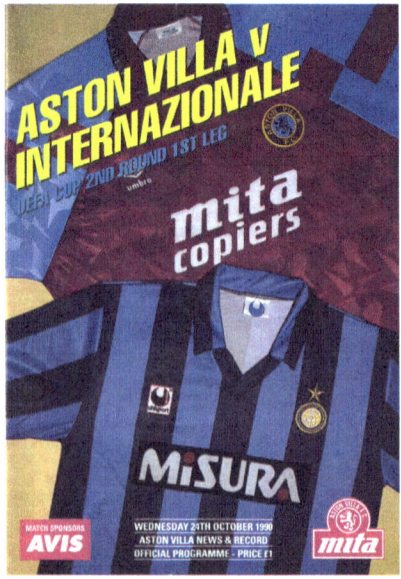

A treasured keepsake of a truly epic Villa Park night

modestly concocted collection of Football League professionals who earned all the plaudits."

Villa's defence, with the inexperienced Andy Comyn playing alongside Kent Nielsen, provided the platform by keeping a tight rein on Klinsmann and Serena for all but a 20-minute spell in the first half; Paul Birch's diligence nullified the threat of Matthaus; Tony Daley's direct running created endless problems for the visitors' back four. And then we had two of the finest goals ever scored down Witton way.

Kent Nielsen is barely visible as he unleashes the stunning volley which left Inter keeper Walter Zenga diving in vain as it thudded into the net for the opening goal against the Italian giants

The first arrived on 14 minutes, following a largely cagey start by both teams. When Platt's shot was charged down, Birch played the ball in to Tony Cascarino, who teed it up for Nielsen to unleash an explosive 30-yard right-foot drive which thudded into the bottom corner of the net as Zenga dived in

Game over – David Platt wheels away after firing past Inter keeper Zenga in the 67th minute to clinch Villa's 2-0 win

vain. When the Danish defender was interviewed after the game, David Moore of the Daily Mirror, used the famous Carlsberg lager advert to suggest it was "probably" the best goal Nielsen had ever scored!

If the opener was stunning, Villa's second, on 67 minutes, was simply sublime. Cowans' beautifully-floated diagonal pass picked out Platt who –

Second round, 1st leg
ASTON VILLA 2 INTERNAZIONALE 0
24th October 1990, Villa Park, Att: 36,461
1-0 NIELSEN (15) 2-0 PLATT (67)

ASTON VILLA
Nigel SPINK, Chris PRICE, Staurt GRAY (c), Andrew COMYN, Derek MOUNTFIELD, Kent NIELSEN, Tony DALEY, David PLATT, Paul BIRCH, Gordon COWANS, Anthony CASCARINO.
INTERNAZIONALE
Walter ZENGA, Giuseppe BERGOMI (c), Andreas BREHME, Nicola BERTI, Riccardo FERRI, Sergio BATTISTINI, Paolo STRINGARA, Fausto PIZZI (Andrea MANDORLINI 71), Jurgen KLINSMANN, Lothar MATTHAUS, Aldo SERENA.

having made a brilliant run – controlled the ball and stroked it deftly inside Zenga's near post before the Inter defence realised what was happening.

Cowans' immaculate display – along with several other impressive performances around that time – certainly caught the eye of his former manager. Graham Taylor, who had brought the midfielder back to Villa from Italian club Bari two years earlier, and was now the England coach. And as Villa headed to Milan for the second leg against Inter, Cowans learnt he had been recalled to the national squad for the European Championship qualifier against the Republic of Ireland in Dublin the following week. As modest as ever, the man known as "Sid" said his call-up had come as a shock and that he probably wouldn't be involved at Lansdowne Road. In the event, he was named in the starting

Inter the fire – Kent Nielsen and Paul McGrath look apprehensive as they step out into the white-hot atmosphere of the San Siro. At least Derek Mountfield manages a smile

Above left: Cutting up rough – the playing surface in Milan is far from ideal as Tony Daley speeds away from Inter's Riccardo Ferri to get in a cross from the left. Above right: Cascarino in the air – Tony Cascarino climbs above Inter skipper Giuseppe Bergomi

line-up against the Irish, winning his 10th and final England cap. Platt also played and scored.

Perhaps that provided some sort of consolation after the bitter disappointment endured by Cowans and his team-mates at the San Siro. It wasn't merely the fact that Villa lost the second leg 3-0 and went out of the UEFA Cup on aggregate; the manner of their defeat left a sour taste which lingered for much of the remainder of the season as Venglos and his players became embroiled in a relegation battle.

Things started to go wrong as early as the seventh minute. Klinsmann, who had promised to make amends for his poor display at Villa Park, did exactly that when he chased a long through ball, leaving Nielsen in his wake. As Mountfield made a last-ditch challenge, the German striker hooked the ball past

Nigel Spink as he fell. It was clearly going to be a long night for Villa. They managed to hold on to their aggregate advantage until just past the hour mark, when they were on the receiving end of the first of two highly dubious decisions. A linesman ruled that Stuart Gray fouled Antonio Paganin, even though the Villa skipper appeared to win the ball fairly, and when

Great support – David Platt acknowledges the Villa fans who travelled to Italy for the second leg

Second round, 2nd leg
INTERNAZIONALE 3 ASTON VILLA 0
7th November 1990, Stadio Giuseppe Meazza, Att: 75,585
1-0 KLINSMANN (6) 2-0 BERTI (61) 3-0 BIANCHI (73)

INTERNAZIONALE
Walter ZENGA, Giuseppe BERGOMI (c), Andreas BREHME, Nicola BERTI (Andrea MANDORLINI 80), Riccardo FERRI, Sergio BATTISTINI (Antonino PAGANIN HT), Alessandro BIANICHI, Fausto PIZZI, Jurgen KLINSMANN, Lothar MATTHAUS, Aldo SERENA.
ASTON VILLA
Nigel SPINK, Chris PRICE, Stuart GRAY (c), Paul McGRATH, Derek MOUNTFIELD (Ian OLNEY 80), Kent NIELSEN, Tony DALEY, David PLATT, Paul BIRCH, Gordon COWANS, Anthony CASCARINO.

Matthaus delivered the free-kick, Nicola Berti's low angled drive left Spink helpless. Now it was a question of whether the visitors could survive a sustained onslaught in front of 75,000 fanatical Italians.

They might well have done, but for another double dose of injustice 15 minutes from the end. It was bad enough that Klinsmann was standing offside as a long pass was played out of Inter's defence but even worse that the ball ran out of play before Fausto Pizzi crossed from the left. Alessando Bianchi, unmarked at the far post, lashed a powerful volley between Spink's legs, and Villa were out. Chairman Doug Ellis was so incensed that he claimed Villa had been cheated out of the competition, adding: "Television shows that Inter's third goal came from a cross after the ball had crossed the byeline. But I shall be making no complaints to UEFA. We are English and we shall just have to keep a stiff upper lip."

HEAVE-HO FOR IVO

It is undoubtedly the most quirky quiz question in Villa's history: Which Villa player scored for the club without ever making a competitive appearance for them? The answer is Ivo Stas, who conceded the own goal which gave Villa a 2-1 victory over Banik Ostrava in Czechoslovakia early in the 1990-91 campaign.

Despite his misfortune, skipper Stas produced a classy "libero" performance in front of the Banik defence which persuaded Villa manager Jo Venglos to sign him.

Unfortunately, Stas injured his Achilles tendon in his first training session in England and was restricted as a result to merely a couple of friendly games, including one against Gornik Zabrze at the 1991 Hanover Tournament in Germany, before heading back to his homeland the following season.

Villa skipper Stuart Gray got to know Stas, who is pictured on the day he signed, a little better than most. As our earlier photo shows, he conducted the pre-match formalities with him at the two legs of the Banik tie.

Andy Comyn is visible in the background (left) as Paul Birch climbs to win a header at home to Inter Milan

BETTER THAN McGRATH!

It was a truly special experience for all Villa's players when they beat Inter Milan in the first leg of the second-round tie.

And for full-back Andy Comyn it was like a scene straight from a Disney film. Just over 12 months earlier he had been competing in non-League football for Alvechurch.

"The change has been phenomenal for me," he said. "The biggest crowd I played in front of before I came here was 1,500 for an FA Cup tie against Bromsgrove. Now I have played in front of nearly 37,000 against Inter Milan. It's a pure fairytale."

The Inter game was one of five consecutive appearances for Comyn as a replacement centre-back for the injured Paul McGrath – and Villa kept a clean sheet in all five. Keeper Nigel Spink said: "The best compliment I can pay Andy is that we have not really missed Paul, which is great credit to him." Comyn (third right) takes a look around the San Siro here with his colleagues on a night on which he was an unused substitute. Also seen (from left) are messrs Gallacher, Cascarino, Ormondroyd, Olney, Daley and Blake.

CHRIS FLIES HIGH

Several players had their first taste of playing a competitive European match on foreign soil when Villa headed for Ostrava for the second leg of their first-round tie against Banik. But right-back Chris Price (right) revealed he had NEVER played abroad in 12 seasons as a professional footballer before joining the club in the summer of 1988. "The first game for me was when we went to Israel for a friendly just before Christmas during my first season here," he said. "At Hereford and then Blackburn, there were no end-of-season tours and we always stayed in this country for pre-season games."

ITALIAN JOB FOR PLATT

Little could David Platt have known, when he stepped out at the San Siro stadium, that he would ply his trade in Italy over the following four seasons. Platt, pictured below winning an aerial battle with Inter's Nicola Berti, had joined Villa from Crewe Alexandra in February 1988 for a £200,000 fee that was described by Graham Taylor as "over the top". In the summer of 1991, though,

Platt netted Villa a club record incoming fee of £5.5m when he moved to Bari. He joined Serie A big hitters Juventus the following year and then had two seasons with Sampdoria before returning to England as an Arsenal player in 1995.

THE HOLTE - IN ALL ITS GLORY

Few have summed up the atmosphere of a big European night on the Holte End better than Jeff Prest. More than a decade after the first leg against Inter Milan, he wrote in the Villa News & Record about "one of those unforgettable nights where every worry and hang-up you bring through the turnstile is seared off by 90 minutes

that reduce your whole world to the size of a football pitch." He added of his experience on that famous terrace (left): "I went to see Inter but ended up watching the Holte End. Stood right at the back, I peered down a shadowy ski slope of frothing humanity as Villa downed a star-studded side to a backdrop of jubilation that drained you just to be part of it." Wonderful!

1993-94

'The best save I've ever seen'

If a week is a long time in football, three years is an eternity. When Villa returned to foreign fields on a competitive basis in September 1993, so much had changed in football and politics. Having enjoyed a reasonably successful first season as manager, Ron Atkinson had guided Villa to runners-up spot behind his former club Manchester United in the FA Premier League's inaugural campaign. These days, that would have been good enough for Champions League qualification; in that era it merely secured a place in the UEFA Cup.

There had been wholesale changes among Villa's personnel since the game against Inter Milan in 1990, and when they set out on their latest UEFA campaign, eight players made their European debuts for the club. Only Nigel Spink, Gordon Cowans, Paul McGrath and Tony Daley remained from the team beaten 3-0 on that controversial night in Milan. And even though Villa headed back to the same part of the continent to where they had played their first-round tie against Banik Ostrava three years earlier, it was now a different country. Slovan Bratislava had finished the previous season third in the Czechoslovakian league but their city had since become part of the independent Republic of Slovakia.

For all that, there was a familiar face on hand to greet them when they arrived at the Tehelne Pole stadium for training on the day before the first leg of their first-round clash. Jozef Venglos had left Villa at the end of the 1990-91 season and had subsequently taken charge of Turkish club Fenerbahce for two years before being appointed Slovakia's national coach. The tie was a perfect opportunity for him to take a look at Slovan's internationals in action against foreign opposition, but he was also delighted at the opportunity of being reunited with some of the Villa players with whom he had ventured into Europe.

The visiting party were accompanied by Peter Withe, Dr Jo's assistant for the second half of 1990-91. He travelled to Bratislava as an expert analyst for BBC Radio, while former defender Gordon Smith – a member of the 1977-78 UEFA Cup side – was there in connection with his new career in stadium

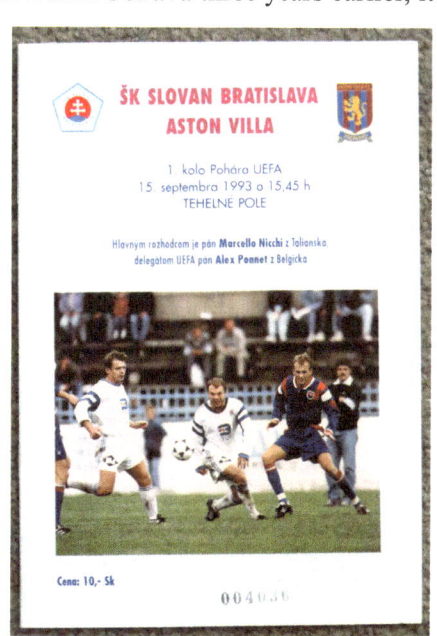

The match-day publication Villa found awaiting them on their return to familiar territory

advertising. Withe and Smith, along with the English media, quickly discovered that while Czech beer is excellent, watching UEFA Cup football in Slovakia can be very expensive. Waiters at the Danube Hotel showed a great deal of interest in the game but when one of them was asked if he would be attending, he explained that ticket prices had been raised from the usual £1 to as much as £5 in some

This way, boys – Dalian Atkinson's pace enables him to leave two Slovan defenders trailing behind him in Bratislava. Left: The San Siro's proper title

areas. "It costs one day's pay to go to this game," he said, "and my little boy needs a new pair of shoes."

The waiter arguably enjoyed better value from his son's new footwear than he would have done by being among those present at the sparsely-populated Tehelne Pole. The game, which kicked off at 2.45pm GMT, was broadcast live at home on ITV and petered out to a largely uneventful goalless draw. That was mainly because of an excellent afternoon's work by Spink, who made some fine saves, although

Villa were convinced they should have been awarded a penalty when Slovan keeper Alexander Vencel barged into Dalian Atkinson after the striker had nudged the ball past him in the 55th minute. A stunned silence among the 10,886 spectators suggested that home supporters feared the worst but there were gasps

First round, 1st leg
SLOVAN BRATISLAVA 0 ASTON VILLA 0
15th September 1993, Tehelne Pole, Att: 10,886

SLOVAN BRATISLAVA
Alexander VENCEL, Tomas STUPALA (c), Marian ZEMAN, Ondrej KRISTOFIK, Vladimir KINDER, Dusan TITTEL, Robert TOMASCHEK, Ludovit LANCZ (Ladislav PECKO 60), Stefan MAIXNER, Fabio NIGRO, Jaroslav TIMKO (Pavol GOSTIC 45).
ASTON VILLA
Nigel SPINK, Earl BARRETT, Stephen STAUNTON, Shaun TEALE, Paul McGRATH, Kevin RICHARDSON (c), Raymond HOUGHTON, Gordon COWANS, Dean Nicholas SAUNDERS, Dalian ATKINSON, Andrew TOWNSEND

of disbelief when Italian referee Marcello Nicchi ignored Villa's appeals. Manager Atkinson later offered the view that the official declined to award a spot-kick because he would also have been forced to send off Vencel for a professional foul.

Overall, a draw was a satisfactory outcome, although the boss still had a warning, both for his team and for fans, before the return match. "In case any supporters believe we can expect the

Tongue-in-cheek – but Dean Saunders is a picture of concentration as he looks for an opening in the Villa Park return against Slovan

formality of an easy ride into the second round, let me put that matter right straight away," he wrote in his programme notes.

"As we prepare for this second leg I shall be reminding our players just how hard they had to work to get themselves into Europe. Having achieved that objective by finishing runners-up to Manchester United in the Premier League there's no way that we should now take progress for granted. A goalless draw away from home is fair enough. But it is not a winning scoreline."

That final paragraph was printed in capital letters, as if to underline the point that a 1-1 outcome at Villa Park would represent an aggregate defeat. Quite simply, Villa had to win, and skipper Kevin Richardson was certainly in no doubt about the size of the task faced by him and his-team mates. Like

First round, 2nd leg
ASTON VILLA 2 SLOVAN BRATISLAVA 1
29th September 1993, Villa Park, 24,461
1-0 ATKINSON (15) 2-0 TOWNSEND (22) 2-1 TITTEL (86)

ASTON VILLA
Nigel SPINK, Neil COX, Stephen STAUNTON, Shaun TEALE, Paul McGRATH, Kevin RICHARDSON (c), Gordon COWANS, Andrew TOWNSEND, Dean Nicholas SAUNDERS, Dalian ATKINSON, Guy WHITTINGHAM.
SLOVAN BRATISLAVA
Alexander VENCEL, Tomas STUPALA (c), Marian ZEMAN, Ondrej KRISTOFIK (Ludivit LANCZ 28), Vladimir KINDER, Dusan TITTEL, Ladislav PECKO, Robert TOMASCHEK, Miroslav CHVILA, Fabio NIGRO, Jaroslav TIMKO (Pavol GOSTIC HT).

Derek Mountfield three years earlier, Richardson had been a member of the Everton title-winning side denied a crack at the European Cup because of the Heysel disaster. Now he was understandably savouring his first taste of European football since being on the bench for the Merseysiders in the 1985 Cup Winners' Cup final.

Dalian Delight – Dalian Atkinson is all set to pounce for the opening goal against Slovan (above left), with team-mates Kevin Richardson and Guy Whittingham sharing his delight as he turns away to celebrate the breakthrough (right)

"A good case could be made for the UEFA Cup being the hardest of the three major European competitions," he said. "In the European Cup it's possible for one of the bigger fish to draw a couple of the weaker nations early on and have relatively few problems in getting to the group stage. But in the UEFA cup you tend to get a stronger cross-section of teams from each country."

Richardson had earlier missed out on a shot at the European Cup when part of Arsenal's title-winning team in 1989, so he was as determined as anyone to take heed of the manager's pre-match warning.

Thankfully it was a determination which was ingrained into the whole team and Villa went about their business impressively. On a night when Neil Cox and Guy Whittingham made their European debuts, the home side began positively and were two-up after 21 minutes. First, Vencel failed to cut out Cox's 14th-minute cross, leaving

Still class – A decade after helping Villa to European Cup and Super Cup glory, Gordon Cowans receives the man-of-the-match award after the home leg against Slovan

Andy Townsend to head on for Whittingham to try an overhead kick. Vencel managed to knock the ball down but Dalian Atkinson was perfectly positioned to volley home. And when Townsend doubled the advantage with a curling left-footer, home fans were already looking forward to the second round.

After that, unfortunately, it was a story of missed chances, most notably when Richardson headed wide from a good position. Atkinson's men then endured a nervous final four minutes after Dusan Tittel's long-range shot was deflected past Spink to make it 2-1. Thankfully there were no further setbacks, and the first leg of the second round offered Villa supporters a trip to the seaside. La Coruna may not be an obvious holiday destination but those who made the journey were enchanted by the resort on the craggy north-west tip of Spain's Galicia region.

Deportivo La Coruna's home, the Riazor Stadium, is unquestionably located in one of the most attractive settings in world football, nestling just

Small measures – Bryan Small's only two European appearances for Villa were the games against Deportivo. The full-back moves in to challenge Mauro Da Silva during the first leg in Spain

behind the western end of the crescent-shaped beach. The venue underwent a total transformation between 1995 and 1998, but when Villa played there it was a typical old-fashioned football ground, albeit with three stands not four. An ornamental tower overlooked one end while the "beach end" was dominated by a huge indoor arena, with neither seating nor terracing. The only people watching from that area were the ball boys who were kept busy at every match. And those youngsters undoubtedly had the best view of what manager Atkinson described as "the best save I have I ever seen."

Just three minutes in, Shaun Teale lunged into a sliding tackle on Javier Manjarin but succeeded only in taking his opponent's legs, leaving referee Marc Batta no alternative but to point to the spot. Brazilian striker Bebeto struck the penalty firmly and waist high towards the left-hand corner, but Mark Bosnich flung himself across his line and was almost horizontal as he clawed the ball away. It was an incredible way for the Australian keeper to mark his European debut, and although he would make numerous other crucial penalty saves during his time at Villa Park, none was quite as spectacular. Bosnich had clearly listened to his manager's advice to wait and watch the taker before making a late decision on which way to go, rather than to guess and commit himself too early. "They were like gunslingers starting each other out," Atkinson commented later. "That save was unreal."

The BIG late breakthrough that had Villa hopes rising in Spain

Dean Saunders holds off a desperate challenge from Jose Ribera (top picture) before slotting a low shot past keeper Francisco Liano (middle photo left) to give Villa the lead in La Coruna. The delight on Deano's face contrasts sharply with the dejected looks of the Deportivo keeper and defender as he picks himself up (bottom left) before racing to celebrate with strike partner Dalian Atkinson (below)

Slippery customer – Tony Daley is all poise as his trickery takes him past his marker at the Riazor Stadium

Bosnich, never a man for modesty, wouldn't have argued with such an appraisal, and the keeper gave an insight into the psychological game he played with the Brazilian ace before the spot-kick was taken. "As Bebeto was placing the ball he glanced briefly to my right and then took a much longer look to my left," he revealed. "Then he looked at me. It could have been a double bluff but I made up my mind that I would go left. I feinted to the right first, and then took off the other way. Luckily it worked out."

Ironically, Bosnich probably wouldn't have played had Steve Staunton been fit. But in the absence of the injured Republic of Ireland international, the manager gave a European debut to Bryan Small and opted to use his Aussie keeper as one of the three non-British players he was allowed under UEFA's regulations, along with Paul McGrath and Andy Townsend. Bozzie's heroics also gave Villa heart against the side who had dared to challenge Spain's elite clubs Barcelona and Real Madrid over the previous couple of seasons. Although Deportivo continued to press forward after the penalty save, Villa held firm and increased in confidence as the game progressed – to the point where they grabbed the lead 12 minutes from the end with their best move of the match.

Dalian Atkinson, whose runs had worried home defenders all night, burst through the middle before playing a perfectly-timed pass to Dean Saunders on his right. The Welsh striker's well-struck shot left keeper Francisco Liano well beaten and Villa were within reach of what would have been an immense result. It didn't quite materialise, substitute Pedro Riesco rescuing a draw for the home side with an 87th-minute equaliser which was all the more galling because it followed a frantic raid which carried none of the finesse Deportivo had displayed earlier.

Second round, 1st leg
DEPORTIVO LA CORUNA 1 ASTON VILLA 1
19th October 1993, Riazor, Att: 11,237
0-1 SAUNDERS (79) 1-1 RIESCO HERRERA (87)

DEPORTIVO LA CORUNA
Francisco LIANO FERNANDEZ, Salvador GONZALEZ MARCO (Marcos VALLES ILLANES 67), Fernando MARTINEZ PERALES, Jose Luis RIBERA URANGA, Miroslav DJUKIC, Mauro DA SILVA GOMEZ, Luis Maria LOPEZ REKARTE, Donato GAMA DA SILVA, Javier MANJARIN PEREDA (Pedro RIESCO HERRERA 77) Francisco Javier GONZALEZ PEREZ (c), Jose Roberto GAMA DE OLIVEIRA.
ASTON VILLA
Mark BOSNICH, Earl BARRETT, Bryan SMALL, Shaun TEALE, Paul McGRATH, Kevin RICHARDSON (c), Andrew TOWNSEND, Gordon COWANS, Dean Nicholas SAUNDERS, Dalian ATKINSON, Tony DALEY.

Still, a 1-1 draw away to one of Spain's top teams was quite an achievement, and Villa arrived back at Birmingham International at 4am optimistic that they could make full use of the home advantage that would be theirs in the return leg two weeks later. In the intervening period, Atkinson's men were highly impressive, recording wins at home to Chelsea and away to Swindon Town to spring up to a pleasing fifth place in the Premier League, as well as running out 4-1 victors at Sunderland in the League Cup on a night when Bosnich once again produced a superlative display.

The keeper was then away on international duty for Australia and missed the match at Swindon,

NO HELP THIS TIME FROM THE GREEN, GREEN GRASS OF HOME

Heading out – Dalian Atkinson climbs to head towards the Deportivo goal at Villa Park. But like the rest of Villa's efforts, it came to nothing

but he was recalled to face Deportivo. This time, sadly, things didn't turn out so well. In the 36th minute, the visitors launched a swift raid which culminated in Javier Manjarin scoring at the far post with a downward header which McGrath could only boot into the roof of the net as he desperately tried to clear. Villa, to put it bluntly, were poor, and when asked afterwards about how the players felt, Atkinson replied: "They should feel ashamed." The manager had good reason to feel aggrieved by his team's exit, having never previously suffered a home defeat in any of the European competitions, although the remainder of the season turned out well for both clubs.

> **Second round, 2nd leg**
> **ASTON VILLA 0 DEPORTIVO LA CORNUA 1**
> **3rd November 1993, Villa Park, Att: 26,737**
> **0-1 MANJARIN PEREDA (36)**
>
> **ASTON VILLA**
> Mark BOSNICH, Earl BARRETT, Bryan SMALL, Shaun TEALE, Paul McGRATH, Kevin RICHARDSON (c), Gordon COWANS (Raymond HOUGHTON 62), Andrew TOWNSEND, Dean Nicholas SAUNDERS, Dalian ATKINSON, Tony DALEY.
> **DEPORTIVO LA CORUNA**
> Francisco LIANO FERNANDEZ, Salvador GONZALEZ MARCO , Fernando MARTINEZ PERALES, Jose Luis RIBERA URANGA, Miroslav DJUKIC, Mauro DA SILVA GOMEZ, Luis Maria LOPEZ REKARTE, Donato GAMA DA SILVA, Javier MANJARIN PEREDA (Pedro RIESCO HERRERA 76), Francisco GONZALEZ PEREZ (c), Jose GAMA DE OLIVEIRA (Marcos VALLES ILLANES 81).

Despite going out to Eintracht Frankfurt in the next round, Deportivo enjoyed another successful campaign in La Liga, missing out on the championship title to Barcelona only when they squandered a penalty in the closing minutes of their final match at home to Valencia. Villa, meanwhile, went on to get back among the honours themselves as they memorably lifted the League Cup by brilliantly beating favourites Manchester United 3-1 in the final at Wembley. And that success meant that European football was back on the claret-and-blue agenda for the 1994-95 campaign.

Not the worst view in the world - the close-up of Gordon Cowans in control that Michael Oakes had from his place among Villa's substitutes for the games against Slovan Bratislava

BENCHMARK FOR OAKES

He hadn't yet made his first-team debut, but Michael Oakes was understandably thrilled to be on the substitutes' bench for both legs of the first-round tie against

113

Slovan Bratislava. The young goalkeeper's unexpected opportunity arose because Nigel Spink was selected as the last line of defence for the tie against the team from Slovakia.. Villa would normally have had Australian Mark Bosnich among their subs but that option was impossible because of UEFA's ruling that no side could choose more than three foreigners in their squad on match nights.

Oakes described the first leg in Slovakia as "a terrific experience just to be with the lads on a trip like that" and added: "I had thought about the prospect of going for a while.I knew there would be a chance because of the three foreigners rule."

ALL SHIVERY FOR THE BACKROOM DUO

It may have been Spain, but two Villa backroom men were laid low by flu after checking out Deportivo La Coruna before the second-round tie. Coach Dave Sexton and chief scout Brian Whitehouse were caught out by the weather while watching Deportivo away to Albacete. "We thought it would be warm over there," said Whitehouse. "But the game didn't finish until 10.45pm and it was freezing."

That wasn't the end of their discomfort. On the 250-mile trip back to Madrid, their driver pulled off the motorway and told them they had a puncture and had run out of fuel. Fortunately, the wheel was changed while local police arranged for a petrol station to open so they could fill the tank.

No weather problems for him - Tony Daley finds that life's a beach as he relaxes on the sand at La Coruna with a slice of cake to celebrate turning 26 the day before the first leg against Deportivo

TONY'S BIRTHDAY ON THE BEACH

Villa's excursion to Spain coincided with a special and happy occasion for England international Tony Daley, who celebrated his 26th birthday on the eve of the first leg against Deportivo. Once the word was out, plans were quickly made for a birthday photo with a difference as the flying winger prepared to tuck into a slice of cake on the beach in La Coruna. Judging by his lightning-quick runs at the Riazor Stadium, it's a fair bet that Daley didn't eat any of his unexpected treat, but it made for an ideal picture before the match.

It turned out to be the last season in claret-and-blue for Daley, who had joined Villa straight from school a decade earlier. He joined Graham Taylor – previously his boss at Villa and with England – at Wolves the following summer but not before helping Villa back into Europe as a member of the 1994 League Cup-winning side.

1994-95

Come hell and high water

It was ironic that Villa's 1994-95 UEFA Cup trail should come to a tame conclusion in the relative calm of their own backyard. By then, they had endured monsoon-like conditions – and had also been to hell and back. There was a touch of irony about the first-round draw, too. Ron Atkinson's team were paired with Inter Milan, the Italian giants who had knocked them out in controversial circumstances at the second-round stage four years earlier.

But there were a few subtle differences this time. Inter, while still formidable opponents – and, indeed UEFA Cup holders – were not quite the force they had been when laden with World Cup stars in 1990; the first leg would, on this occasion, take place at the San Siro - although the atmosphere in the imposing stadium was nowhere near as intimidating it had been for Villa's previous visit. The reason was simple. Back in 1990-91, Dr Jo Venglos's Villa side had had to contend with a baying crowd of more than 75,000 as well as Inter's highly talented line-up. Now, the attendance failed to reach 23,000.

The drop-off was put down to various factors. Inter had lost at home to Roma a few days earlier, ticket prices were high, there was a public transport

Spot the San Siro crowd – but it's business as usual for a business-like Dalian Atkinson and he seems none too concerned by the unexpected backdrop as he takes on Inter's Mirko Conte

115

strike in Milan – and many of the locals must have wondered if the game might be postponed after the torrential rain and electric storms which had swept across the city 24 hours earlier. Villa's party had been given a taste of the dreadful conditions even before touching down at Malpensa airport the previous afternoon. The flight was already 90 minutes late because the club's charter plane had been struck on the runway by a catering vehicle and departure had been delayed while a replacement aircraft was found.

Many of those on board, including the author, thought the substitute plane had landed when it dropped with a sudden thud in the violent storms over northern Italy, but as it was buffeted by another bout of turbulence it became evident it was still in the air, with lightning flashing all around us. It was too much for a couple of reporters on the official flight. Ray Matts of the Daily Mail and Peter White of The Sun were notoriously bad fliers, even in the best of conditions, and had both downed several glasses of brandy, both during the delay at Birmingham International and on the plane to calm their nerves.

As the plane approached Milan in that storm, even seasoned air travellers had tight, nervous looks across their faces, while Ray and Peter, for all the Cognac which had earlier given them rosy complexions, were positively ghost-like. The conditions eased slightly during the coach journey from the airport to the hotel, but by the time a group of us headed to the San Siro that night to check out Villa's training session, the rain was bucketing down. The taxi driver pulled up as close as possible to a side door which an official was holding open for us, but in the few seconds it took to step from the cab and inside the stadium – no more than a couple of yards – we were absolutely soaked. You've heard of Rochdale on a wet Tuesday night? Milan on a wet Wednesday evening isn't exactly appealing, either.

At least we were under cover as we watched the session. As rain cascaded down off the roof of the deserted stadium, parts of the pitch were flooded and the first dozen rows of seats were saturated. It was certainly no fun for the players, who could barely move in areas where the surface had become waterlogged. Manager Atkinson sensibly decided to call a halt, sending his troops back to the sanctuary of a dry dressing room. There seemed every likelihood that the match would be postponed but the weather the following day couldn't have been more different. Thursday dawned bright and sunny, although the match was something of an anti-climax. Villa, with only Nigel Spink and Paul McGrath remaining from the previous visit to this vast arena, defended doggedly, with right-back Earl Barrett and the relatively inexperienced Ugo Ehiogu making some superbly-timed tackles. For all that, the most dangerous

No joy – Dean Saunders unleashes a shot which came to nothing

moment of the opening period was a fierce Steve Staunton shot which forced Italy's national goalkeeper Gianluca Pagliuca to make an excellent one-handed save.

By the 75th minute Spink, back in the team because Mark Bosnich was injured, had also made only one save of note, such was the visitors' discipline and resolve.

First round, 1st leg
INTERNAZIONALE 1 ASTON VILLA 0
15th September 1994, Stadio Giusesppe Meazza, Att: 22,639
1-0 BERGKAMP pen (76)

INTERNAZIONALE
Gianluca PAGLIUCA, Giuseppe BERGOMI (c), Mirko CONTE, Andrea SENO, Gianluca FESTA, Giovanni BIA (Massimo PAGANIN 71), Alessandro BIANCHI, Wim JONK, Nicola BERTI, Dennis BERGKAMP, Ruben SOSA (Marco DELVECCIO 83).
ASTON VILLA
Nigel SPINK, Earl BARRETT, Stephen STAUNTON, Ugochuku EHIOGU, Paul McGRATH, Kevin RICHARDSON (c), Andrew TOWNSEND, John FASHANU (Raymond HOUGHTON 79), Dean Nicholas SAUNDERS, Dalian ATKINSON, Philip Geoffrey KING.

But when the keeper dived at the feet of Ruben Sosa and the striker fell, Danish referee Peter Mikkelsen pointed to the spot and Dutch striker Dennis Bergkamp planted the penalty past Spink for the only goal of the night.

A 1-0 defeat was a considerable improvement on the 3-0 setback Villa had suffered at the same

On target – Dalian Atkinson gets in a shot (left) despite the close attention of Giovanni Bia and the striker also produces a leap of faith to avoid a challenge from Inter defender Gianluca Festa at the San Siro stadium

Man-marking – Giovanni Bia (No 6) ensures that Dean Saunders is kept at bay as Giuseppe Bergomi prepares to clear in Milan

venue nearly four years earlier and one which offered Atkinson's men a fighting chance on home soil in the return. Even so, there was a strong feeling that Sosa had taken a dive to earn the penalty. "There was no physical contact when the gentleman fell over," insisted Spink, with a barely-disguised touch of sarcasm. "When I came out I got a slight flick on the ball and he theatrically fell over me. That's not a penalty in my book." Atkinson, meanwhile, smiled ruefully when questioned on the subject in the post-match press conference. "I thought we were very, very unlucky," he said. "Nigel definitely had a touch on the ball before Sosa went over."

Two weeks later, Atkinson called for patience as his team attempted to transform their one-goal deficit into an aggregate victory. "We can't go off to the sound of the trumpets and expect to grab two quick goals," he wrote in his programme column. "This one has to be played with the heads as well as the hearts." The players took their boss at his word. With the upper tier of the Holte End still under construction, the attendance was limited to 30,533, but the atmosphere was electric. Villa's players were positive from the outset, producing a performance of controlled aggression and no little skill to record a 1-0 win which took the tie to extra-time and then penalties.

There were a couple of scares along the way, Nicola Berti's seventh-minute shot rattling the

All-square – Ray Houghton celebrates levelling on aggregate

woodwork while substitute Davide Fontolan was guilty of a dreadful late miss. But generally Villa were outstanding, matching their opponents in every department and making the breakthrough four minutes before half-time. Kevin Richardson's cross from the right deflected off Massimo Paganin as he was challenged by Dalian Atkinson and the ball fell invitingly to Ray Houghton eight yards out. The highly experienced Republic of Ireland international lashed it home with the outside of his right foot as Pagliuca dived the wrong way, and Villa were very much back in business.

Towards the end of normal time, substitute Guy Whittingham almost made it 2-0 with a delightful chip that hit the bar, but after an additional 30 minutes the aggregate scores were still level and it was down to penalties – Villa's second shoot-out in a matter of months. In February, Mark Bosnich's saves had carried them to a dramatic win over Tranmere Rovers in the League Cup semi-final; this showdown would prove to be equally nerve-tingling.

The first six kicks were all converted – Giovanni Bia, Bergkamp and Andre Seno for Inter; Garry Parker, Steve Staunton and Andy Townsend for the home side. Then Fontolan nervously sent his penalty over the bar, only for Villa's delight to turn to despair as Whittingham's effort was saved by Pagliuca. Sosa was next up, with a shot which was too powerful for Spink but which crashed against the bar. Advantage Villa, once again – one more conversion and they could celebrate victory over one of the biggest clubs in world football.

So who better to take the next penalty than a player Inter had probably never heard of? Phil King, a cheerful, happy-go-lucky

Dutch master – Dennis Bergkamp on the ball at Villa Park, with Phil King in close attendance

You're the penalty king! Ray Houghton has no doubt that Phil King is the right man for the job as his team-mate makes his way, under intense pressure, to take the crucial spot kick

full-back, had joined Villa from Sheffield Wednesday that summer for £250,000 – a fraction of what most of Inter's players had cost. In the midst of all the tension, King stood joking with his team-mates before striding up to the spot to face Pagliuca, who had cost a world record for a goalkeeper of £7m from Sampdoria that summer after becoming the first keeper to save a penalty in a World Cup final shoot-out. Paglucia had kept out Marcio Santos's kick in the final in Los Angeles, only for Italy to lose the shoot-out to Brazil. Now he faced the boy from Bristol –

No problem, job done! King raises his arms in triumph after despatching his kick past Gianluca Pagliuca

First round, 2nd leg
ASTON VILLA 1 INERNAZIONALE 0 (aet)
(Villa won 4-3 on penalties)
29th September 1994, Villa Park, Att: 30,533
1-0 HOUGHTON (41)
Penalties: 0-1 BIA 1-1 PARKER 1-2 BERGKAMP 2-2
STAUNTON 2-3 SENO 3-3 TOWNSEND 4-3 KING

ASTON VILLA
Nigel SPINK, Earl BARRETT, Stephen STAUNTON,
Ugochucku EHIOGU, Paul McGRATH, Kevin
RICHARDSON (c) (Garry PARKER 99), Raymond
HOUGHTON, Andrew TOWNSEND, Dean Nicholas
SAUNDERS (Guy WHITTINGHAM 19), Dalian ATKINSON,
Philip Geoffrey KING.
INTERNAZIONALE
Gianluca PAGLIUCA, Giueseppe BERGOMI (c), Mirko
CONTE (Angelo ORLANDO 97), Massimo PAGANIN,
Gianluca FESTA, Giovanni BIA, Andrea SENO, Nicola
BERTI, Darko PANCEV (Davide FONTOLAN 61), Dennis
BERGKAMP, Ruben SOSA

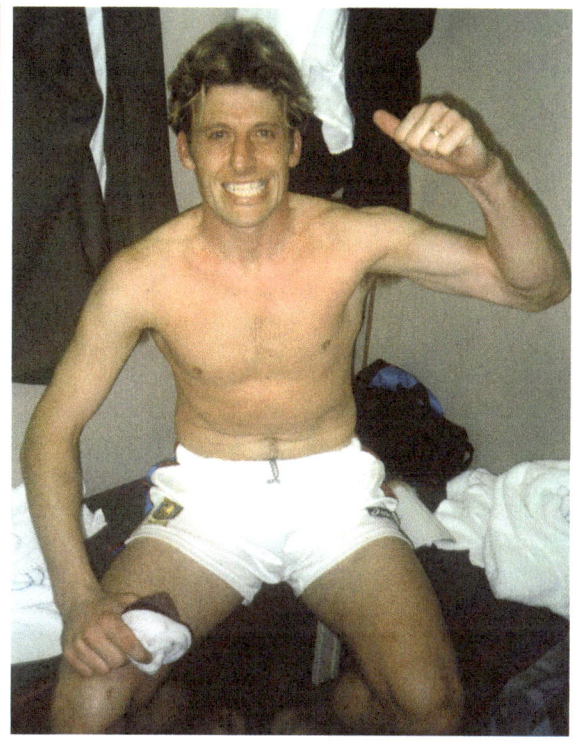

Above: The vital extended statistics from an epic Villa
Park night. Right: We're Inter the next round – Andy
Townsend celebrates in the dressing room

and dived in vain to his right as the ice-cool King drove his shot straight down the middle. Villa had won 4-3 on penalties and Villa Park erupted.

As the TV cameras homed in on Atkinson, the manager described his team's achievement as "as good a European night as I have known," adding: "I asked for a big, big performance and those lads have been great. They have given a hell of a performance."

It was to hell that Villa were next required to travel. Or at least that was how supporters of Trabzonspor described their run-down Avni Aker Stadium in the Turkish outpost of Trabzon. Villa had faced intimidating situations before, notably when visiting Istanbul in 1977 and 1982, but this time the mind games began even as they touched down on the day before the first leg of their second-round tie. The official party were greeted at the airport by a group of Trabzonspor fans holding a banner which declared: "WELCOME TO HELL".

On the night of the game, the banner was again on display inside a stadium that was packed to capacity, while fans unable to gain admission clung to trees and other vantage points around the ground. Drums beat relentlessly and firecrackers were let off, while at one point a flare was thrown on to the pitch behind Steve Staunton as he was making a clearance.

"The noise level wasn't as great as against Besiktas, but it was a far more dangerous situation," recalled former Villa secretary Steve Stride. "When I went to Trabzon to make arrangements for our official party and supporters, I was told that any coins, pens or anything else that might be thrown on the pitch would be confiscated at the turnstiles. We passed on this information to our supporters but it soon became apparent that home fans didn't have the same strict regulations. We could hear shots being

Not so Hell-ish – Despite warnings of the hostile reception they might receive, these Villa supporters found time to soak up the Turkish sunshine as they lined up for a souvenir group

fired into the air from the terraces. Coins and pens might have been banned but there seemed to be no objection to guns!"

It was a volatile situation to say the least, but thankfully the small band of Villa fans who made the trip were not subjected to any violence and the match passed without incidents in the crowd. Unfortunately for the visitors, it was a similar story on the pitch. Villa were excellent in the first half, with Whittingham hitting the bar and Houghton firing straight at keeper Victor Grichko when he might have scored. In the 77th minute, however, Orhan Kaynak rose to meet an inswinging corner from the right with a firm six-yard header which gave Spink no chance, leaving Villa with a miserable five-hour flight home through the night.

The 1-0 result left Atkinson's men with exactly the same second-leg scenario they had faced against Inter, although the manager warned that no-one should be lulled into thinking a home game against lesser-known opposition would provide a less daunting task. "There could be a feeling among some supporters," he said, "that because the name Trabzonspor is little-known in this country they will be an easier hurdle than the Italians. Anyone

Second round, 1st leg
TRABZONSPOR 1 ASTON VILLA 0
18th October 1994, Huseyin Avni Aker, Att: 23,000
1-0 KAYNAK (76)

TRABZONSPOR
Viktor GRISCHKO, Lemi CELIK, Ogun TEMIZKANOGLU, Kemal SERDAR, Tolunay KAFKAS, Abdullah ERCAN, Cengiz ATILA, Unal KARAMAN (c), Soner BOZ, Hami MANDIRALI (Hamdi ASLAN 88), Orhan KAYNAK (Kakhi KACHARAVA 89).
ASTON VILLA
Nigel SPINK, Earl BARRETT, Stephen STAUNTON, Ugochucku EHIOGU, Paul McGRATH, Kevin RICHARDSON (c), Raymond HOUGHTON, Andrew TOWNSEND, Dean Nicholas SAUNDERS, Guy WHITTINGHAM, Philip Geoffrey KING.

who believes that is on entirely the wrong lines."

How right he was. Villa were on top for most of the match but just as they had during the first half in Turkey, they squandered a number of good chances before Dalian Atkinson marked his 100th appearance for the club by opening the scoring on 77 minutes. The striker's drive was deliberately handled by Ogun Temizkanoglu, an offence which earned the defender a red card and Villa a

Determined Deano – Saunders make a forceful run in the first leg against Trabzonspor

penalty. Staunton's spot-kick was charged down by Grichko and most spectators were convinced Ugo Ehiogu's shot from the rebound crossed the line before it was scrambled away, although there was no time to debate the point before Atkinson smashed the ball home for the goal which brought the aggregate scores level.

Suddenly, the prospect of extra-time and possibly another penalty shoot-out loomed large, but right at the death Trabzonspor, despite being down to 10 men, consigned Villa to the hell they had threatened

Turk them on - Dalian Atkinson at the heart of the action in the second leg against Trabzonspor. Unusually, Villa are not the team in claret and blue

two weeks earlier. The game had entered stoppage time when Orhan, scorer of the first-leg decider, sent a rising shot on the turn into the roof of the net after a left-wing corner had not been cleared. That meant Villa were all but out, now needing to score twice in the few seconds that remained. Amazingly, they still managed one goal, Ehiogu stabbing home a low shot from close range after a mistake in the visitors' defence but that

Dalian on the charge against the Turks once more – but the night ended in frustration

merely intensified the agony. It clinched a 2-1 victory on the night and took the aggregate to 2-2, but wasn't enough to prevent Trabzonspor going through on the away goals rule.

FIDDLER ON THE ROOF

Villa's longest-established celebrity fan Nigel Kennedy travelled on the official flight to Milan for the first leg against Inter – accompanied by the instrument which has made him famous all over the world. The virtuoso violinist helped to pass the time with a couple of tunes as players, officials and supporters waited for their luggage to be unloaded onto the carousel at Malpensa Airport.

And he was happy to put on another impromptu performance (left) at a reception on the rooftop restaurant of the city's British Consulate the following lunchtime. Club officials and members of the press enjoyed excerpts from Vivaldi's Four Seasons plus a rendition of the Match of the Day theme as they wined and dined in glorious sunshine.

Kennedy revealed that

the violin he used wasn't exactly vintage, having been made in 1991. But he added: "It's a historic exhibit because it has all the Villa players' signatures from the team that went to Spain last year."

BLACK AND BLUE - ALL WHITE?

Villa wore their regular kit for the first leg against Inter in Milan, while Inter switched from their usual blue and black stripes to an all-white outfit, UEFA rules stating that whenever there is a colour clash, the home side should change. With that in mind, Villa commissioned a special one-off strip of all white with a claret-and-blue trim before the second leg. As it was, the kit wasn't needed on this occasion. Referee Joel Quinon and the UEFA delegate assigned to the game decided there was no need for either team to change from their usual colours.

The kit didn't go to waste, though. Villa used it for the home leg of their second-round tie against Trabzonspor, when the visitors wore their traditional claret-and-blue striped shirts.

Kitted out as per usual - Steve Staunton forces his way past Inter captain Giuseppe Bergomi to shoot

'I THOUGHT I'D BEEN KIDNAPPED'

Villa took their own chef and provisions to Turkey for the visit to Trabzonspor – and poor Steve Burton feared he was the subject of a kidnap. After landing at Trabzon airport and being greeted by a "Welcome to Hell" banner, the players went directly to the stadium for training and their coach had a police escort. But former Savoy Hotel chef Steve was directed to a pick-up truck with two skips of food plus Villa's match kit. After a short distance the driver, who spoke no English, pulled to the side of the road – and waved goodbye to Steve, who was left on his own in the middle of nowhere.

"I just thought I'd been kidnapped," he said. "I was really frightened. I thought 'this isn't supposed to be happening'. I had visions of a news report saying the Kurds in the hills were living off Villa's bacon, sausage and pasta." Thankfully a replacement driver arrived after a while, and Steve eventually arrived at the hotel kitchen to perform his culinary duties.

We have to score!

The instruction is the most basic in football. Unfortunately it was delivered too late to make any impact – and Villa paid a heavy price. Just four minutes remained when Tommy Johnson was sent on as a substitute for Savo Milosevic against Helsingborgs IF, and the Geordie striker carried more on to the pitch than merely a pair of fresh legs.

The first leg at Villa Park had ended 1-1, now it was goalless at the tiny Olympia Stadium in the Swedish port of Helsingborg. And it suddenly dawned on the players that they had been under a misapprehension about the competition rules. "When Tommy came on he told us we had to score," said Alan Wright. "Otherwise we were out. Most of us had thought the away goals rule only came into force after extra-time, so we suddenly realised we had to do something very quickly."

The dependable left-back certainly took his team-mate at his word. Almost immediately, Wright unleashed a powerful 25-yard drive which looked good enough to take Villa into round two – until keeper Sven Andersson stretched to tip the ball on to the woodwork. As the saying goes, though, it was

Swede smiles – The travelling fans are in high spirits before the second leg in Sweden, although it was a sombre trip home after Villa were knocked out by the part-timers

Early breakthrough – The ball nestles in the Helsingborgs net after Tommy Johnson had opened the scoring with his powerful low drive

too little too late, which was all the more galling because Villa had launched this particular European adventure with arguably their strongest squad for years.

The previous season, with new signings Gareth Southgate, Mark Draper and Milosevic, they had finished fourth in the Premiership, which would have been good enough in its own right to secure UEFA Cup qualification if they hadn't already done so by winning the League Cup. Now they were even stronger – on paper, at least. Portuguese right-back Fernando Nelson had been recruited from Sporting Lisbon, while Milosevic's Serbia international colleague Sasa Curcic had eclipsed him as the club's record signing when the midfielder arrived from Bolton Wanderers for £4m. There was certainly an air of great optimism when Villa were drawn against the part-timers of Helsingborgs in the opening round, particularly as they were lying fourth in the table when the first leg rolled around.

The prospect of building a decent lead looked entirely realistic when Brian Little's side went ahead inside a quarter of an hour. Johnson, back in the side because Curcic was ineligible until the third round, was the man who made the early breakthrough, sending a blistering drive past Andersson from the edge of the penalty area after Andy Townsend had nodded down Mark Draper's floated cross. With Draper having already fired a long-range shot against the bar, it seemed merely a question of how many Villa would score. But Helsingborgs, whose line-up included former Sheffield Wednesday defender Roland Nilsson, proved to be stubborn opponents. Every time Villa moved forward, the visitors got as many men behind the ball as possible, forcing Little's players to constantly move the ball sideways.

The outcome was that strikers Dwight Yorke and Milosevic received very little service, and with 10 minutes remaining, subdued home supporters seemed to have reluctantly accepted their team would

First round, 1st leg
ASTON VILLA 1 HELSINGBORGS IF 1
10th September 1996, Villa Park, Att: 25,818
1-0 JOHNSON (14) 1-1 WIBRAN (79)

ASTON VILLA
Michael OAKES, Stephen STAUNTON, Gareth SOUTHGATE, Andrew TOWNSEND (c), Mark DRAPER, Savo MILOSEVIC, Dwight Eversley YORKE, Thomas JOHNSON, Alan WRIGHT, Fernando Nelson JESUS VIERA ALVES, Ugochucku EHIOGU.
HELSINGBORGS IF
Sven ANDERSSON, Ola NILSSON, Roland NILSSON(c), Andreas JAKOBSSON, Christer FURSTH, Peter WIBRAN. Magnus POWELL (Martin PRINGLE 52), Mattias JONSSON, Jan ERIKSSON, Ulrik JANSSON. Jesper LJUNG.

be taking only a one-goal lead to Sweden two weeks later. Then it got worse. Up to that point, one of the game's few positives was that young keeper Michael Oakes, who had deputised for the injured Mark Bosnich since the start of the season, was on course to keep a clean sheet on his European debut. The notion, sadly, was dispelled when the unmarked Peter Wibran drilled home an equaliser that not only gave the visitors a 1-1 draw but also a vital away goal.

The importance of Wibran's strike became evident right from the kick-off in the return match. Helsingborgs, aware that a 0-0 draw would carry them into the second round, were clearly happy to settle for that particular outcome, even though their coach Reine Almqvist insisted afterwards that the decision to go for a goalless stalemate wasn't taken until half-time. That questionable explanation of his team's negative tactics was scant consolation for 300 Villa supporters in the attendance of just over 10,000, who watched in frustration as Helsingborgs once again retreated behind the ball in numbers, with Villa simply unable to break them down.

As usual in such situations, there were at least a couple of slices of misfortune for the losers to bemoan. Andersson's late save from Wright was one, while Little's troops were convinced they should have been awarded a penalty when Ola Nilsson appeared to handle inside the area as he was challenged

All set for take-off – Steve Staunton, Mark Draper, Alan Wright and Michael Oakes are in jovial mood as they make their way to the boarding gate. It wasn't such a happy return flight

Good to see you again – Andy Townsend and Helsingborgs captain Roland Nilsson, the former Sheffield Wednesday and Coventry City defender, exchange pennants before the second leg

by Yorke in the 55th minute. Instead of pointing to the spot, though, Luxembourg referee Roger Philippi penalised the astonished Villa striker for a foul. Had a penalty been awarded, Yorke would have had the

opportunity to send his team into the next round and end a personal goal drought which had lasted for the opening nine games of the campaign. Ironically, he ended his barren spell with a vengeance in the following game, netting a hat-trick at Newcastle six nights later. Not that it gave him any great satisfaction as he also had another perfectly good effort disallowed at St James' Park and Villa lost 4-3.

The ones that counted on Tyneside were the first three of Yorke's 20-goal league and cup total for the season. If only he had started scoring a little earlier...

> **First round, 2nd leg**
> **HELSINGBORGS IF 0 ASTON VILLA 0**
> **24th September 1996, Olympia, Att: 10,103**
>
> **HELSINGBORGS IF**
> Sven ANDERSSON, Ola NILSSON, Roland NILSSON (c), Andreas JAKOBSSON, Christer FURSTH (Jesper LJUNG 83), Peter WIBRAN, Magnus POWELL (Martin PRINGLE 57), Matthias JONSON, Jan ERIKSSON, Ulrik JANSSON, Marcus LANTZ (Anders JONSSON 87).
> **ASTON VILLA**
> Michael OAKES, Stephen STAUNTON, Gareth SOUTHGATE, Andrew TOWNSEND (c), Ian TAYLOR, Mark DRAPER, Savo MILOSEVIC (Thomas JOHNSON 83), Dwight Eversley YORKE, Alan WRIGHT, Fernando Nelson JESUS VIERA ALVES (Paul McGRATH 59), Ugochucku EHIOGU.

Helsingborgs hold-up. Dwight Yorke tries to crack a stubborn home defence

NOT A FIRST

Anyone who felt Villa broke new ground when they faced Helsingborgs were wrong. They had faced the same club on a six-match tour of Sweden and Norway at the end of their Second Division title-winning campaign of 1959-60.

In the second match of the tour, on 12th May 1960, Joe Mercer's team beat Helsingborgs 3-2 with two goals from Gerry Hitchens and one from Peter McParland.

NO ROOMS AT THE INNS

Helsingborgs left hotel arrangements for the first leg in Villa's hands and caused them a major headache. A trade show was taking place in Birmingham, just as in 1981 when Valur stayed in Stoke before Villa's first European Cup tie. Eventually, accommodation for the visiting Swedes was found at the Hilton Hotel near the Nottingham exit of the M1 at the junction with the M42 – around 40 miles from Villa Park.

NO WAYWARD SHOOTING TODAY, LADS.....LET'S KEEP OUR FEET DRY

Sea view – Villa's players couldn't have wished for a more picturesque setting for training before the second leg against Helsingborgs. When the Swedes were in the Midlands, they had Nottingham as a backdrop

1997-98

The B road to Madrid

Villa had been in the surreal situation, just under 17 years earlier, of losing a match and then celebrating famously. In March 1998, they achieved a tremendous victory – and felt little more than misery and dejection.

The visitors' dressing room at Highbury in May 1981 had been awash with champagne when Ron Saunders' team discovered they were champions despite slipping to a 2-0 defeat against Arsenal in their final game of the season. This time, in the home dressing room at Villa Park, the mood was sombre and reflective. Despite having just beaten Spanish giants Atletico Madrid, Villa had missed out on a UEFA Cup semi-final place because of the away goals rule. For all that, it was an amazing night which is etched on the memory of everyone who was there – not to mention one of the players involved. Stan Collymore has been going to Villa Park since 1977, initially as a young supporter, then as a player and latterly as a radio commentator. And he reckons he has never known the claret-and-blue faithful generate quite so much noise as they did on the evening Atletico came to town.

"The place erupted when I scored the goal which gave us victory on the night," Collymore said. "Unfortunately, it wasn't enough to see us through to the semi-finals but it was a moment which I will always remember. I never tire of watching the footage. The atmosphere was incredible, although I think most of us believed it was all over when Atletico took the lead in the first half. That put them 2-0 ahead on aggregate and meant we had to score three."

Collymore had been watching from the bench up to that juncture, having just recovered from the toe injury which had resulted in him being taken off in the first leg in

It's a screamer – Stan Collymore's delight is all too evident after his powerful rising shot has given Villa a 2-1 lead on the night. Sadly, it wasn't quite enough

High kicks – Dwight Yorke strives to make a breakthrough during a goalless first half at Villa Park

Madrid. But seven minutes after half-time at Villa Park, he went on as a substitute for Savo Milosevic and John Gregory's side started to claw their way back into contention. Dwight Yorke had a shot blocked, then hit the bar with a header as Villa increased the tempo, and in the 71st minute Ian Taylor fired home a low drive for the equaliser after good work by Lee Hendrie and Julian Joachim. Two minutes later Hendrie was involved again as Villa stormed into the lead.

"Lee knocked the ball inside to me just outside the penalty area," said Collymore. "It flashed across my mind that we needed something special, so I let fly with a right-foot shot which was as good as any I ever hit." Indeed, the ball was still rising and would possibly have reached the top of the Holte End's upper tier if it hadn't been on target. But Collymore's aim was as true as his shot was powerful and the ball thudded into the roof of the net before keeper Jose Molina could move.

Villa led 2-1 on the night and were level on aggregate. Despite pressing forward relentlessly, though, they were unable to find that elusive third goal as Atletico survived the barrage. As I wrote in the following morning's Birmingham Post: "The great Euro adventure is over but Aston Villa were magnificent ambassadors for English football as they reached the end of the UEFA Cup road."

It had been very much a B road which carried Villa to the quarter-finals, the draws for the first three rounds pairing them with opponents from Bordeaux, Bilbao and Bucharest, starting with a dogged, disciplined performance in the beautifully-warm south west of France in mid-September. Despite signing Collymore from Liverpool for a club record £7m, Villa had made their worst-ever start to a season, losing the first four league games, but thankfully the rot had been stopped before they headed to the world's most famous wine region. A 1-0 home win over Leeds United was followed by a 3-0 success away to Premiership new boys Barnsley, so that when Brian Little's men lined up at the Parc Lescure, their confidence was well on the way to repair and they were ready for battle against the not inconsiderable talents of Girondins de Bordeaux.

The home side's starting line-up included two players, Sylvain Wiltord and Lilian Laslandes, who would go on to play in the Premiership, plus another who is regarded as one of France's finest players of all time. Jean-Pierre Papin was approaching his 34th birthday but the mere presence of the former European Footballer of the Year gave the visitors' defence plenty to think about. They coped well, though, and although les Girdondins enjoyed greater possession and created the better opportunities, Villa held firm for a creditable goalless draw which offered them every hope for the return leg. Towards the end, Papin slipped past Steve Staunton and at his peak would surely have aimed for the far corner. Instead he opted for pure power and allowed Mark

Images of Bordeaux .... optimistic supporters in form (right) amid the warmth of the Parc Lescure and (below) the entry of the teams

First round, 1st leg
GIRONDINS DE BORDEAUX 0 VILLA 0
16th September 1997, Stade Chaban-Delmas
Att: 13,000

BORDEAUX: Ulrich RAME, Paulo Sergio GRALAK, Nisa SAVELJIC, Kizito MUSAMPA, Lilian LASLANDES, Michel PAVON, Sylvain WILTORD, Peter Bernard LUCCIN (Lassina DI-ABATE 84), Francois GRENET (Romain FER-RIER 73), Kodjo AFANOU, Jean-Pierre PAPIN (Kaba DIAWARA 84).

VILLA: Mark BOSNICH, Stephen STAUNTON, Gareth SOUTHGATE (c), Ugochucku EHIOGU, Ian TAYLOR, Mark DRAPER, Dwight Eversley YORKE, Stanley Victor COLLYMORE, Alan WRIGHT, Fernando Nelson VIERA ALVES, Simon GRAYSON (Sasa CURCIC 52).

Tenacious Tayls – Ian Taylor evades the challenge of Romain Ferrier to fire a shot at goal in Bordeaux

Bosnich to charge the ball away as it hurtled towards his near post.

There was speculation Papin may miss the second leg because his daughter was ill but he duly landed in Birmingham two weeks later. As ever on these occasions, the media turned out in force to interview visiting players and officials but there wasn't an English-speaker to be found, so Thierry Vautrat, a sports journalist with the Sud-Ouest newspaper, faced the TV cameras. Thierry discovered a soft spot for the boys in claret and blue during that trip and in recent years he has visited Villa Park at least once a season. If their local reporter had more than mastered our language, however, Bordeaux were far from the masters of Villa Park. True, they were more adventurous than we had been led to believe but it was a night on which Villa imposed themselves on the game and were worthy winners, even if they had to wait until extra-time before breaking the French resistance.

With only nine minutes of the additional 30 left and a pulsating tie edging towards penalties, Villa produced the move of the night.

Shadow man – Fernando Nelson keeps a close watch on Girondins midfielder Francois Grenet in Villa's away first leg

Super Savo! It's ecstasy as the Serbian striker celebrates his late winner with Dwight Yorke

Stan Collymore, enjoying the most effective game since his summer move from Merseyside, delivered a magnificent 30-yard pass to substitute Gary Charles on the right. When the defender crossed hard and low, Milosevic got in front of his marker to turn the ball past keeper Ulrich Rame from close range. It was no more than the home side deserved and it was a huge relief to the Serb, who had been handed a place in the starting line-up for only the third time that season after enduring what he described afterwards as a "nightmare" start to the campaign.

First round, 2nd leg
VILLA 1 GIRONDINS DE BORDEAUX 0 (aet)
30th September 1997, Villa Park, Att: 33,072
1-0 MILOSEVIC (111)

VILLA: Mark BOSNICH, Stephen STAUNTON, Gareth SOUTHGATE (c), Ugochucku EHIOGU, Ian TAYLOR, Savo MILOSEVIC, Dwight Eversley YORKE, Stanley Victor COLLYMORE, Alan WRIGHT, Fernando Nelson VIERA ALVES (Gary CHARLES 106), Simon GRAYSON.

BORDEAUX: Ulrich RAME, Paulo Sergio GRALAK, Nisa SAVELJIC, Michel PAVON, Johan MICOUD (Peter Bernard LUCCIN 106), Lilian LASLANDES (Kaba DIAWARA 82), Sylvain WILTORD, Francois GRENET, Kodjo AFANOU, Lassina DIABATE, Jean-Pierre PAPIN (Kizito MUSAMPA 63).

Milosevic was re-established as a regular by the time the first leg of the second round rolled around. Indeed, it was his striking partner Collymore who had a problem before the game against Athletic Bilbao

The bench in Bilbao – Villa's subs in the first leg. Pictured from the left at the San Mames are Michael Oakes, Julian Joachim, Simon Grayson, Sasa Curcic, Lee Hendrie and Ugo Ehiogu

at the San Mames Stadium. As usual, a small number of reporters dutifully attended the team's training session at the stadium on the evening before the game. In truth, we would have preferred to have been enjoying a San Miguel or two with our less-diligent colleagues, particularly as watching the players in training invariably failed to provide anything worthy of inclusion in the following day's paper. Not this time, though. After a while it became evident that Collymore was experiencing some difficulty, although

he certainly didn't appear to be injured. As he walked over to where we were standing near the dug-out, the reason for his discomfort became apparent – one of his favourite boots had ripped, rendering the pair useless.

Thankfully Villa managed to get it repaired the following morning, leaving them to concentrate on the main task in hand, Little opting to employ a 3-5-2 formation which regularly reverted to 5-3-2 as wing-backs Fernando Nelson and Alan Wright shuttled back to help quell the pressure exerted by Athletic. With a 39,000 crowd offering partisan support from the steeply rising stands of an arena nicknamed The Cathedral, there was no shortage of hard work for Villa.

As it turned out, the more clear-cut chances in a compelling goalless stalemate fell to Little's side, none better than in the 39th minute when Collymore combined superbly with Dwight Yorke, who frustratingly fired

Second round, 1st leg
ATHLETIC CLUB 0 ASTON VILLA 0
21st October 1997, San Mames, Bilbao, Att: 39,713

ATHLETIC CLUB
Imanol ETXEBERRIA EGANA, Rafael ALKORTA MARTINEZ, Yosu URRUTIA TELLERIA (c), Jose Angel ZIGANDA, Carlos GARCIA GARCIA, Joseba ETXEBERRIA, Bittor ALKIZA FERNANDEZ, Mikel LASA GOICECHEA (Aitor LARRAZABAL BILBAO 61), Inigo LARRAINZAR SANTAMARIA, Francisco GONZALEZ GOMEZ (Mario BERMEJO CASTANEDO 76), Roberto RIOS PATUS.

ASTON VILLA
Mark BOSNICH, Stephen STAUNTON, Gareth SOUTHGATE (c), Ian TAYLOR (Simon GRAYSON HT), Mark DRAPER, Savo MILO-SEVIC, Dwight Eversley YORKE, Stanley Victor COLLYMORE, Alan WRIGHT, Fernando Nelson VIERA ALVES, Riccardo SCIMECA

wide from a good position. Simon Grayson, a half-time substitute after Ian Taylor suffered a hamstring strain, was also cursing when his perfectly-placed header was cleared off the line 20 minutes from the end. At the whistle, though, the visitors had every reason to feel satisfied with a composed, disciplined performance, even if the manager

Stan Collymore takes a throw against the backdrop of the Bilbao floodlights (top) and battles with Roberto Rios

Breakthrough – Ian Taylor fires home the opening goal at Villa Park after Bilbao keeper Imanol Etxeberria had dropped Savo Milosevic's left-wing cross

offered no more than a cautious comment that "the tie is evenly-balanced" when asked about the return match.

He was spot on, even when Villa established a 2-0 lead by the 50th minute at Villa Park. It could have been more, Milosevic twice putting the ball in the net in the opening stages, only to see his first effort disallowed for a foul and his second ruled out because he had handled and was offside anyway. The striker's petulance after the second decision earned him a yellow card, although his contribution to the opening goal was immense.

Controlling Steve Staunton's long, high pass with a sublime touch, Milosevic turned cleverly away from Francisco Ferreira before delivering a fine cross from the left. Athletic keeper Imanol Etxeberria, possibly distracted by Yorke's close attendance, momentarily lost concentration and allowed the ball to slip from his grasp. Taylor, who had also ventured into the penalty area, could barely believe his luck as he was left with a simple tap-in from six yards to give Villa a 27th-minute lead.

The advantage was doubled five minutes after the interval. Wright and Taylor worked the ball in neatly from the left and when Yorke hesitated briefly, it looked as if he would push it sideways to the overlapping Mark Draper. But as Draper's run provided the perfect decoy and threw the Bilbao defence off balance, Yorke unleashed a fierce low shot with the minimum of backlift to claim his first goal since the end of August.

If Yorke's goal gave the home side some breathing space, it also spurred Athletic into the sort of inventive football which had resulted in them being beaten just once since the start of the season. Five good chances were created in as many minutes, Mark Bosnich making four excellent saves while a shot from Ismael Urzaiz flashed narrowly wide. A Bilbao goal looked increasingly inevitable and it arrived on 70 minutes, when Taylor's headed clearance went only as far as sub Javier Gonzalez, whose shot from the edge of the area took a deflection off Gareth Southgate as it flew into the corner of the net.

> **Second round, 2nd leg**
> **ASTON VILLA 2 ATHLETIC CLUB 1**
> **4th November 1997, Villa Park, Att: 35,915**
> **1-0 TAYLOR (28) 2-0 YORKE (50) 2-1 GONZALEZ GOMEZ (70)**
>
> **ASTON VILLA**
> Mark BOSNICH, Gary CHARLES, Stephen STAUNTON, Gareth SOUTHGATE (c), Ian TAYLOR, Mark DRAPER, Savo MILOSEVIC, Dwight Eversley YORKE, Alan WRIGHT, Fernando Nelson VIERA ALVES (Simon GRAYSON 85), Riccardo SCIMECA.
> **ATHLETIC CLUB**
> Imanol ETXEBERRIA EGANA, Rafael ALKOTRA MARTIZEZ, Yosu URRUTIA TELLERIA (c) (Franciso Javier GONZALEZ GOMEZ 68), Jose Angel ZIGANDA (Julen GUERRERO LOPEZ 53), Aitor LAR-RAZABAL BILBAO, Francisco Anton FERREIRA COLMENERO (Mikel LASA GOICOECHEA 50), Joseba ETXEBRRIA, Bittor ALKIZA FERNANDEZ, Ismael URZAIZ ARANDA, Inigo LARRAINZAR SAN-TAMARIA, Roberto RIOS PATUS

That left the home side on edge for the 20 minutes that remained, their nerves heightened by the knowledge that a second Athletic goal would take the Basque outfit through on the away goals rule. But it was Villa who went closer to scoring, Staunton's 30-yard free-kick being tipped over by Etxeberria before the keeper clawed away a close-range Milosevic shot after a delightful move involving Yorke, Gary Charles and Taylor. Even so, there was huge relief when the final whistle sounded. Villa had managed to hold their lead and were through to the third round for the first time in 20 years.

Next up was a trip to Romania to face Steaua Bucharest, the club with an army background, who had won the European Cup 11 years earlier. It wasn't the most appealing of prospects in the last week of November, particularly in raw temperatures and on a pitch which was heavy and bumpy. It didn't help, either, that Villa went into the first leg depleted by the absence of Southgate, who was injured, and Bosnich – on international duty with Australia.

The keeper's absence meant a rare European outing for Michael Oakes, who had the misfortune of presenting Steaua with their opening goal. Oakes was beaten by a 29th-minute Cristian Ciocoiu shot which rebounded off the post onto the back of his outstretched hand and into the net. Three minutes later, Oakes had no chance as Ciocoiu's acrobatic overhead kick left him helpless and made it 2-0.

Bucharest-bound Dwight Yorke at Birmingham Airport before the flight to Romania

Third round, 1st leg
STEAUA BUCURESTI 2 ASTON VILLA 1
25th November 1997, Steaua Stadium, Bucharest, Att: 19,500
1-0 OAKES og (30) 2-0 CIOCOIU (32) 2-1 YORKE (55)

STEAUA BUCURESTI
Zoltan RITLI, Laurentiu Aurelien REGHECAMPF, Ilie Iulian MIU, Iosif ROTARIU, Valeriu RACHITA, Marius Mihai LACATUS (c) (Marius Sebastian LUCA 88), Damian MILITARU, Cristian CIOCOIU (Narcis Claudiu RADUCAN 76), Constantin Catalin MUNTEANU, Erik LINCAR (Ion Lavi HRIB 70), Tiberiu CSIK.
ASTON VILLA
Michael OAKES, Stephen STAUNTON (c), Ugochucku EHIOGU, Ian TAYLOR, Mark DRAPER, Savo MILOSEVIC, Dwight EVERSLEY YORKE, Stanley Victor COLLYMORE, Alan WRIGHT, Fernando Nelson VIERA ALVES (Gary CHARLES 70), Riccardo SCIMECA.

Over my shoulder – Stan Collymore flicks a header over a Steaua defender during the first leg in Bucherest

Villa's prospects at that stage were as grim as the spartan Stadionul Steaua, and things almost grew worse still when Catalin Munteanu's angled drive crashed against the bar early in the second half. Having survived that potential crisis, however, the visitors were back in contention on 54 minutes when Milosevic crossed from the left and Yorke headed home at the far post. Suddenly, the whole complexion of the tie changed. From being down and almost out, Villa now had a vital away goal, and the knowledge that if there was no more scoring on the night, a 1-0 win in the second leg would be enough to take them through to the quarter-finals.

In the event, they made doubly sure with a 2-0 success at Villa Park. Despite struggling to find their best form in the Premiership, Villa seemed to have a happy knack of turning on the style for European

Third round, 2nd leg
ASTON VILLA 2 STEAUA BUCURESTI 0
9th December 1997, Villa Park, Att: 35,102
1-0 MILOSEVIC (71) 2-0 TAYLOR (86)

ASTON VILLA
Mark BOSNICH, Gary CHARLES, Stephen STAUNTON, Gareth SOUTHGATE (c), Ugochucku EHIOGU, Ian TAYLOR, Mark DRAPER (Fernando Nelson VIERA ALVES 82), Savo MILOSEVIC, Stanley Victor COLLYMORE, Alan WRIGHT, Simon GRAYSON (Lee HENDRIE 62).

STEAUA BUCURESTI
Zoltan RITLI, Laurentiu Aurelien REGHECAMPF, Ilie Iulian MIU, Adrian MATEI, Iosif ROTARIU, Valeriu RACHITA (Erik LINCAR 87), Marius Mihai LACATUS (c) (Marius Sebastian LUCA 68), Damian MILITARU, Cristian CIOCOIU (Ion Lavi HRIB 77), Constantin Catalin MUNTEANU, Tiberiu CSIK.

Above: Ian Taylor sends a header at the Steaua goal. Below: Savo's hot again – Stan Collymore and Milosevic salute the Holte End after the Serb's breakthrough goal

nights and they dominated from start to finish – even if they had to wait until the 71st minute for the breakthrough.

It arrived when Milosevic – always a star performer on the Euro stage – broke Steaua's stubborn resistance as he controlled Staunton's long through-ball with his left foot before drilling a powerful shot past keeper Zoltan Titli with his right. That would have been enough to ensure progress on the away goals rule but four minutes from the end Taylor made sure when he moved on to a deft pass from substitute Lee Hendrie, darted through the middle and calmly slotted low past Ritli.

By the time the quarter-final against Atletico rolled around in March, much had changed at Villa Park. Although Collymore scored his first goals for the club in a 4-1 Boxing Day victory over Tottenham, the side's league form dipped in the opening weeks of 1998. Then Milosevic was transfer-listed after spitting towards supporters during a woeful 5-0 defeat at Blackburn; and three days after a 2-1 setback against Wimbledon which left Villa looking anxiously over their shoulders towards the relegation zone, Little resigned.

The club certainly didn't drag their heels in finding a replacement. Within 24 hours of the manager's departure, former Villa midfielder John Gregory – who had previously been on Little's coaching staff – was lured away from the dug-out at Wycombe Wanderers and installed at Villa Park. The appointment was greeted with cynicism in the media, one tabloid headline reading simply: "John who?" because of Gregory's lack of managerial experience. A week later, the critics had been silenced as Villa beat Liverpool 2-1 in Gregory's first match in charge and restricted Atletico to a single-goal lead in the first leg of the UEFA Cup quarter-final.

Not for the first time, Villa encountered problems before kick-off in Spain. It was bad enough that five players – Gareth Southgate, Ian Taylor, Dwight Yorke, Stan Collymore and Steve Staunton – had been booked in previous ties. That meant another caution for any of the quintet would rule them out of the second leg. And minutes after touching down in Madrid, Yorke and Mark Bosnich were threatened with an immediate return to Birmingham because they were non-EU nationals and didn't have the correct documentation with them. Frantic negotiations took place at the airport and thankfully Villa's pleas were accepted by the Spanish officials. The two players completed visa applications and were allowed into the country.

It was just as well that Bosnich overcame the administrative hitch, the keeper making some excellent saves as Villa were almost totally outplayed in the first half at the Estadio Vicente Calderon. Bosnich was beaten just

Atletico – or Real? Ex-Villa striker Alan McInally takes a break from his media duties in Madrid

Quarter-final, 1st leg
ATLETICO DE MADRID 1 ASTON VILLA 0
3rd March 1998, Estadio Vicente Calderon, Att: 47,000
1-0 VIERI pen (42)

ATLETICO DE MADRID
Jose Franciso MOLINA JIMENEZ, Antonio MUNOZ GOMEZ, Andrei FRASCASERLLI, Santiago DENIA SANCHEZ (c), Juan VIZCAINO MORCILLO, Christian VIERI, Milinko PANTIC (Avi NIMNI 74), Jose Maria ROMERO POYON (Veljko PAUNOVIC 61), Carlos AGUILERA MARTIN, Francisco Miguel NARVAEZ MOCHON, Jose Luis PEREZ CAMINERO
ASTON VILLA
Mark BOSNICH, Gareth SOUTHGATE (c), Ugochucku EHIOGU, Ian TAYLOR, Mark DRAPER, Dwight Eversley YORKE, Stanley Victor COLLYMORE (Julian JOACHIM 50), Alan WRIGHT, Simon GRAYSON, Lee HENDRIE, Riccardo SCIMECA (Stephen STAUNTON 42)

Under pressure – Jose Molina punches clear as Ian Taylor leaps to challenge the Atletico keeper in the Vicente Calderon Stadium

once, Italian striker Christian Vieri converting a 41st-minute penalty after Ian Taylor had fouled Jose Luis Caminero, and in the second half Villa took the game to Atletico. But four minutes from the end Yorke must have wished he hadn't been allowed entry into Spain at all as he displayed uncharacteristically poor control after Julian Joachim had skipped past three opponents to provide an inviting cross for the unmarked Trinidad & Tobago international. The chance of a vital goal had gone begging, and Villa paid the ultimate price two weeks later. Instead of progressing to the semi-finals, they were left to reflect on a glorious failure as they won narrowly on the night to make it 2-2 on aggregate but went out on the away goals rule.

There was still a memorable conclusion to the campaign, though. Villa won nine of their last 11 games to finish a highly pleasing seventh. When

Quarter-final, 2nd leg
ASTON VILLA 2 ATLETICO DE MADRID 1
17th March 1998, Villa Park, Att: 38,500
0-1 PEREZ CAMIENRO (28) 1-1 TAYLOR (71) 2-1 COLLYMORE (73)

ASTON VILLA
Mark BOSNICH, Stephen STAUNTON, Gareth SOUTHGATE, Ugochucku EHIOGU, Ian TAYLOR, Mark DRAPER (Fernando Nelson VIERA ALVES 53, Gary CHARLES 84)), Savo MILOSEVIC (Stanley Victor COLLYMORE 53), Dwight Eversley YORKE, Julian JOACHIM, Alan WRIGHT, Lee HENDRIE.
ATLETICO DE MADRID
Jose Francisco MOLINA JIMENEZ, Andrei FRASCARELLI (Daniel PRODAN 59), Santiago DENIA SANCHEZ (c), Juan VIZCAINO MORCILLO, Christian VIERI, Milinko PANTIC (Jorge LARDIN CRUZ 58), Carlos AGUILERA MARTIN (Antonio MUNOZ GOMEZ 79), Francisco Miguel NAVAREZ MOCHON, Delfin GELI ROURA, Jose Luis PEREZ CAMINERO, Radek BEJBL.

No translator required - assistant manager Allan Evans and striker Stan Collymore take a breather before extra-time against Bordeaux and use it for one or two reminders

Chelsea beat Stuttgart in the Cup Winners Cup final, an extra UEFA Cup place became available for English clubs and Villa could start preparing for Europe once again.

WARNING.....NO DRUNKEN FISH!

Villa had more to worry about than just their opponents when they faced Girondins de Bordeaux in the first round. They also had to contend with blood-sucking insects and drunken fish! Humidity in France resulted in a swarm of mosquitoes invading the Parc Lescure, both during training and in the first leg. "When we got back to the dressing room," said striker Stan Collymore, "everyone was covered in bites."

For the second leg, the Villa News & Record included a welcome to visiting supporters in French, plus a seven-point list of safety regulations, including a warning that it was prohibited to take alcohol into Villa Park. But instead of the words 'boissons alcolics' being used, a misprint resulted in the programme announcement referring to 'poissons alcolics', the meaning of which is: alcoholic fish!

THE DRINKS ARE ON US

Many supporters made the trip to Bilbao by road, and they could barely believe their eyes when their coaches pulled into a street near the San Mames stadium.

"I have never experienced anything like it as a football fan," said Phil Harris from Halesowen, a Villa supporter since 1972. "The street was full of Bilbao fans and when that the coaches contained Villa supporters they all stood and applauded as we went past. It was amazing; we never met anything but kindness anywhere on the trip."

THE CAPTAIN'S LOG...

If Gareth Southgate hadn't been a footballer, his most likely career path would have been journalism – and he would clearly have been just as successful. During the build-up to the first leg against Athletic Bilbao, Villa's captain was commissioned by the Villa News & Record to write a diary outlining the

Determined defending from the diarist – Gareth Southgate is in full flight against the backdrop of a mass of Athletic fans as keeper Mark Bosnich positions himself well to deal with any danger

team's preparations. The outcome was a fascinating read in the programme for the home game against Athletic. A couple of Southgate's entries unnderline the fact that the skipper was very much the thinking man's footballer:

Monday October 20: Our hotel in Bilbao is in the centre of the city; so hopefully the locals won't do anything to keep us awake all night! The night before any European tie the away side is entitled to train at the stadium and so we get our first look at 'The Cathedral', as the San Mames stadium is known. My first impression is that it is like a larger scale of The Dell, very tight with the stands rising straight up from the pitch."

Tuesday October 21: The morning of the game – and we are awakened by the din from a pneumatic drill right outside the hotel window. I'm quite sure this is all a coincidence, but sometimes you wonder.

A DIPLOMATIC WISH

Respected football writer Dennis Shaw had quite a surprise when he introduced himself to Britain's vice-consul to Romania on the evening before the away leg against Steaua Bucharest. Sarah Spencer's first question to the former Birmingham Evening Mail scribe was: "How is Gareth Southgate's injury coming on?" Sarah, it transpired, was originally from Acocks Green – and had been brought up as a Villa supporter.

BOZZIE BOMBARDED

There were times when Mark Bosnich could be impetuous on the pitch, but the controversial keeper was certainly hard done-by when he was shown a yellow card during the first leg of the quarter-final against Atletico. Bozzie was booked by referee Stefano Braschi for time wasting – despite having been bombarded by home supporters with a series of objects, including cigarette lighters, batteries and even a couple of bottles.

"All I was doing was shifting stuff which had fallen into the path of my run-up to take a goal-kick," said the Aussie keeper. "I drew it to the referee's attention because I didn't want to tread on anything and possibly cause myself an injury. But the ref said he had to keep the game going. If it had been near the end, I could have understood him thinking I was time wasting, but it happened early in the first half. There was no way I was messing about to kill time."

1998-99

'Score a couple - and win it!'

It is fondly remembered as the time when Villa made the best start to a season in their history. By the middle of November, John Gregory's men hadn't suffered a single league defeat and were sitting at the top of the Premiership after a 12-match unbeaten sequence. What shouldn't be overlooked, though, is that the impressive start also included three UEFA Cup victories. Sadly, there was also a defeat which ended their hopes of emulating the previous season's run to the quarter-final.

After overcoming the Norwegian part-timers of Stromsgodset in the first round, Villa's hopes of making the third round were sky high after a 1-0 first-leg success away to Celta Vigo. But Celta were not one of Spain's top teams for nothing. Although Gregory's boys went into the second leg with a precious away goal, they were outclassed at Villa Park. As the match report in the 1999 Aston Villa Review painfully pointed out, Villa received "a lesson in poise from silky Celta."

That didn't come as a total surprise to those who had witnessed Celta's quality during the first game in which Villa made what amounted to a smash-and-grab raid to lead on aggregate. Indeed, there had been much a bigger surprise in the home first leg of the opening-round tie against Stromsgodset. Villa had started the season with a draw and four wins but they suffered an attack of European stage fright when faced with what looked by far their easiest task to date. The Norwegians took a 21st-minute lead through Anders Michelsen and Villa were still coming to terms with that totally unexpected development when substitute Christer George slotted home a second goal two minutes later. Home supporters could barely believe what they were seeing, while the small contingent of visiting supporters celebrated noisily in a corner of the Doug Ellis stand. Try as they might, Villa simply couldn't get a foothold in the game as half-time came and went.

In the 56th minute, in fact, it could well have been game over, when Michelsen was sent racing through with

---

First round, 1st leg
ASTON VILLA 3 STROMSGODSET 2
15th September 1998, Villa Park, Att: 28,893
0-1 MICHELSEN (22) 0-2 GEORGE (24) 1-2 CHARLES (83) 2-2 VASSELL (90) 3-2 VASSELL (90)

ASTON VILLA
Mark BOSNICH, Gary CHARLES, Alan WRIGHT, Gareth SOUTHGATE (c), Mark DRAPER (Riccardo SCIMECA 66), Alan THOMPSON, Julian JOACHIM, Gareth BARRY, Simon GRAYSON (Ian TAYLOR 37), Lee HENDRIE, Darren BYFIELD (Darius VASSELL 80).
STROMSGODSET
Glenn Arne HANSEN, Thomas WAEHER , Kenneth Wideman KARLSEN (c), Sander SOLBERG, Ousman NYAN, Rune HAGEN, Hans-Erik ODEGAARD (Christer GEORGE 10, Vegard STROM 70), Lars GRANAAS, Anders MICHELSEN (Lasse OLSEN 87), Pal SKISTAD, Morten KIHLE.

only Mark Bosnich to beat. The goalkeeper spread himself and managed to divert the ball for a corner and avert what would have been a disastrous situation. But even having survived that near miss, Villa still hadn't managed a response as the game approached its 80th minute. Then Gregory made a substitution which turned the match on its head. Young striker Darius Vassell, who had made late appearances in the recent Premiership wins against Middlesbrough and Newcastle United, was handed another cameo role – and rarely has a player made a more effective European debut.

With seven minutes left, Villa were thrown the lifeline of a close-range goal from right-back Gary Charles but as the game reached the end of the 90 minutes the visitors still led 2-1. Since the 68th minute, though, they had been reduced to 10 men following skipper Kenneth Karlsson's red card for use of his elbow against Riccardo Scimeca, and in stoppage time they finally submitted to the increasing pressure. When Vassell had gone on to replace Darren Byfield, coach Steve Harrison had told him: "Get yourself out there, score us a couple of goals and win us the game." Which is precisely what the 18-year-old did.

Comeback Charles – Villa right-back Gary Charles reduces the deficit with just seven minutes remaining at home to Stromsgodset (above) before saluting the Holte End

Well done, son – Stoppage-time hero Darius Vassell is congratulated by Ian Taylor

First, Alan Wright hoisted a cross to the far post for Scimeca to head back across the face of goal. Lee Hendrie mis-hit his shot but Vassell was perfectly positioned to guide the ball into the roof of the net left-footed from a couple of yards. The youngster was even closer to the goal when he stabbed the ball over the line three minutes later after Ian Taylor's pass had set up Alan Thompson for a fierce low drive which goalkeeper Glenn Arne Hansen could only parry. In the space of a surreal period of added time, Holte Enders had found themselves a new hero. Thanks to Vassell, as club journalist Jeffrey Prest observed, Villa were heading to Norway "with a toe in the second round instead of one foot in the grave."

Villa were based in Oslo for the return, making the short journey to the port of Drammen, home of Stromsgodset's tiny Marienlyst Stadium. The ground has been rebuilt over the past few years but in 1998 it was basic in the extreme. Even with temporary seats installed for Villa's visit, the attendance didn't reach 5,000 but the mountains in the distance at least provided a pleasant backdrop.

Warming up – Ian Taylor and Simon Grayson run out before going through their pre-match preparations in Drammen

Tunnel vision – The teams emerge from behind the goal at the tiny Maryienlyst ground in Drammen. Gareth Southgate leads out Villa, followed by Mark Bosnich, Stan Collymore and Ian Taylor

There was a bizarre start, the home side kicking off with 10 men because Rune Hagen had worn a T-shirt during the warm-up and left his number 10 shirt in the dressing room. It certainly amused Peter Withe, who was working as Villa's chief European scout and was in Norway as a co-commentator for TV coverage of the game. "I've seen some things in football," he said. "but nothing like that. I know some players have phobias about not wearing their shirts when they go out on the pitch before a game. But it comes to something when you leave it in the dressing room." Hagen was able to join the action barely 30 seconds after it started but even with a full complement of players, the home side were no match for a Villa side determined to avoid a repeat of their early discomfort in the first leg.

The visitors were ahead after 10 minutes, former Chelsea defender Erland Johnsen failing to cut out Mark Draper's pass and allowing Stan Collymore to cut inside him on the left before sending a stunning right-foot angled drive into the far corner. In the 24th minute the tie was as good as over, Draper flicking on a Gary Charles pass for Ian Taylor to unleash a cross-shot from the right. It was too hot for keeper Hansen, who palmed it into Collymore's path and he calmly stroked home from eight yards.

The rest of the match was a formality, and Collymore became only the third player to score a European hat-trick for Villa with a clinical close-range conversion after Julian Joachim had got behind Erik Hagen to deliver low from the right in the 64th minute.

First round, 2nd leg
STROMSGODSET 0 ASTON VILLA 3
29th September 1998
Marienlyst, Dremmen
Att: 4,845
0-1 COLLYMORE (11) 0-2 COLLYMORE (24) 0-3 COLLYMORE (64)

STROMSGODSET
Glenn Arne HANSEN, Thomas WAEHER, Sander SOLBERG (Vegard STROM 85), Ousman NYAN, Rune HAGEN, Jostein FLO (c), Christer GEORGE (Lasse OLSEN 67), Erland JOHNSEN, Lars GRANAAS, Erik Bjurnstad HAGEN (Hans-Erik ODEGAARD 67), Pal SKISTAD.
ASTON VILLA
Mark BOSNICH, Gary CHARLES (Riccardo SCIMECA 51), Alan WRIGHT, Gareth SOUTHGATE (c), Ugochucku EHIOGU, Ian TAYLOR (Fabio FERRARESI 70), Mark DRAPER, Stanley Victor COLLYMORE, Alan THOMPSON, Julian JOACHIM (Darius VASSELL 67), Simon GRAYSON.

That's another fine mess you have got us out of, Stanley!

Three steps to round two for Villa....

Top – That's one! Stan Collymore turns away after opening the scoring in the second leg against Stromsgodset

Middle – A precise left-foot shot gives Collymore his second at the Maryienlest to put Villa two-up

Below left – Collymore taps home from close range in the 64th minute before celebrating his hat-trick

Below – My ball! Collymore proudly shows off his keepsake while indicating how many he had scored

From the relative serenity of Drammen, Villa's next port of call was another, more bustling port, the city of Vigo on Spain's north-west coast, just a couple of hours' drive from La Coruna, where they had performed so well five years earlier. Their display against Celta at Estadio de Balaidos was even better than the one which had earned a 1-1 draw against Deportivo in 1993. Villa were ahead in the 15th minute, courtesy of Julian Joachim's

Julian Joachim is denied as Celta substitute Tomas heads clear in Spain - but jubilant below after hitting Villa's first-leg winner

first European goal. Despite the best efforts of the opposition, who oozed class and who were on top for long periods, Gregory's side held firm, defending deeper and deeper as the game progressed.

The all-important goal was instigated by Collymore, whose pace and fine pass enabled Joachim to slip through the middle and beat advancing keeper Richard Dutruel with a low shot, although no-one was under any illusions that winning the away leg would be enough to ensure a passage to the third round. Villa's domestic form since the first leg had faltered, too. They had needed a 68th-minute Ugo Ehiogu goal to salvage a 1-1 home draw with Leicester City and slumped to a 4-1 defeat at Chelsea in the League Cup before the return for a Premiership fixture at Stamford Bridge four days later was postponed because of a waterlogged pitch.

It wasn't exactly the ideal

> **Second round, 1st leg**
> **CELTA DE VIGO 0 ASTON VILLA 1**
> **20th October 1998, Balaidos, Att: 28,000**
> **0-1 JOACHIM 14**
>
> **CELTA DE VIGO**
> Richard Philippe DUTRUEL, Miguel Angel SALGADO FERNANDEZ, Fernando Gabriel CACERES ZAYA. Iomar DO NASCIMENTO (c), Valeriy KARPIN (Jorge Paulo SANTOS REIS CADETE 83), Haim Michael REVIVO (Juan SANCHEZ MORENO HT), Luboslav PENEV, Goran DJOROVIC, Aleksander MOSTOVOY, Jose Maria LOPEZ ECHEVARRA (Tomas Alberto HERVAS GIRON 62), Claude MAKELELE.
> **ASTON VILLA**
> Michael OAKES, Gary CHARLES, Alan WRIGHT, Gareth SOUTHGATE (c), Ugochucku EHIOGU, Mark DRAPER, Stanley Victor COLLYMORE, Julian JOACHIM, Gareth BARRY, Lee HENDRIE, Riccardo SCIMECA.

preparation for a second leg against the team who had dared to threaten Barcelona and Real Madrid's supremacy in La Liga, and Villa suffered accordingly. Collymore was unfortunate to have an early header ruled out for offside before the visitors went ahead on 26 minutes when Juan Sanchez fired home from what looked a more blatant offside position. Three minutes later, Collymore equalised from the penalty spot after Mazinho had handled in the area but Celta were back in front when Russian midfielder Alexandr Mostovoi steered a 25-yard free kick beyond Michael Oakes' despairing dive and into the bottom corner.

The aggregate score was level once again, and had it stayed 2-1 the visitors would have gone through on away goals. As it was they made absolutely sure three minutes after the interval, Luboslav Penev putting the ball in the roof of the net from almost point-blank range after Oakes had spilled a Sanchez header. Just like five years earlier, Villa had been unable to capitalise on a fine first-leg display in Spain, and as Gregory admitted: "They looked better-balanced and kept the ball better than us."

> **Second round, 2nd leg**
> **ASTON VILLA 1 CELTA DE VIGO 3**
> **3rd November 1998, Villa Park, Att: 29,910**
> **0-1 SANCHEZ MORENO (27) 1-1 COLLYMORE (30 pen) 1-2 PENEV (35) 1-3 MOSTOVOY (48)**
>
> **ASTON VILLA**
> Michael OAKES, Gary CHARLES (Mark DRAPER HT), Alan WRIGHT, Gareth SOUTHGATE (c), Ugochucku EHIOGU, Ian TAYLOR, Stanley Victor COLLYMORE, Alan THOMPSON (Simon GRAYSON 83), Julian JOACHIM, Gareth BARRY (Darius VASSELL 65), Lee HENDRIE.
> **CELTA DE VIGO**
> Richard Philippe DUTRUEL, Miguel Angel SALGADO FERNANDEZ, Rafael BERGES MARIN (c) , Fernando Gabriel CACERES ZAYA, Iomar DO NASCIMENTO, Valeriy KARPIN (Tomas Alberto HERVAS GIRON 70), Luboslav PENEV (Jorge Paulo SANTOS REIS CADETE 75), Juan SANCHEZ MORENO (Dan EGGEN 56), Goran DJOROVIC, Aleksander MOSTOVOY, Claude MAKELELE.

'EAT HERE!'

The owner of the backstreet Vigo bar must have thought he had won the Spanish lottery. On a quiet Monday night in October, the streets were pretty much deserted and a solitary customer kept him company while sipping a beer that would last for an hour or more. It was a night when it hardly seemed worth opening, so imagine his delight when his

Seaside stroll – Villa's players soak up the sunshine in Vigo as part of their training schedule ahead of the first leg against Celta. They weren't the only ones to enjoy the build-up......

establishment was suddenly invaded by a dozen or so English reporters, all flush with expense accounts from their newspapers. And when, after a couple of beers, his unexpected clientele enquired where they might find a decent restaurant, his smile widened still further. "Here," he beamed. "You can eat here!"

He was right. While we were initially a little apprehensive as he led us up the stairs to a darkened room, it transpired that this was, indeed, his restaurant as well as his bar. We dined like kings on king prawns, succulent steaks and a host of other delicious dishes, all washed down with countless bottles of wine. At the end of the night, we couldn't quite believe how reasonable the bill was – and our host could barely believe he had catered for such a large dinner party of English journalists.

'RAMBO RIDES AGAIN'

Alan McInally was among the media representatives in Oslo for the Stromsgodset clash. The Scot, there for Sky Sports, is pictured being introduced to manager John Gregory by Jim Walker, the physio who nursed him through injury during his early Villa days. 'Rambo' never played for Villa in Europe but helped them to promotion from the Second Division in 1988 and his goals were a major factor in Graham Taylor's men surviving a top-flight relegation battle the following season.

2000-01

The man in a muddle

The football season always got under way in September during the game's pioneering days in the Victorian era. After the First World War, it was moved forward to August. And, as the 21st century dawned, Aston Villa made their earliest-ever start to a campaign. It was a record which would be beaten just 12 months later but on Sunday 16th July 2000, Villa played a competitive game earlier than at any time in the club's history.

Many supporters were still lying on beaches when John Gregory and his players headed to the Czech Republic for their first taste of Intertoto Cup football. The much-maligned summer competition had actually been in existence since the 1960s but it was only in 1995 that it was officially acknowledged, and used as a "back door" route into the UEFA Cup. Some clubs started out in the third week of June but Villa were at least spared that inconvenience when they qualified for the first time by virtue of a sixth-place Premier League finish the previous season, when they had also reached the FA Cup final.

Victory over Chelsea in the last final at the old Wembley Stadium would have provided an automatic passage to the UEFA Cup but a 1-0 defeat meant they had to take the Intertoto route. At least they were spared having to play in the first two rounds, and the club's quest for UEFA Cup qualification began with a third-round tie in the Czech mining town of Pribram. The name of their opponents – Marila Pribram – was unknown to many of us, which perhaps wasn't altogether surprising. The club had previously existed as Dukla Prague 50 kilometres away in the Czech capital. They had been a dominant

Intertoto Cup
Third round, 1st leg
MARILA PRIBRAM 0 ASTON VILLA 0
16th July 2000, Na Litavce, Att: 7,000

MARILA PRIBRAM
Michal SPIT, Marcel MACHA, Radek MYNAR, Rudolf OTEPKA (Robert NOVAK 82), Michal SEMAN (Daniel SMEJKAL 56), Jaroslav SCHINDLER, Jiri RYCHLIK, Damir GRLIC, Tomas KUCERA (Jan ZUSTAK 63), Lukas JAROLIM (c), Marek KULIC.
ASTON VILLA
David JAMES, Mark DELANEY, Alan WRIGHT, Gareth BARRY, Ugochuku EHIOGU, George BOATENG, Ian TAYLOR, Jlloyd SAMUEL, Dion DUBLIN, Paul MERSON (c), Steven STONE (Darius VASSELL 71).

force in Czech football, winning 11 league titles between 1953 and 1982 but had relocated to Pribram in 1997, and shortly before Villa's visit they had dropped the Dukla title in favour of Marila.

The town in which political prisoners had once been slave labourers in a uranium mine was hardly the most auspicious setting for Villa's Intertoto debut, although the small number of supporters who made the trip had no complaints about savouring the renowned Czech beer at 50p a pint. At least the cheap alcohol eased the tedium of a goalless draw which was only marginally more interesting than a pre-season friendly. The home side threatened briefly just after half-time but Villa were generally the better side and Paul Merson had an effort disallowed for offside before Darius Vassell's volley was kept out by keeper Michal Spit, who also made two decent saves to deny Dion Dublin. If it was a largely tepid affair, however, the game boiled over 10 minutes from the end when defender Mark Delaney was sent off for retaliation following a collision with Spit as they contested a Merson free-kick.

A different kind of home debut! Luc Nilis emerges from the tunnel at The Hawthorns for his first Villa game

Six days later, Villa staged their earliest competitive home fixture, although it wasn't at Villa Park. The old Trinity Road stand had been demolished that summer and work on the new one was still in progress, so the the second leg was staged four miles away at The Hawthorns. It was a strange experience to see Villa play a home game at West Bromwich Albion's stadium and the attendance of just 8,200 reflected the fact that it was still holiday time for many supporters. And to add to the unreal atmosphere, the kick-off had to be brought forward to 2pm because of a wedding reception which was taking place at the ground later that afternoon.

Third round, 2nd leg
ASTON VILLA 3 MARILA PRIBRAM 1
22nd July 2000, The Hawthorns, Att: 8,000
1-0 DUBLIN (8) 1-1 KULIC (20) 2-1 TAYLOR (57) 3-1 NILIS (61)

ASTON VILLA
David JAMES, Gareth BARRY, Alan WRIGHT, Gareth SOUTHGATE (c), Ugochucku EHIOGU, George BOATENG (Lee HENDRIE 56), Ian TAYLOR, Luc NILIS (Julian JOACHIM 75), Dion DUBLIN (Darius VASSELL 65), Paul MERSON, Steven STONE.
MARILA PRIBRAM
Michal CALOUN, Marcel MACHA, Radek MYNAR (Michal NEHODA 83), Jaroslav SCHINDLER, Daniel SMEJKAL, Jiri RYCHLIK, Damir GRLIC, Robert NOVAK (Rudolf OTEPKA 68), Tomas KUCERA, Lukas JAROLIM (c), Marek KULIC (Michal SEMAN 72).

Not that it took Dublin much time to claim Villa's first goal of the season. Less than eight minutes had elapsed when the striker rose to head home a Merson corner and be saluted by supporters on the Birmingham Road End, which had effectively become the Holte End for the day. The lead lasted barely five minutes before Marek Kulic tucked

Brummie Road or the Holte? The claret-and-blue faithful take over the Birmingham Road End for the home leg against Marila – and celebrate Dion Dublin's goal after eight minutes

home an equaliser from close range – and it wasn't until just after half-time that Villa resumed their control. Two minutes into the second period, summer signing Luc Nilis sent a 25-yard free-kick thudding against a post, and in the 50th minute Ian Taylor prodded the ball past keeper Michael Calhoun to restore Villa's lead. This time they had no intention of letting it go, and on the hour Belgium international Nilis showed just why Gregory had signed him on a Bosman transfer. He was a picture of composure as he calmly fired home his first Villa goal following Gareth Barry's deep cross.

Sadly, Nilis would only score once more – a stunning left-foot volley against Chelsea – before his career was tragically ended by multiple fractures to his right leg in an horrific collision with Ipswich

Best man? John Gregory poses with the happy couple whose wedding reception followed Villa's win at The Hawthorns

keeper Richard Wright in early September. But even before that dreadful incident at Portman Road, we were aware there would be no UEFA Cup football on Villa's agenda that season. That notion was destroyed by a second knockout blow in less than two years at the hands of Celta Vigo. There was no success at the Balaidos this time, either, and the second leg must surely rank as the most farcical match in Villa's history.

The game in Spain was Villa's third in 11 days before the month of July was out and it was one to forget for David James. The former Liverpool keeper, whose mistake had presented Roberto Di Matteo with Chelsea's Cup Final winner in May, was again guilty of a costly fumble as Benni McCarthy pounced to give Celta a 1-0 win which, ironically, would have been more emphatic but for some fine saves from James earlier in the contest. A 1-0 deficit obviously wasn't insurmountable, even allowing for the fact that Villa again had to play the second leg at The Hawthorns. But the evening started with a pre-match ticking-off because the AVFC logo appeared twice on Villa's socks and it went downhill from there, with Gregory's boys fighting a losing battle from the 12th minute, when McCarthy opened the scoring. After Merson had seen a penalty saved by Jose Pinto, Gareth Barry equalised with a spot-kick on the stroke of half-time but McCarthy's second goal just short of the hour mark left Villa 2-1 down on the night, 3-1 behind on aggregate and effectively out of the competition.

While there were few complaints about the outcome, though, the spotlight was very much on Dieter Schoch, the Swiss official whose abject performance brought refereeing into disrepute. Schoch had taken charge of Villa's 3-0 away success against Stromsgodset a couple of years earlier but there was no indication that night in Norway about how woeful he would turn out to be in West Bromwich. A headmaster by profession, his penchant for discipline was

Semi-final, 1st leg
CELTA DE VIGO 1 ASTON VILLA 0
26th July 2000, Balaidos, Att: 9,550
1-0 McCARTHY (17)

CELTA DE VIGO
Jose Manuel PINTO COLORADO, Juan VELASCO DAMAS, Fernando Gabriel CACERES ZAYA, Everton GIOVANELLA, Tomas Alberto HERVAS GIRON (Jesus Antonio MORA NIETO 61), Valeriy KARPIN (c) (Pablo COIRA LOJO 90), Juan Francisco GARCIA, Dorival GHIDONI JUNIOR, Benedict Saul McCARTHY, Sergio FERNANDEZ GONZALEZ, Pablo GONZALEZ COUNAGO (Jose Maria MENA GARCIA 72).
ASTON VILLA
David JAMES, Steven STONE, Alan WRIGHT, Gareth BARRY, Jlloyd SAMUEL, George BOATENG (c), Ian TAYLOR, Luc NILIS (Darius VASSELL 19, Julian JOACHIM 90), Dion DUBLIN, Lee HENDRIE, Alan THOMPSON

never more evident than in that Villa v Celta game; it was more fitting to a classroom than a football pitch. Despite one shocking challenge from Juan Garcia, whose wayward boot left Steve Stone needing 17 stitches in a head wound, it was a game that never came remotely close to getting out of control. Yet Schoch somehow contrived to show a dozen yellow cards plus three red – for Villa's Ian Taylor and Alan Thompson, and Celta's Juan Velesco.

Thompson's dismissal was justified after the midfielder reacted angrily to another heavy Garcia challenge, this time on George Boateng, but the other two red cards were harsh in the extreme and Taylor's second caution was for diving when he was clearly jumping to avoid being clattered by a late tackle. Several of the other yellow cards were also brandished too enthusiastically, yet in the midst of all this, Garcia wasn't even booked for the challenge which left Stone's head bleeding copiously. Schoch also failed to punish Gustavo Lopez

Ouch! A distressed Steve Stone is led off by physio Jim Walker at The Hawthorns

for an elbow-led push on Gareth Southgate and then, to top it off, he blew the final whistle when there were a few minutes remaining – and had no option but to re-start the game when his error was pointed out to him. No wonder he was described in one report as the "man in the muddle".

While that blunder provided a comical finale, the ref was later heavily criticised by Gregory for his overall handling of the tie. "He was an embarrassment to UEFA," said the Villa boss. "I don't know where they got this guy from. They must have thrown him into the Intertoto from a local youth league. He was totally out of his depth. He was also unbelievably petty. Both teams wore their normal kits in the first leg but we had to change for this game because he said they clashed."

In hindsight, it could be argued that the match official was within his rights to order the change of kit and, indeed, to insist that the rules be followed implicitly regarding the logo on the socks. But those were merely irritants, rather

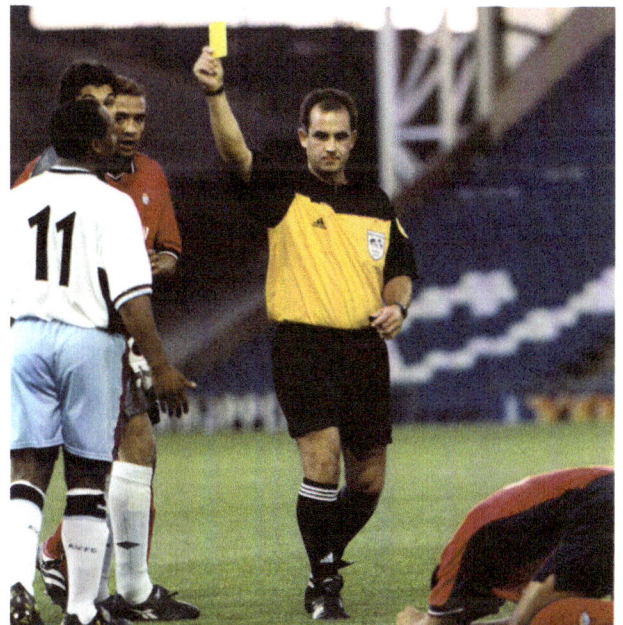

More cards than Clinton's – Dieter Schoch books Julian Joachim. He wasn't the only one

One-off – Striker Richard Walker (centre) and midfielder Stephen Cooke played their only European games in the second leg against Celta

than the core of the issue. Gregory wasn't alone in claiming Schoch had been an embarrassment to European football's governing body and Villa duly submitted an official protest to UEFA officials. The following year, the man known in Switzerland as "Red Didi" lost his FIFA badge and in 2002 he blew the final whistle on his refereeing career.

Semi-final, 2nd leg
ASTON VILLA 1 CELTA DE VIGO 2
2nd August 2000, The Hawthorns, Att: 11,909
0-1 McCARTHY (11) 1-1 BARRY (48 pen) 1-2 McCARTHY (59)

ASTON VILLA
David JAMES, Steven STONE (Alan THOMPSON 48), Alan WRIGHT, Gareth SOUTHGATE (c), Gareth BARRY, George BOATENG, Ian TAYLOR, Jlloyd SAMUEL (Lee HENDRIE 33), Richard WALKER, Paul MERSON, Julian JOACHIM (Stephen COOKE 74).
CELTA DE VIGO
Jose Mauel PINTO COLORADO, Juan VALESCO DAMAS, Fernando Gabriel CACERES ZAYA, Everton GIOVANELLA, Tomas Alberto HERVAS GIRON (Goran DJOROVIC 31, Pablo COIRA LOJO 51), Valeriy KARPIN (c), Gustavo Adrian LOPEZ PABLO (Jesus Antonio MORA NIETO 74), Juan Francisco GARCIA, Dorival GHIDONI JUNIOR, Benedict Saul McCARTHY, Sergio FERNANDEZ GONZALEZ.

LUC'S BONUS GAME

Luc Nilis's time in claret and blue was short-lived and mired in misfortune, but it would have been even shorter had it not been for a change of heart by UEFA. The Belgium international was initially ruled out of Villa's Intertoto Cup tie with Marila Pribram because he needed to be registered by 7th June to be eligible - a scenario that looked highly unlikely because his contract with his former club PSV Eindhoven was not due to come to an end until the final day of the month.

But UEFA altered the rule, putting the registration deadline back by a week. That development meant he could have played in both matches against Marila but, as it was, manager John Gregory left him out of the first leg in the Czech Republic in order to give him more time to acclimatise to his unfamiliar surroundings. Instead, Nilis made his debut for the club in the return fixture at The Hawthorns.

Nilis, who is pictured right during his goal-scoring appearance in the 3-1 home win over Marila Pribram, also found the target when he was handed his Villa Park debut in the Premier League encounter with Chelsea, but played only five games before suffering the injury which ended his career.

2001-02

Tragedy, triumph, Angel delight

Before July 2001, Villa had never faced Croatian opposition. By the end of September that year they had played two ties against teams from that country – in different competitions. For the second year running, the club's European adventure began in the pre-season Intertoto Cup. And after overcoming Slaven Belupo at the third-round stage, John Gregory's side went on to become one of the competition's three winners that summer by beating Stade Rennais of France in the semi-final and Swiss club Basel in the final.

Delight over the club's third European triumph was, sadly, short-lived. Although Villa's Intertoto success provided a route into the UEFA Cup, that episode came to an abrupt end elsewhere in Croatia, in a tie overshadowed by one of the most appalling events in history. The first leg of the first-round tie against NK Varteks was scheduled to take place at Villa Park on the evening of Thursday 13th September, but just over 48 hours earlier the world was stunned by news that al-Qaeda terrorists had crashed two hijacked passenger aircraft into the

Villa in Varazdin – The players line up before the second leg against Varteks. Left to right: Peter Schmeichel, Alan Wright, George Boateng, David Ginola, Lee Hendrie, Moustapha Hadji, Alpay, Bosko Balaban, Mark Delaney, Olof Mellberg, Hassan Kachloul. Top photo: Ginola and Boateng step out at the Stadion Varteksa.

First round, 1st leg
ASTON VILLA 2 NK VARAZDIN 3
20th September 2001, Villa Park, Att: 27,132
0-1 BJELANOVIC (43) 1-1 ANGEL (53) 1-2 KARIC (63) 2-2 ANGEL (70) 2-3 BJELANOVIC (85)

ASTON VILLA
Peter Boleslaw SCHMEICHEL (c), Mark Anthony DELANEY, Alan WRIGHT, Erik Olof MELLBERG, Alpay Fehmi OZALAN, George BOATENG, Juan Pablo ANGEL ARANGO, Steven STONE (David GINOLA 64), Moustapha HADJI, Darius VASSELL, Hassan KACHLOUL (Gareth BARRY 76).
NK VARAZDIN
Danijel MADARIC, Danijel HRMAN (Andrija BALAJIC 90), Matija KRISTIC, Ivan REZIC, Devis MUKAJ, Veldin KARIC, Miljenko MUMLEK (c), Sasa BJELANOVIC, Goran GRANIC, Silvester SABOLCKI, Zoran KASTEL

twin towers of the World Trade Centre in New York and another into the Pentagon in Washington, killing thousands. In the light of what had happened and with the resulting anxiety worldwide, no-one was in the mood for football and UEFA immediately postponed all ties scheduled for the remainder of that week, with Villa's first leg against Varteks put back until the following Thursday.

When the game did take place Juan Pablo Angel scored two excellent goals, converting a low cross from Steve Stone in the 53rd minute and heading home Hassan Kachloul's deep cross 13 minutes later. On each occasion, though, the Colombian merely cancelled out goals for Varteks: by Sasa Bjelanovic on the stroke of half-time and Veldin Karic on 63 minutes. And when Bjelanovic sent a deft volley past Peter Schmeichel, the isolated pocket of 30 visiting supporters were celebrating a 3-2 success they could hardly have envisaged.

But the business of having to win by two clear goals in the second leg wasn't Villa's only worry. The effect of the US terrorist attacks became evident the following Wednesday, when the Villa party gathered at Birmingham International Airport for the flight to Croatia. Security was more vigilant than anyone on board had ever experienced, and David Ginola had an item from his toilet bag confiscated before being allowed to board the plane. After his hand luggage had passed through the X-ray machine, he was told he must hand over a pair of nail-cutters because they constituted a potential danger. Ginola, though, was more than happy to comply with the regulations. "I don't think my nail-clippers could be regarded as any kind of weapon," he said. "But it's good to see the security people taking this so seriously."

At least Ginola was able to fly, which was more than could be said for Hyder Jawad, the newly appointed football correspondent of the Birmingham Post. Hyder found he had forgotten his passport and by the time he had fetched it and returned to the airport, the flight to Zagreb had departed. He immediately made alternative

First round, 2nd leg
NK VARAZDIN 0 ASTON VILLA 1
27th September 2001, Stadion Varteksa, Att: 8,000
0-1 HADJI (90)

NK VARAZDIN
Danijel MADARIC, Danijel HRMAN (Antun ANDRICEVIC 90), Matija KRISTIC, Ivan REZIC, Devis MUKAJ, Veldin KARIC (Oscar DROBNE 90), Miljenko MUMLEK (c) (Andrija BALAJIC 58), Sasa BJELANOVIC, Goran GRANIC, Silvester SABOLCKI, Zoran KASTEL.
ASTON VILLA
Peter Boleslaw SCHMEICHEL (c), Mark Anthony DELANEY, Alan WRIGHT, Erik Olof MELLBERG (Steven STONE 45), Alpay Fehmi OZALAN, George BOATENG, David GINOLA, Lee HENDRIE, Bosko BALABAN (Juan Pablo ANGEL ARANGO HT), Moustapha HADJI, Hassan KACHLOUL (Dion DUBLIN 64)

Keep it close – Hassan Kachloul holds off a challenge from Silvester Sabolcki in the away leg against Varteks

travel arrangements via Munich, and arrived in Zagreb as his fellow reporters were heading out for dinner that evening.

On arrival in Croatia the focus was very much on Villa's new striker Bosko Balaban, who had recently been signed from Dinamo Zagreb for £5.8m. Balaban had watched the first leg from the subs' bench but his return home generated enormous interest in the city where he had shot to prominence as a prolific scorer. He was constantly the centre of attention for the local media as TV, radio and newspaper reporters requested interviews. Unfortunately, Balaban did all his talking off the pitch. Although he was included in the starting line-up at the compact Varazdin Stadium, an hour's drive from the capital, he was so ineffective that he was replaced at half-time by Angel. Not that the substitution made a great deal of difference on a night when Villa were nowhere near their best. Going into stoppage time, the aggregate score remained 3-2 to Varteks, which made it all the more galling that Mustapha Hadji's superb dipping shot in the first minute of added time should give Villa a 1-0 win on the night. At least the goal briefly silenced 9,500 vociferous home supporters but three minutes later the final whistle blew and the Croatians were celebrating a place in the second round.

Too little, too late - Mustapha Hadji's stunning long-range shot is on its way into the Varteks net. But the Moroccan midfielder's late strike wasn't enough to prevent Villa going out on the away goals rule

Villa had also been based in Zagreb at the start of that European venture, a first round Intertoto tie against Slaven Belupo. The club's first match against Croatian opposition was played in blazing sunshine at the tiny Gradski Stadium in Koprivnica on the second Saturday of July. The conditions certainly weren't ideal for the team's first action

Third round, 1st leg
SLAVEN KOPRIVNICA 2 ASTON VILLA 1
14th July 2001, Gradski Stadium, Att: 3,000
1-0 CRNAC (61) 1-1 GINOLA (87) 2-1 GERSAK (89)

SLAVEN KOPRIVNICA
Ivica SOLOMUN, Petar BOSNJAK, Frano AMZIC, Pavo CRNAC (Zdravko MEDIMOREC 80), Stipe BOSNJAK, Hasan KACIC, Roy FERENCINA, Mario KOVACEVIC, Renato JURCEC (c) (Miljenko KOVACIC 49), Damir MUZEK (Goran GERSAK 58), Marijo DODIK.
ASTON VILLA
Peter ENCKELMAN, Mark Anthony DELANEY, Alan WRIGHT, Gareth BARRY (David GINOLA 71), Alpay Fehmi OZALAN, George BOATENG, Stephen STAUNTON, Lee HENDRIE, Dion DUBLIN (Darius VASSELL 52), Paul MERSON (c), Steven STONE (Jlloyd SAMUEL 77).

of the season and the players undeniably toiled in the unforgiving heat. As the match report in the Aston Villa Review suggested, it was a case of "Slaven away at a cooker." With the exception of the Turk Alpay Ozalan, Villa's defenders were uneasy throughout the match, although just over an hour had elapsed before Slaven managed a breakthrough, Pavo Crnac taking advantage of the visitors' hesitancy

Stretching out – Substitute Darius Vassell warms up on the touchline before replacing Dion Dublin in the first leg against Slaven Belupo

to burst through and score with a powerful shot. That was how it stayed until the final minute, when Ginola produced a piece of magic. His fine curling shot caught keeper Ivica Solomun completely by surprise as it flew into the far corner – only for Slaven to respond immediately with a winner from substitute Goran Gersak.

The weather was considerably milder for the second leg the following Saturday, when club officials were slightly taken aback by the size of the crowd. Attendances for the club's first two "home" matches in this competition – both played at The Hawthorns 12 months earlier – had been modest. But the arrival of summer signings Peter Schmeichel, Moustapha Hadji and Hassan Kachloul had clearly sparked supporters' imagination and 27,850 turned up at Villa Park for the Slaven game. They were rewarded with an authoritative performance which earned John Gregory's side a 2-0 victory. Lee Hendrie never scored a Villa hat-trick, although he was desperately close on this occasion. The young midfielder opened the scoring on 19 minutes, blasting in a cross from Hassan Kachloul, and six

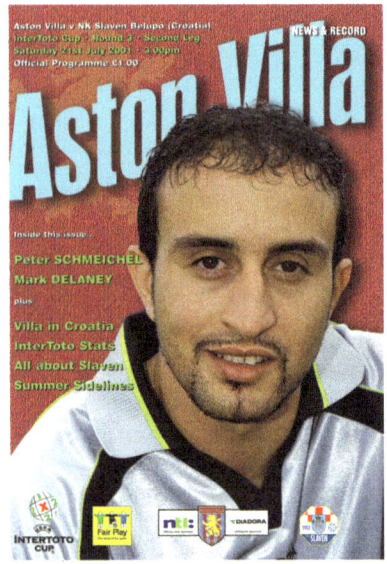

Cover star – New signing Hassan Kachloul featured on the cover of the Villa News & Record (left) for the home leg against Slaven

minutes before the interval he doubled the lead by prodding the ball home in a crowded goalmouth. Then, on 62 minutes, he was all set to celebrate number three as he lined up a shot for what looked a certain goal, only to have the ball whipped off his toe by a defender.

Nevertheless, those two first half strikes were enough to see Villa through 3-2 on aggregate, and three days later they were on their way across the Channel for a second-round, first-leg tie against Stade Rennais. As in the previous away leg, a last-minute goal threw Gregory's boys a lifeline, this time after the hosts had established a two-goal lead and had looked capable of increasing it every time they attacked.

The French outfit were ahead through Lucas Severino in the 20th minute and when Cyril Chapuis doubled their advantage mid-way through the second half it looked very much like Villa's interest in the Intertoto would end at the semi-final stage for the second year running. Indeed, they would surely have been putting their passports away but for a crucial Peter Enckelman save after a weak George Boateng back-pass had presented the hosts with an almost certain third goal. Having survived that scare, however, the visitors grew more confident during the latter stages, and when Darius Vassell climbed to head home a Ginola free-kick right at the end, the deficit suddenly looked much less daunting.

The importance of Vassell's last-gasp goal became evident a week later. Ginola had started the first leg on the bench but he was in the starting line-up at Villa Park and made his presence felt after just five minutes by delivering a teasing low cross which a stretching Dion Dublin side-footed into the net. Another sizeable crowd –

Semi-final, 2nd leg
ASTON VILLA 1 STADE RENNAIS 0
1st August 2001, Villa Park, Att: 30,700
1-0 DUBLIN (5)

ASTON VILLA
Peter ENCKELMAN, Mark Anthony DELANEY, Alan WRIGHT, Gareth BARRY, Alpay Fehmi OZALAN, George BOATENG, Hassan KACHLOUL, Dion DUBLIN, Paul MERSON (c) (Moustapha HADJI 57), Lee HENDRIE (Steven STONE 75), David GINOLA (Darius VASSELL 85).
STADE RENNAIS
Eric DURAND (c), Gregory PAISLEY, Yoann BIGNE, Lamine DIATTA, Stephane GREGOIRE, Julien ESCUDE, Olivier MONTERRUBIO (Frederic PIQUIONNE 77), Cyril YAPI, Gael DANIC, Cyril CHAPUIS (Severino LUCAS 51), Vanderson MARQUES PEREIRA (Christophe LEROUX 58).

30,782 – settled down in anticipation of an emphatic victory, but it failed to materialise. When the final whistle sounded, Dublin's early goal was all that separated the teams on the night. It was 2-2 on aggregate – and Vassell's late header in France became invaluable.

Villa were through on the away-goals rule, and there was another first for the club in the final. When they lined up for the first leg against Basel, it was the first time Villa had faced Swiss opposition in a competitive fixture. The match at St Jakob-Park proved far less testing than the games against the men from Rennes in the semi-final. Despite the backing of fervent fans, Basel's raids carried only minimal threat, and even when the home side managed to find a way through Villa's well-organised defence, goalkeeper Enckelman was equal to anything they could offer. Just before half-time, the visitors were close to scoring when Hadji just failed to convert Dublin's knock-down from close range, and in the 59th minute Villa took the lead. Kachloul's drive from the left was too strong for Pascal Zuberbuhler and when the goalkeeper could only block it, Paul Merson was perfectly positioned for a tap-in. For just over a quarter-of-an-hour Villa looked set to head for home clutching that more than useful lead, only for the notion to be dispelled when Christian Gimenez equalised with a goal of some similarity after Enckelman had blocked a fierce drive from home substitute Carlos Varela.

Having played

MATCH REPORT • FC Basel 1 Aston Villa 1

Swiss rolled by Merson as Villa move nearer

Knock-out competitions are supposed to intensify the further they progress, but after Villa notch a valuable away goal for the third round in succession, courtesy of captain Paul Merson, they are entitled to feel that the steeper slopes of this tournament are already behind them.

Against a Basel side which f...

sped clear of Mark Delaney in the 44th minute to try his luck once more, but the Finn was once again quickly out to block the shot with his knees.

Gimenez and Ergic saw good first-half chances go wide and their team quickly heard the frustration of their fans, which would have been considerably worse had Moustapha Hadji converted Dion Dublin's knock-down from just a few feet out, after 15 minutes. Dublin's header was onto the Moroccan before he knew it, though, and he stabbed a shot narrowly past the post.

Villa finally broke the deadlock shortly before the hour mark, when Hassan Kachloul tried a shot from the left that was too hot to handle for Zuberbühler, whose block sent the ball ...

● Merson's moment... Paul Merson's 59th minute tap-in hands Villa the lead.

Final, 1st leg
BASEL 1893 1 ASTON VILLA 1
7th August 2001, St Jakob-Park, Att: 25,879
0-1 MERSON (58) 1-1 GIMENEZ (74)

BASEL 1893
Pascal ZUBERBUHLER, Alexandre QUENNOZ, Oliver KREUZER (c), Jean-Michel TCHOUGA, Hakan YAKIN (Sebastien BARBERIS 72), Christian GIMENEZ, Murat YAKIN, Yao AZIAWONOU, Mario CANTALUPPI (Carlos VARELA PEREZ 57), Ivan ERGIC.
ASTON VILLA
Peter ENCKELMAN, Mark Anthony DELANEY, Alan WRIGHT, Gareth BARRY, Alpay Fehmi OZALAN, George BOATENG, Hassan KACHLOUL, Dion DUBLIN (Steven STONE 79), Paul MERSON (c) (Darius VASSELL 65), Lee HENDRIE.

five Intertoto games in just over three weeks, Villa turned their attention to domestic action the following weekend when they creditably drew at Tottenham Hotspur in their opening Premiership game of the 2001-02 campaign. While they drew a blank at White Hart Lane, Gregory's boys were in irrepressible mood when Basel arrived at Villa Park for the second leg of the Intertoto final three nights later. What's more, the home team had to overcome the shock of falling behind to a goal from Aussie Scott Chipperfield on the half-hour.

Once again, it was Ginola who provided the lifeline, just as he had in the previous two European ties. A minute before half-time his clever flick, following a Boateng pass, enabled Vassell to smash home the equaliser and from that juncture the outcome was never in doubt. Ten minutes after the interval, the Frenchman swung a free-kick towards the near post and Angel, who had scored just once since his £9.5m

On the level – Darius Vassell hits Villa's equaliser at home to Basel on the stroke of half-time

Because I'm worth it – The hair made famous by a L'Oreal advert is flowing freely, and so is David Ginola, who scored the fourth goal against Basel. Below: Job done – Angel makes his way back to the dressing room after being substituted by Dion Dublin in the 77th minute against Basel. The striker had just scored his second goal to put Villa 3-1 up

record transfer from River Plate of Argentina, arrived perfectly for a header which put Villa in front.

Angel had gone part-way to Holte End hero status with his goal against Coventry City on the final day of the previous season and this was another nudge in the right direction. On 77 minutes, a slice of good fortune enabled the Colombian striker to enhance his relationship with the claret-and-blue faithful when his shot took a deflection to establish a 3-1 lead and effectively put the game beyond the Swiss team's reach. Six minutes from the end, Ginola crowned a scintillating display by sprinting from the left to stroke a low shot into the corner of the net.

Final, 2nd leg
ASTON VILLA 4 BASEL 1893 1
21st August 2001, Villa Park, Att: 39,593
0-1 CHIPPERFIELD (30) 1-1 VASSELL (45) 2-1 ANGEL (55) 3-1 ANGEL (78)
4-1 GINOLA (84)

ASTON VILLA
Peter Boleslaw SCHMEICHEL (c), Mark Anthony DELANEY, Stephen STAUNTON (Jlloyd SAMUEL 68), Gareth BARRY, Alpay Fehmi OZALAN, George BOATENG, Steven STONE, Lee HENDRIE (Hassan KACHLOUL 65), Darius VASSELL, David GINOLA, Juan Pablo ANGEL ARANGO (Dion DUBLIN 80).
BASEL 1893
Pascal ZUBERBUHLER, Philippe CRAVERO, Alexandre QUENNOZ, Oliver KREUZER (c) (Ivan KNEZ 86), Benjamin HUGGEL, Carlos VARELA PEREZ, George KOUMANTARAKIS, Hakan YAKIN (Sebastien BARBERIS 68), Christian GIMENEZ (Herve TUM 83), Murat YAKIN, Scott CHIPPERFIELD.

We've won the cup – Villa's players gather for a photo after being presented with the Intertoto Cup. Back row: Jonathan Bewers, Lee Hendrie, Dion Dublin, Peter Schmeichel, Aplay Ozalan, Darius Vassell, Hassan Kachloul, Peter Enckelman, Gareth Barry, Mark Delaney, David Ginola. Front: Moustapha Hadji, Steve Staunton, George Boateng, Steve Stone, Paul Merson (with the trophy), Jlloyd Samuel

Villa had beaten Bayern Munich in the 1982 European Cup final and Barcelona in the Super Cup the following year. Now they could boast a third European trophy, albeit one that wasn't quite as prestigious as the previous two. It was time for the celebrations to begin.

IN IT TO WIN IT

Dion Dublin is proud to have won a European trophy with Villa – and it doesn't bother him in the slightest that the success was achieved in a much-maligned competition. Many clubs took part almost reluctantly in the Intertoto Cup, which involved starting in June for those involved in the early rounds before the summer tournament was merged into the new Europa League in 2009. Villa, thankfully, avoided any ridiculously early starts, and Dublin is convinced a strong mental approach helped them to win the 2001 tournament. "A lot of people didn't take the Intertoto Cup seriously," said the striker who secured Villa's passage to the final at the expense of Stade Rennais. "But we had a good side and we were in it to win it. The gaffer picked strong sides and we had some great leaders – players like Paul Merson, Peter Schmeichel and George Boateng. When you look at the players in that squad it's amazing we didn't achieve more. On paper, as individuals, we were very strong. I'm proud to say I won a trophy with Villa, albeit one which a lot of people weren't interested in. Our attitude towards the competition was certainly better than most."

GET HERE EARLY!

Villa stayed in Zagreb for both of their 2001 games in Croatia. And secretary Steve Stride found himself with nearly seven hours to kill before the Intertoto Cup tie against Slaven Belupo. While everyone else enjoyed a lie-in on the morning of the match, Steve had to be up at 7.30am for the trip to Slaven's stadium, an hour and 45 minutes away. He was required to attend the pre-match meeting organised by UEFA, at which officials from the two clubs can iron out any problems.

These meetings usually last at least an hour, but not on this occasion. He recalls: "It was a case of 'Good morning, allow me to introduce everyone. Are both teams happy? Are the kit colours in order? Excellent.' The whole thing lasted all of five minutes!" At least Stride was subsequently able to ensure that officials of other clubs got their money's worth from pre-match gatherings. After leaving Villa in 2007, he was appointed a UEFA delegate and has travelled all over Europe to organise such meetings.

BOAZ THE BAG MAN

Young keeper Boaz Myhill flew to France for the day – to sit on the bench and help lug the team's kit bags around. With Peter Schmeichel doubtful after suffering a calf injury, Myhill received a call on the day before the match against Stade Rennais, requesting him to join the squad. That presented a problem, because California-born Myhill couldn't find his passport. He eventually located it at Villa Park, chief scout Ross MacLaren having accidentally kept it following the team's return from Croatia for the Slaven game. While Peter Enckelman took Schmeichel's place between the posts, Myhill was among the substitutes in Rennes – and then he helped kit man Jim Paul, a task which was nothing new to him. On Villa's return to Birmingham, he quipped: "Sometimes I think I'm going to spend the rest of my life moving kit bags around with Jim!"

DOCTOR – OR BALL-BOY?

Villa's medical officer Dr Barrie Smith was made redundant from his "part-time" job as Villa prepared for the away leg of the UEFA Cup tie against Varteks. When not attending to the players' medical needs, he regularly volunteered to retrieve balls at the club's vast training ground. But the team's warm-up session in Croatia took place in the shadow of Dinamo Zagreb's Maksimar Stadium, on a pitch edged by high fencing. It also took place on a heavy surface, ensuring that wayward shots didn't travel far.

"I regard myself unofficial ball-boy at Bodymoor Heath," said Barrie as he watched the 75-minute work-out in Zagreb. "But there's clearly no need for my services here!"

CHRISTIAN v LIONS

It was a case of Christian against the Lions when Villa faced Basel in the Intertoto Cup final. The Swiss club were managed by Christian Gross, the former Tottenham Hotspur manager, and he must have had a feeling of déjà vu after the second leg. Shortly after his appointment by the London club in 1997, he had brought Spurs to Villa Park for a Boxing Day fixture – and ended up on the wrong end of a 4-1 scoreline. Little could he have known it would be the same story for Basel nearly four years later...

Happy Alpay, happy Villa – That was a catchphrase often used by Alpay Ozalan, and it was certainly true when the Turk acknowledged supporters following the victory over Basel. In the background are two of the side's international stars, Paul Merson (left) and keeper Peter Schmeichel

FULL-TIME VILLAN

The European ties in 2001 were featured in the new *Full-time Villan* publication.. The double-sided A4 sheet (below) provided a souvenir of every game that season, plus other editions to mark the arrival of new signings. It was available in the club shop for 50p but disappointing sales resulted in it being discontinued after just one season.

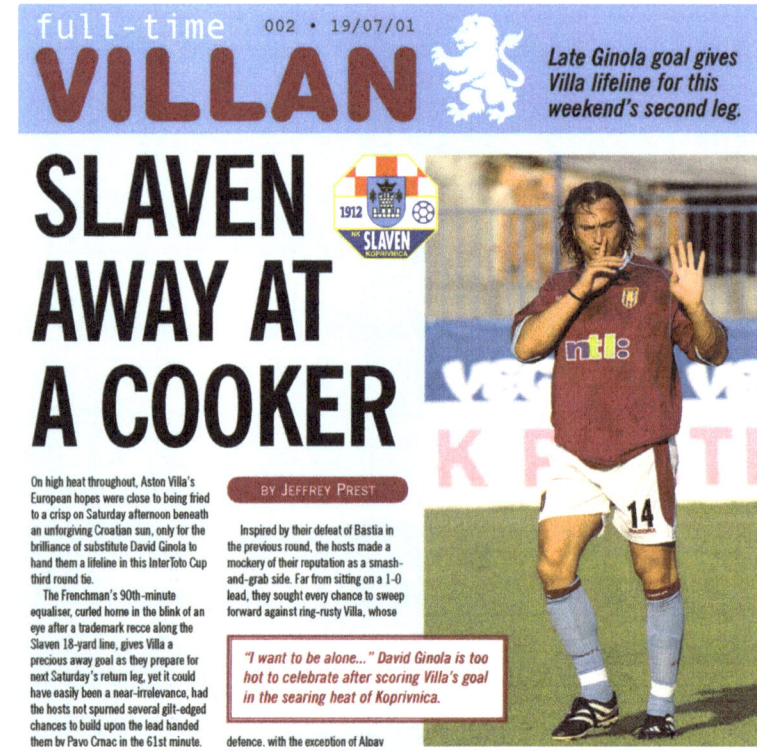

full-time 002 • 19/07/01

VILLAN

Late Ginola goal gives Villa lifeline for this weekend's second leg.

SLAVEN AWAY AT A COOKER

BY JEFFREY PREST

On high heat throughout, Aston Villa's European hopes were close to being fried to a crisp on Saturday afternoon beneath an unforgiving Croatian sun, only for the brilliance of substitute David Ginola to hand them a lifeline in this InterToto Cup third round tie.

The Frenchman's 90th-minute equaliser, curled home in the blink of an eye after a trademark recce along the Slaven 18-yard line, gives Villa a precious away goal as they prepare for next Saturday's return leg, yet it could have easily been a near-irrelevance, had the hosts not spurned several gilt-edged chances to build upon the lead handed them by Pavo Crnac in the 61st minute.

Inspired by their defeat of Bastia in the previous round, the hosts made a mockery of their reputation as a smash-and-grab side. Far from sitting on a 1-0 lead, they sought every chance to sweep forward against ring-rusty Villa, whose defence, with the exception of Alpay

"I want to be alone..." David Ginola is too hot to celebrate after scoring Villa's goal in the searing heat of Koprivnica.

2002-03

Swiss roll – but no French fancy

There's an old saying that sport and religion don't mix. Villa's players willingly endorsed that sentiment when their 2002-03 Intertoto Cup campaign looked certain to be over almost before it had begun. Once again, they entered the competition at the third-round stage, and the venue for the first leg of their tie against Zurich had to be switched. The Swiss club's own stadium was hosting a Jehovah's Witness convention.

Consequently, the match was played at the Stadion Hardturm, home of Zurich's neighbours, Grasshoppers. And even though the home side didn't have genuine home advantage, they emerged 2-0 winners, leaving Villa with a Swiss mountain to climb in the second leg. It certainly wasn't what manager Graham Taylor had in mind as he led the club in European competition for the first time. During

Dublin' up – Dion Dublin and Gareth Barry pressure Zurichs defence but Villa lost 2-0 in Switzerland

Third round, 1st leg
ZURICH 2 ASTON VILLA 0
21st July 2002, Hardturm, Att: 4,500
1-0 KEITA (32) 2-0 YASAR (83)

ZURICH
Miroslav KONIG, Alain NEF, Wilco HELLINGA, Stephan KELLER, Daniel TARONE (Luca IODICE 58), Urs FISCHER (c), Ursal YASAR, Kanga Gauthier AKALE, Yvan QUENTIN, Alhassane KEITA (Daniel GYGAX 47), David PALLAS REY (Tariq CHIHAB 77).
ASTON VILLA
Peter ENCKELMAN, Mark Anthony DELANEY, Alan WRIGHT, George BOATENG, Dion DUBLIN (c), Jlloyd SAMUEL, Steven STONE, Michael BOULDING (Moustapha HADJI 58), Peter James CROUCH, Thomas HITZLSPERGER (Lee HENDRIE 73), Gareth BARRY (Hassan KACHLOUL 81).

his first spell in charge, Taylor had taken Villa to First Division runners-up spot behind Liverpool in 1989-90 but had missed out on sampling UEFA Cup football the following season by accepting the FA's offer to become Bobby Robson's successor as England manager.

Now, having returned for a second spell in the dug-out following John Gregory's departure, he was hoping Villa could repeat their Intertoto success of 12 months earlier and earn another "back door" passage into the UEFA Cup. It just wasn't Villa's night in Switzerland, though, and perhaps understandably so, given that six players – Olof Mellberg, Marcus Allback, Darius Vassell, Steve Staunton, Alpay Ozalan and Bosko Balaban – were all taking a well-earned break following their involvement in that summer's World Cup finals in South Korea and Japan. A combination of those absentees and the fact that Zurich had already played four matches in earlier rounds, gave the hosts a telling edge. Even so, Villa created a number of decent openings and looked more likely to score in the opening half hour, when Thomas Hitzlsperger had a stinging left-foot effort tipped away by keeper Miroslav Konig.

It came as a shock when Zurich took the lead just past the half-hour mark, Alhassane Keita taking Peter Enckelman by surprise with a low shot from the edge of the penalty area which squeezed past the keeper and into the net. There was no further score until seven minutes from the end when a slip by Dion Dublin – playing at the back because of

PETER **CROUCH** FEELS THE WEIGHT OF STEPHAN **KELLER'S** CHALLENGE

It's not how you start...

Ask most fans of Premiership clubs at Christmas how their heroes fared in the first pre-season outing and they will not have a clue.

High scoring draws at the local non-League club or defeat on tour against a team of Swedish part-timers will long have been forgotten. Not so this 2-0 defeat in Zurich.

But, as Graham Taylor said after a disappointing first-leg, the big disadvantage of the InterToto Cup is that you are under pressure to produce results from day one. These games matter.

How Villa's programme reflected on events in Zurich

Villa's lack of central defenders – allowed Ursal Yasar to double the home side's advantage. In between the goals, Villa had rarely been under any threat and even the home side could scarcely believe they were suddenly in such a commanding position. Yasar's celebration, in fact, was so demonstrative that he was sent off. Unfortunately, any notion that Villa might capitalise on having an extra player was dispelled a minute later when Jlloyd Samuel also saw red for a second bookable offence, although substitutes Mustapha Hadji and Hassan Kachloul went close to reducing the deficit in the closing stages.

The match in Zurich brought a debut for Michael Boulding, a former tennis professional who had recently been signed from Grimsby Town. It wasn't the most auspicious of starts, Boulding being replaced by Hadji 12 minutes into the second half. But Taylor offered his new boy another starting appearance in the second leg at Villa Park, and the young midfielder repaid the manager's faith by opening the scoring. As expected, Villa pressed from the outset and should really have been more than a single goal ahead at the

Third round, 2nd leg
ASTON VILLA 3 ZURICH 0
27th July 2002, Villa Park, Att: 18,349
1-0 BOULDING (32) 2-0 ALLBACK (48) 3-0 STAUNTON (77)

ASTON VILLA
Peter ENCKELMAN, Mark Anthony DELANEY, Gareth BARRY, Erik Olof MELLBERG, Stephen STAUNTON (c), Thomas HITZLSPERGER, Ian TAYLOR, Lee HENDRIE, Peter James CROUCH, Marcus ALLBACK (Stefan MOORE 71), Michael BOULDING (Paul MERSON HT).
ZURICH
Miroslav KONIG, Alain NEF, Wilco HELLINGA, Stephan KELLAR, Mario RAIMONDI (Daniel TARONE 74), Urs FISCHER (c), Tariq CHIHAB (David PALLAS REY 63), Kanga Gauthier AKALE, Yvan QUENTIN, Luca IODICE, Alhassane KEITA (Daniel GYGAX HT)

One-nil – or maybe fifteen-love? Michael Boulding marks his home debut by serving up his first Villa goal

interval, although they were grateful for Boulding's awareness as he slid in to convert from point-blank range after Gareth Barry's deep free-kick had been headed across the goalmouth by towering striker Peter Crouch.

If the home side were indebted to Boulding for that predatory finish, it also has to be said his departure at half-time had a bearing on the second goal, which put Villa two-up on the day and level on aggregate. Three minutes into the second period, home fans were furious when no free-kick was awarded after Lee Hendrie was scythed down on the halfway line, but substitute Paul Merson responded with

the sort of magic which epitomised his outstanding career. As Hendrie crashed to the ground, Merson collected the loose ball and darted through the middle before delicately lifting it into Allback's path. The Swedish striker, who had signed from Dutch club Heerenveen just before the World Cup, marked his Villa debut with a stunning right-foot volley which went in off the underside of the bar.

While the two new boys

On the mark – Villa level (above) with Marcus Allback's fierce drive via the bar. Super Steve (below) – the skipper savours the goal that gave Villa a 3-2 aggregate win, much to sub Stefan Moore's delight

marked their first Villa Park appearances with goals, it was fitting that Villa's third – the one which carried Taylor's men into the semi-finals – should come from a less likely source. Skipper Steve Staunton hadn't scored since a third-round FA Cup tie at Portsmouth more than two-and-half years earlier but when Hitzlsperger delivered a fine corner from the right, the Republic of Ireland international produced a perfectly-placed header to clinch a 3-2 aggregate success.

Villa had overcome Swiss opposition for the second year running, having beaten Basel in the previous season's final, and when they flew across the Channel three days later the squad were optimistic they could do likewise against French opponents. Having travelled to Brittany in 2001, their destination this time was the delightful northern city of Lille, which had been nominated European City of Culture for 2004. There was a slight problem for Taylor when he faced the media on the day before the first leg because most of the reporters didn't speak any English, but help was at hand from David Chatfield, an Englishman who had lived in France since 1973. While Chatfield translated for the manager, there was no such problem for Mustapha Hadji, who had spent most of his life in France and happily chatted to the local journalists in French.

The players and club officials made the trip by air, and around 100 supporters arrived in two coaches on the day of the match in time to soak up the mid-afternoon sun and enjoy a few beers outside a bar on the main square before heading to the Stade Grimonprez-Jooris, a very basic arena which had been opened in 1975 but which would be bulldozed less than two years after Villa's visit. If it was hardly state-of-the-art, though, the tiny stadium was a pleasant enough setting for the first leg of the semi-final and the visitors had every reason to feel satisfied with a workmanlike performance that earned a draw which should really have been a win. With Mellberg and Staunton in commanding

Marcus Allback - and Villa's award-wining match-day programme - on the ball

Semi-final, 1st leg
LILLE OSC 1 ASTON VILLA 1
31st July 2002, Grimonprez-Jooris, Att: 14,437
0-1 TAYLOR (75) 1-1 D'AMICO (90)

LILLE OSC
Gregory WIMBEE (c), Abdelilah FAHMI, Philippe BRUNEL (Nicolas BONNAL 61), Matt MOUSSILOU (Hector Santiago TAPIA URDILE 71), Stephane PICHOT, Mile STERJOVSKI, Gregory TAFFOREAU, Mathieu CHALME (Djezon BOUTOILLE 71), Matthieu DELPIERRE, Sylvain N'DIAYE, Patricio D'AMICO.
ASTON VILLA
Stefan POSTMA, Mark Anthony DELANEY, Jlloyd SAMUEL, Erik Olof MELLBERG, Stephen STAUNTON (c), Thomas HITZLSPERGER, Ian TAYLOR, Moustapha HADJI (Darius VASSELL 70), Peter James CROUCH, Marcus ALLBACK (Steven STONE 81), Gareth BARRY.

form at the back, the visitors took the sting out of Lille's frequent attacks and created a few chances of their own before deservedly taking a 76th-minute lead. Mellberg met Hitzlsperger's corner with a header which was parried by keeper Gregory Wimbee and Ian Taylor was perfectly positioned to stab home the rebound from a couple of yards.

It didn't rank among his best goals ,but as the 90-minute mark passed, it looked certain to provide a perfect platform for the second leg. Then, just as Stefan Postma was ready to celebrate a clean sheet on his debut, Villa's new keeper was beaten in the second minute of stoppage time when Fernando D'Amico flung himself forward to head the equaliser from six yards.

If that was a disappointing finale, it still seemed merely a minor inconvenience when Villa lined up on home soil a week later, looking to book a place in the final for the second year running. The signs were promising as they kicked off with an away goal in the bank; surely they could look forward to a final against either VfB Stuttgart or Slaven Belupo, the side they had overcome in the third round 12 months earlier? The manager wasn't quite so sure. "Even if we had been 1-0 up from the first game, there would still be a second leg," he pointed out. "What we have to do is give Lille more problems but we certainly don't underestimate them."

Taylor was right to be cautious. Even a single-goal success in France wouldn't have been enough as Villa were right out of sorts against a resolute side who had Champions League experience from a year earlier.

> **Semi-final, 2nd leg**
> **ASTON VILLA 0 LILLE OSC 2**
> **7th August 2002, Villa Park, Att: 26,147**
> **0-1 FAHMI (45) 0-2 BONNAL (47)**
>
> **ASTON VILLA**
> **Peter ENCKELMAN, Mark Anthony DELANEY, Stephen STAUNTON (c), Erik Olof MELLBERG, Dion DUBLIN (Lee HENDRIE HT), Thomas HITZLSPERGER, Ian TAYLOR (Moustapha HADJI 57), Darius VASSELL, Peter James CROUCH (Stefan MOORE 80), Marcus ALLBACK, Gareth BARRY.**
> **LILLE OSC**
> **Gregory WIMBEE (c), Abdelilah FAHMI, Rafael SCHMITZ, Nicolas BONNAL (Benoit CHEYROU 62), Philippe BRUNEL (Djezon BOUTOILLE 69). Matt MOUSSILOU (Mile STERJOVSKI 81), Gregory TAFFOREAU, Mathieu CHALME, Matthieu DELPIERRE, Christophe LANDRIN, Sylvain N'DYIAYE.**

French resistance – Peter Crouch is unable to break down the visitors' defence during the second leg against Lille at Villa Park

Lille were equally bereft until, in first-half stoppage time a free-kick from Abdelilah Fahmi deflected off Allback to leave Enckelman wrong-footed. A minute into the second half, Nicolas Bonnal side-footed home after the keeper pushed aside Philippe Brunel's fierce drive, so Taylor's men needed to score three - an incline resembling the French Alps. Despite their non-stop endeavour they barely gained a foothold.

A SHIRTY GRANDSON

Graham Taylor could be seen gazing up at the Trinity Road stand after the 3-0 home victory over Zurich, but he wasn't seeking approval from chairman Doug Ellis. The manager was trying to spot his five-year-old grandson Jake, who had watched from the directors' box. The youngster was wearing the new replica shirt, complete with his name on the back, which Taylor's wife Rita had purchased. "It would have been lovely to see him in his new shirt but I couldn't spot him," said Taylor."

LILY THE PINK

Villa's media team faced a sizeable problem when they were compiling the programme for the home leg against Lille. The opposition section in the Villa News & Record comprised the regular pen pictures, plus five paragraphs describing what excellent progress Lille had made.

A short, snappy headline was required, and designer Phil Lees came up with a classic. Suddenly recalling the novelty 1960s hit record by The Scaffold, he said: "Got it – Lille in the pink!" We'll drink-a-drink-a-drink to that...even if it was the visitors who were celebrating at the end of match.

Lille in the pink

By comparison with the likes of Monaco, Marseille, Bordeaux and Paris St Germain, Lille Olympic Sporting Club are not one of the glamour clubs of French football, but they have achieved a satisfying degree of success during their short history.

Formed in 1944, they have been champions twice (also for the last time in 1954) and won the cup on two occasions.

In fairness, they have also had a number of spells in the second division, but there is no question that they have been heading in the right direction since being promoted as champions two years ago.

In their first season back in the top flight, they finished third to clinch a European Champions League place, although the limited capacity of their Grimonprez-Jooris stadium meant they had to play their home matches at nearby Lens.

Nevertheless, they gave a good account of themselves in all three of their group home matches, drawing 1-1 against both Manchester United and

Eyes left – or right, as far as Darius Vassell is concerned. Like the rest of his team-mates, the striker's night ended in massive disappointment thanks to a 2-0 early-August defeat. It was a result that helped justify the imaginative headline drummed up (left) by a member of Villa's media department

2008-09

Fairy tales from a great Dane...

Whenever people recall the truly great European nights at Villa Park, the games which immediately spring to mind are Barcelona in 1978 and 1983, Dynamo Kiev and Anderlecht in 1982, Inter Milan in 1990 and 1994, and Atletico Madrid in 1998. On Wednesday 23rd October 2008, another Euro classic was added to the list. It was the first time Villa had been involved in the group stages of a European competition, which had been introduced to the UEFA Cup four years earlier. Whatever the outcome of the opening game, there would still be an opportunity to progress to the knockout stages, with each of the five teams playing two fixtures at home and two away.

But Villa were still anxious to make a flying start, and their first game in Group F was a daunting test against Ajax. The very name of the famous Amsterdam club produced an air of anticipation around the stadium which created a truly spine-tingling atmosphere. And it got better still when goals from skipper Martin Laursen and Gareth Barry clinched a 2-1 victory which gave Martin O'Neill's men a

Danish delight – Martin Laursen has just given Villa the perfect start against Dutch giants Ajax, and the Danish defender's delight is all too evident. The same can be said of James Milner and Carlos Cuellar

positive kick-start towards qualification. Barry, in fact, claimed there had been only one night during all his years at the club to compare with it – and he had been a ball-boy at the time! In March 1998, six weeks before Barry made his first-team debut, Villa had beaten Atletico 2-1 in pulsating quarter-final, only to go out on the away goals rule.

"That was special," said the midfielder. "Our coach Tony McAndrew used to get the younger players to act as ball-boys in those games, so it

Back in front – Gareth Barry has just restored the lead against the Dutch giants

was a good way to sample the atmosphere; it was amazing. Another one which stands out was when Darius Vassell scored those two late goals against Stromsgodset. There was a fair bit of noise at the end of that one because the crowd were so relieved we had won after being two-down. But that was nothing compared to the Ajax win. The cheer at the end of the game was one of the loudest I've heard, which showed how much it meant to the fans." Laursen was equally ecstatic, declaring: "Sometimes it's possible to achieve perfection in football and for me it happened that night. It was a great honour to be captain of Villa for such a big occasion. To score the opening goal in a famous victory was just incredible. I got a good idea of how Kent Nielsen must have felt when he scored at the same end against Inter Milan."

Like his fellow Dane, Laursen was on target at the Holte End, and although his goal bore no resemblance to Nielsen's stunning volley, the crowd reaction was every bit as rapturous. There had been an electric atmosphere all around Villa Park from the outset and the place simply erupted when the blond defender climbed in front of goalkeeper Kenneth Vermeer to meet Ashley Young's left-wing corner with a firm downward header. The home side were rocked by a 22nd-minute

---

Group F, match1
ASTON VILLA 2 AJAX 1
23rd October 2008, Villa Park, Att: 36,657
1-0 LAURSEN (8) 1-1 VERMAELEN (22) 2-1 BARRY (45)

ASTON VILLA
Bradley Howard FRIEDEL, Luke Paul YOUNG, Martin LAURSEN (c), Gareth BARRY, Ashley YOUNG, James MILNER, Gabriel AGBONLAHOR (Curtis DAVIES 90), Stiliyan PETROV, Nigel REO-COKER (Craig GARDNER 81), Nicky SHOREY, Carlos Javier CUELLAR JIMENEZ.
AJAX
Kenneth VERMEER, Bruno SILVA BARONE, Oleguer PRESAS RENOM (Gregory VAN DER WIEL 78), Thomas VERMAELEN, Jan VERTONGHEN, Rasmus LINDGREN, Urby Vitorrio Diego EMANUELSON, Dirk Klaas Jan HUNTELAAR (c), Luis Alberto SUAREZ DIAZ (Leandro Vitor SANTIAGO 60), Gabriel GARCIA DE LA TORRE, Jeffrey Nana Darko SARPONG (Dario CVITANICH 55)

Another view of the glee surrounding Laursen's goal, this time with Milner and Barry close at hand.

Thomas Vermaelen equaliser, although the lead was restored just before the interval when Barry stroked a left-foot shot into the bottom corner after Young's cross had been partially cleared. Both sides had chances in the second half but there was no question about Villa's entitlement to victory. "Both goals came at important times," said Barry. "Martin's header let them know we meant business after they had had a lot of early possession and the second goal would have killed them because it came just before half-time. I knew the keeper wasn't expecting the ball to fall to me, so I just got my head down and concentrated on putting it in the other side of the goal."

Great start – Just seven minutes have elapsed and Villa's campaign is off to a flier with a John Carew goal against Odense

That memorable night heralded Villa's return to big-time European football, although they had already been forced to negotiate three hurdles to reach the group stage, starting in July with a trip to Denmark for the first leg of a third-round Intertoto Cup tie against Odense. Laursen almost enjoyed a fairy-tale ending that afternoon in the birthplace of Hans Christian Andersen. Appointed skipper for the game against his countrymen, the central defender rose to meet Young's free-kick two minutes from the end, and his header looked certain to clinch a 2-1 win until

Third round, 1st leg
ODENSE 2 ASTON VILLA 2
19th July 2008, Odense Stadion, Att: 11,393
0-1 CAREW (7) 1-1 SIDWELL og (25) 1-2
LAURSEN (76) 2-2 CHRISTENSEN (90)

ODENSE
Arkadiusz ONYSZKO, Atle Roar HALAND, Hans Henrik ANDREASEN, Anders Moller CHRISTENSEN, Thomas HELVEG, Henrik Hallenberg HANSEN, Baye Djiby FALL, Bjorn RUNSTROM (Christian BOLANOS 79), Johan ABSALONSEN, Esben Mathias HANSEN (Eric Daniel DJEMBA DJEMBA 28), Chris SORENSEN (c).
ASTON VILLA
Stuart TAYLOR, Wilfred BOUMA, Steven SIDWELL (Wayne ROUTLEDGE 82), Martin LAURSEN (c), Ashley YOUNG, John Alieu CAREW, Gabriel AGBONLAHOR, Zatyiah KNIGHT, Stiliyan PETROV, Nigel REO-COKER, Craig GARDNER.

Fairy-tale time – Laursen is tangled in the net after scoring Villa's second goal in his home country

Anders Christensen popped up with a last-gasp equaliser. Still, a 2-2 draw on foreign soil was a satisfactory start to the campaign, John Carew's powerful seventh-minute drive having been cancelled out by an own goal by new signing Steve Sidwell mid-way through the opening period.

Seven days later, on the final Saturday of July, more than 31,000 turned up at Villa Park for the return clash, which was very much a bitter-sweet occasion. Young's stunning 20-yard volley early in the second half was enough to ensure Villa's progress but the afternoon was marred by a dreadful injury

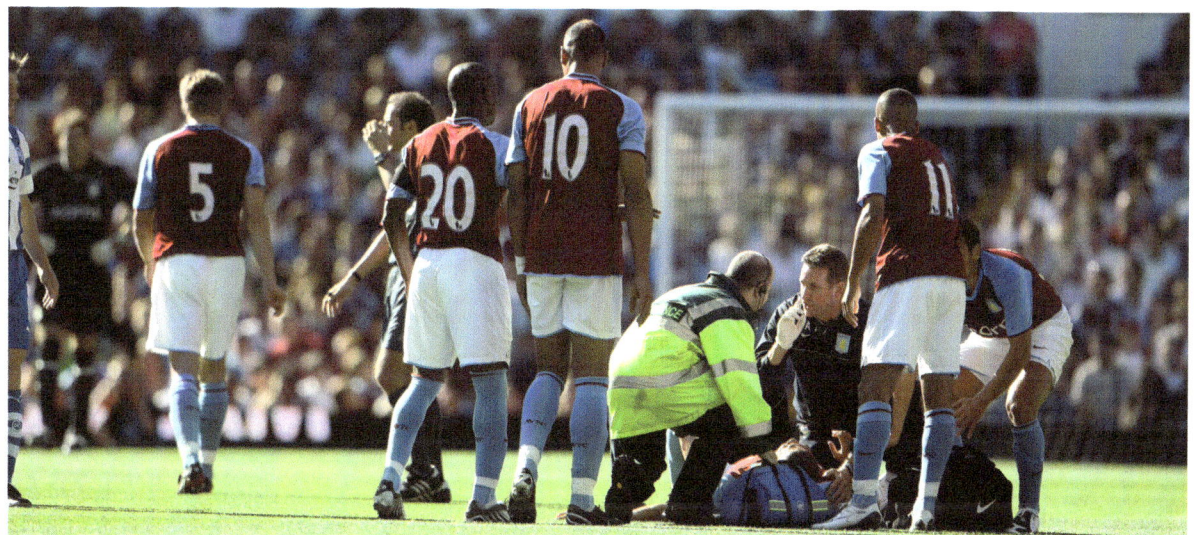

Sickening moment – Villa's players look totally dejected as the seriousness of Wilfred Bouma's injury becomes apparent

Third round, 2nd leg
ASTON VILLA 1 ODENSE 0
26th July 2008, Villa Park, Att: 31,423
1-0 YOUNG (50)

ASTON VILLA
Stuart TAYLOR, Wilfred BOUMA
(Gareth BARRY 15), Steven SIDWELL,
Martin LAURSEN, Ashley YOUNG, John
CAREW, Gabriel AGBONLAHOR, Zatyiah
KNIGHT, Stiliyan PETROV, Nigel REO-
COKER (c), Craig GARDNER.
ODENSE
Arkadiusz ONYSZKO, Atle Roar HALAND,
Hans Henrik ANDREASEN (Christian
BOLANOS 74), Thomas HELVEG (Espen
RUUD HT), Henrik Hallenberg HANSEN,
Baye Djiby FALL, Bjorn RUNSTROM
(Anders Kvindebjerg JACOBSEN 81),
Johan ABSALONSEN, Chris SORENSEN
(c), Jonas TROEST, Eric Daniel DJEMBA.

to full-back Wilfred Bouma, who suffered a dislocated ankle early in the game and was clearly in agony as he was carried off on a stretcher. At least the aggregate success ensured progress to the second qualifying round of the UEFA Cup, in which Villa's players found themselves retracing the steps of the Class of 1981-82 with a trip to the Icelandic capital, Reykjavik.

This time the opponents were FH Hafnarfjordur and, like Valur all those years earlier, they were no match for a team from English football's top flight. The tie, in fact, was as good as over by the 38th minute of the first leg at the Laugardalsvöllur Stadium. Villa made a flying start in the Land of Ice and Fire, Barry catching the home side cold in the fourth minute when he fired past keeper Gunnar Sigurdsson as FH struggled to clear a Young cross. And three minutes later the visitors were firmly in control, Young cutting inside from the left to score with an angled drive. Gabby Agbonlahor, who had netted a hat-trick against Manchester City in the opening Premier League match of the season, added number three when he beat two defenders before slotting the ball past Sigurdsson, and there were other chances before Matthias Gudmundsson raised Icelandic hopes by reducing the deficit just before the interval. But Laursen's perfect header from Young's 64th-minute cross ensured Villa brought home a comfortable lead plus four away goals, making the second leg a formality.

Young gun – with just seven minutes played, Ashley Young is congratulated by Marlon Harewood after doubling the lead

Second qualifying round, 1st leg
FH 1 ASTON VILLA 4
14th August 2008, Lugardalsvollur, Att: 8,686
0-1 BARRY (4) 0-2 YOUNG (7) 0-3 AGBONLAHOR (38) 1-3
GUDMUNDSSON (45) 1-4 LAURSEN (64)

FH
Gunnar SIGURDSSON, Hoskuldur EIRIKSSON (Gudmundur
SAEVARSSON 75), Dennis Michael SIIM, Tommy
Fredsgaard NIELSEN, David Thor VIDARSSON (c) (Asgeir
Gunnar ASGEIRSSON 63), Tryggvi GUDMUNDSSON,
Matthias VILHJAMSSON, Atli GUDNASON (Jonas Grani
GARDASSON 75), Matthias GUDMUNDSSON, Bjorn Daniel
SVERRISSON, Hjortur Logi VALGARDSSON.
ASTON VILLA
Bradley Howard FRIEDEL, Martin LAURSEN (c), Gareth
BARRY, Ashley YOUNG (Wayne ROUTLEDGE 71), Marlon
HAREWOOD, Gabriel AGBONLAHOR (Nathan
DELFOUNESO 76), Curtis DAVIES, Stiliyan PETROV
(Moustapha SALFOU 66), Nigel REO-COKER, Nicky
SHOREY, Craig GARDNER.

Perhaps it was too much of a formality, because the game at Villa Park petered out into a tame 1-1 draw. Home supporters might just have expected another goal feast when Craig Gardner's rising left-foot effort opened the scoring shortly before the half hour but within two minutes FH were level through Atli Bjornsson and that's how it stayed through the second half. At least it was an evening to savour for the tiny 30-strong band of Icelandic supporters who had accompanied their team to Birmingham. And the fact that several of Hafnarfjordur's part-time players were seen taking

Cool finish – Gabby Agbonlalor's left-foot shot makes it 3-0 before the interval

photographs after the game suggested that their ambition had never seriously extended to the possibility of winning a place in the next round.

Instead, it was O'Neill's men who made the flight to Bulgaria for the first leg of a first-round tie

Craig's cracker – Midfielder Craig Gardner sets himself before unleashing the rising shot which put Villa ahead in the home leg against FH

Second qualifying round, 2nd leg
ASTON VILLA 1 FH 1
28th August 2008, Villa Park, Att: 25,415
1-0 GARDNER (27) 1-1 BJORNSSON (30)

ASTON VILLA
Bradley Howard FRIEDEL, Gareth BARRY, Marlon HAREWOOD, Gabriel AGBONLAHOR (Nathan DELFOUNESO 62), Curtis DAVIES, Zatiyah KNIGHT, Moustapha SALIFOU, Wayne ROUTLEDGE, Nigel REO-COKER (c), Craig GARDNER, Isaiah OSBOURNE.
FH
Gunnar SIGURDSSON, Dennis Michael SIIM, Tommy Fredsgaard NIELSEN, Asgeir Gunnar ASGEIRSSON, David Thor VIDARSSON (c), Tryggvi GUDMUNDSSON (Gudmundur SAEVARSSON 83), Matthias VILHJAMSSON, Matthias GUDMUNDSSON, Atli Vidar BJORNSSON (Atli GUDNASON 58), Bjorn Daniel SVERRISSON (Jonas Grani GARDARSSON 85), Hjortur Logi VALGARDSSON.

against Litex Lovech. It was a journey into the unknown for Villa, who had never previously faced Bulgarian opposition, although the situation was helped considerably by the fact that midfielder Stiliyan Petrov was able to act as unofficial tour guide and interpreter on his return to his home country. The official party were greeted by an electrical storm on their arrival in Eastern Europe, with conditions so bad that they were unable to have the stadium training session which is afforded to all visiting teams in European competition. Instead, they used one of Litex's training pitches and thankfully, there was no adverse effect when they got

First round, 1st leg
LITEX LOVECH 1 ASTON VILLA 3
18th September 2008, City Stadium, Att: 5,500
1-0 POPOV (10) 1-1 REO-COKER (45) 1-2 BARRY (72 pen)
1-3 PETROV (90)

LITEX LOVECH
Uros GOLUBOVIC, Cedric CAMBON, Mihail Angelov VANKOV, Wellington Brito DA SILVA (Emil Rosenov ANGELOV 85), Alessandro CORREA, Stanislav MANOLEV, Wilfried NIFLORE (Jeremy ACEDO 74), Plamen NIKOLOV, Carlos Eduardo DE SOUZA TOME (Alexandre BARTHE 62), Ivelin Ivanov POPOV (c), Dzemal BERBEROVIC.
ASTON VILLA
Bradley Howard FRIEDEL, Luke Paul YOUNG, Martin LAURSEN (c), Gareth BARRY (Moustapha SALFOU 78), James MILNER, Gabriel AGBONLAHOR, Stiliyan PETROV, Nigel REO-COKER (Wayne ROUTLEDGE 74), Nicky SHOREY, Carlos Javier CUELLAR JIMENEZ, Craig GARDNER (Marlon HAREWOOD 68).

down to business at the Gradski Stadium, despite a playing surface which cut up badly following the previous day's downpour and left the normally precise Barry visibly frustrated after one of his passes fell well short of its intended target. There was also a more serious setback to deal with when Nigel Reo-Coker was harshly adjudged to have brought down Brazilian Sandrinho in the 10th minute, allowing Ivelin Popov to put Litex ahead with a curling free-kick.

But a dramatic turn of events in first-half stoppage time proved to be the turning point. One minute the visitors were breathing a sigh of relief as Wilfried Niflore hit the side netting when he might easily have given Litex a 2-0 interval lead, the next they were back on level terms. Barry's probing pass had the home defence in a state of total confusion as keeper Uros Golubovic miskicked on the edge of the penalty area and the ball rebounded off Cedric Cambon's heel to leave Reo-Coker with a simple tap-in that more than made amends for his earlier

Leaning back in Lovech – but Nigel Reo-Coker puts Villa level against Litex just before half-time

Spot on – Gareth Barry is a picture of concentration as he steps up (above) to put Villa head in Bulgaria with a well-taken penalty. Right: High-fives – but Stiliyan Petrov keeps a low profile in his homeland as he is congratulated by Marlon Harewood after scoring the third goal

misfortune. After that Villa were comfortable against a side reduced to nine men by the dismissal of Campon for two yellow cards and Mihail Yankov for handling on the line. Barry calmly converted the penalty, and 2-1 became 3-1 right at the end when Petrov – once on the receiving end of an 8-0 drubbing with CSKA Sofia at this venue – tapped home from close range after his initial shot had been parried by the keeper.

Just as they had in the qualifying round, Villa approached the second leg needing to do little more than go through the motions and once again the home game turned out to be something of an anti-climax. Marlon Harewood's clinical 27th-minute finish, when the striker turned away from his marker to drill a superb angled shot beyond keeper Todor Todorov's reach, effectively clinched Villa's passage. Niflore partially made up for his miss in Bulgaria by equalising with a penalty seven minutes after the break and that was that; 1-1 on the night, 4-2 on aggregate.

First round, 2nd leg
ASTON VILLA 1 LITEX LOVECH 1
2nd October 2008, Villa Park, Att: 27,230
1-0 HAREWOOD 1-1 NIFLORE (53 pen)

ASTON VILLA
Bradley HOWARD FRIEDEL, Luke Paul
YOUNG, Ashley YOUNG (Isaiah OSBOURNE
85), James MILNER, Marlon HAREWOOD,
Zatyiah KNIGHT, Moustapha SALIFOU,
Wayne ROUTLEDGE, Stiliyan PETROV (c),
Nicky SHOREY, Carlos Javier CUELLAR
JIMENEZ.
LITEX LOVECH
Todor Tankov TODOROV, Alexandre
BARTHE, Wellington Brito DA SILVA (Emil
Rosenov ANGELOV 78), Alessandro
CORREA, Stanislav MANOLEV, Wilfried
NIFLORE, Plamen NIKOLOV, Petar Dimitrov
ZANEV, Carlos DE SOUZA TOME (Momchil
TSVETANOV HT), Ivelin Ivanov POPOV (c)
(Eduardo Roberto DOS SANTOS 85),
Dzemail BERBEROVIC.

Hard-hitter – Villa scorer Marlon Harewood blasts a shot towards the Litex goal in the second leg at Villa Park

And so to pastures new in the form of the UEFA Cup group stages, which kicked off with that unforgettable victory over Ajax and continued with an equally impressive 1-0 win away to Slavia Prague in the second game. That result was arguably even more impressive, in fact, given that Slavia had

Group F, match 2
SLAVIA PRAGUE 0 ASTON VILLA 1
6th November 2008, Stadion Eden, Att:
20,322
0-1 CAREW (26)

SLAVIA PRAGUE
Martin VANIAK, Mickael TAVARES, Erich
BRABEC (c), David HUBACEK (Zdenek
SENKERIK 66), Marek JAROLIM, Vladimir
SMICER (Dusan SVENTO 41), Marek
SUCHY, Matej KRAJCIK, Ladislav
VOLESAK (Tijani BELAID HT), Tomas
NECID, Jaroslav CERNY.
ASTON VILLA
Bradley GUZAN, Steven SIDWELL, Ashley
YOUNG, John Alieu CAREW (Nathan
DELFOUNESO 90), Gabriel AGBONLAHOR
(Gareth BARRY 89), Curtis DAVIES (c),
Zatyiah KNIGHT, Moustapha SALIFOU,
Nicky SHOREY, Carlos Javier CUELLAR
JIMENEZ, Craig GARDNER.

Sidwell sizzler – Steve Sidwell celebrates with Zat Knight after the only goal against Slavia Prague. Facing page bottom: On parade in Prague are (back row): Ashley Young, John Carew, Gabby Agbonlahor, Carlos Cuellar, Zat Knight, Brad Guzan. Front: Craig Gardner, Nicky Shorey, Steve Sidwell, Curtis Davies, Moustapha Salifou

previously been unbeaten at their new Eden Arena since its opening in May that year – and that Villa had played a Barclays Premier League match at Newcastle just three nights before the game in the Czech capital. In view of the short recovery time, O'Neill made seven changes for the Slavia match but such was the depth of Villa's squad that it was barely noticeable. Curtis Davies, appointed captain for the night, was rock solid alongside Zat Knight, while Sidwell, Gardner, Moustapha Salifou and Carlos Cuellar all slotted in seamlessly. And Brad Guzan, making only his second appearance since his summer move across the Atlantic from Chivas USA, was simply unbeatable between the posts. The keeper, whose only previous game had been a 1-0 League Cup defeat against Queens Park Rangers, made a series of incredible saves to underline just how reliable a deputy he was to fellow American Brad Friedel.

While all the replacements performed admirably, though, the winner was scored by one of Villa's regulars, even if he probably knew very little about it. In the 25th minute, Sidwell let fly with a powerful long-range drive, and Carew deflected the ball past Martin Vaniak for his second goal in three European appearances.

That left Villa top of Group F with two wins and needing just one point from their remaining two fixtures to qualify for the knockout stages, although it was as well they had made such a good start. By way of a gentle reminder that nothing can be taken for granted in European football, MSK Zilina, supposedly much weaker opponents, came to Villa Park and won 2-1, while Villa also lost their final

Nice one, Nathan! Despite a 2-1 home defeat by MSK Zilina, teenager Nathan Delfouneso had the thrill of scoring on his full debut

Group F, match 3
ASTON VILLA 1 MSK ZILINA 2
4th December 2008, Villa Park, Att: 28,797
0-1 LEITNER (16) 0-2 STYVAR (19) 1-2 DELFOUNESO (28)

ASTON VILLA
Bradley GUZAN, Luke Paul YOUNG, Ashley YOUNG, Marlon HAREWOOD, Nathan DELFOUNESO (Gabriel AGBONLAHOR 76), Zatyiah KNIGHT, Moustapha SALIFOU (Gareth BARRY 68), Nigel REO-COKER (c), Carlos Javier CUELLAR JIMENEZ, Craig GARDNER, Isaiah OSBOURNE (James MILNER 65).
MSK ZILINA
Dusan PERNIS, Mario PECALKA, Benjamin VOMACKA, Zdenko STRBA (c), Vladimir LEITNER, Evandro DA SILVA ADAUTO (Admir VLADAVIC 60), Peter PEKARIK, Robert JEZ (Lucas TESAK 90), Peter STYVAR (Emil RILKE 86), Jozef PIACEK, Ondrej SOUREK.

game, going down 3-1 in Hamburg. The Zilina game at least had its compensations in the form of a magnificent goal from 17-year-old Nathan Delfouneso on his full debut and the post-match news of Hamburg's victory over Slavia that night meant Villa had qualified for the last 32 despite slipping to defeat at the hands of the Slovakians. Delfouneso's special moment arrived after MSK had plundered a shock two-goal lead, the teenager scoring with a superb left-foot volley from the edge of the penalty area after Harewood had chested down Reo-Coker's searching high ball.

Delfouneso's liking for UEFA Cup football continued in Hamburg, where his close-range effort seven minutes from the end provided a small consolation in a comprehensive defeat, although the German trip a week before Christmas is better remembered for the eve the game than for the match itself. Reporters accompanying the team had learnt that Nigel Kennedy, famous for his virtuoso violin playing and support of Aston Villa, was in Hamburg and had arranged an impromptu jazz gig at the city's Stage Club. As the scribes prepared to venture from the warmth of their hotel into the chill night air, O'Neill announced he would like to join them. They arrived just as Kennedy was finishing his first set, and O'Neill later ended up on stage in front of 250 jazz lovers before going backstage to congratulate the maestro on his performance. Kennedy informed his audience that Villa would deliver a similar "masterclass" the following night but he was out of tune with his prediction.

Unfortunately, it was O'Neill who was out of tune – with Villa supporters – when the round of 32 rolled around the following February. The team's outstanding league form – including a club record seven consecutive away wins – had continued through the winter months, and as they prepared for the tie against CSKA Moscow, Villa occupied a top-four position. Even so, the manager's popularity among the claret-and-blue faithful nosedived when he effectively sacrificed the chance of UEFA Cup glory to concentrate on securing a place in the bigger and more lucrative Champions League the following season. The tie against the Russians was on a knife-edge following a 1-1 draw in the first leg at Villa Park, when a vibrant, noisy, flag-waving crowd chanted "Istanbul" – the venue for the 2009 final. Despite falling behind to a 14th-minute goal from Brazilian striker Vagner Love, the home side drew level in the 69th-minute when Carew met Gardner's cut-back with a powerful low shot which had Holte Enders in raptures. It meant Villa were the first team to avoid defeat by CSKA in that

> **Group F, match 4**
> **HAMBURGER SV 3 ASTON VILLA 1**
> **17th December 2008, Hamburg Arena, Att: 49,121**
> **1-0 PETRIC (18) 2-0 OLIC (30) 3-0 OLIC (57) 3-1 DELFOUNESO (83)**
>
> **HAMBURGER SV**
> **Frank ROST, Bastian REINHARDT, Joris MATHIJSEN, Marcell JANSEN, Mladen PETRIC (Thiago NEVES 78), Ivica OLIC (Jose Paolo GUERRERO GONZALES 67), David JAROLIM (c), Piotr Artur TROCHOWSKI (Anis BEN-HATIRA 89), Jerome BOATENG, Collin BENJAMIN, Dennis AOGO.**
> **ASTON VILLA**
> **Bradley GUZAN, Luke Paul YOUNG, Steven SIDWELL, Marlon HAREWOOD, Nathan DELFOUNESO, Zatyiah KNIGHT, Moustapha SALIFOU, Nigel REO-COKER (c), Nicky SHOREY, Carlos Javier CUELLAR JIMENEZ, Craig GARDNER (Barry BANNAN 61)**

> **Round of 32, 1st leg**
> **ASTON VILLA 1 CSKA MOSKVA 1**
> **18th February 2009, Villa Park, Att: 38,038**
> **0-1 SILVA DE SOUZA (14) 1-1 CAREW (69)**
>
> **ASTON VILLA**
> **Bradley GUZAN, Luke Paul YOUNG, Gareth BARRY (c), Ashley YOUNG, John CAREW, Gabriel AGBONLAHOR, Curtis DAVIES, Zatyiah KNIGHT, Stiliyan PETROV, Nicky SHOREY, Craig GARDNER.**
> **CSKA MOSKVA**
> **Igor AKINFEEV (c), Sergey IGNASHEVICH, Alexey BEREZUTSKIY, Vagner SILVA DE SOUZA, Milos KRASIC, Yury ZHIRKOV (Caner ERKIN 90), Evgeny ALDONIN (Pavel MAMAEV 90), Vasiliy BEREZUTSKIY, Elvir RAHIMIC, Georgy SHCHENNIKOV, Alan DZAGOEV (Daniel DA SILVA CARVALHO 80).**

All-square – John Carew drives home Villa's equaliser against CSKA following Craig Gardner's cut-back

season's competition and Villa really should have won.

There was certainly no reason to write off their chances in the Russian capital eight nights later, but that was essentially what the manager did by handing full debuts to youngsters Marc Albrighton and Barry Bannan, and playing Delfouneso as a lone striker. The outcome, sadly, was inevitable. Although Villa's weakened team battled bravely and doggedly on a bitterly cold night, any hope of a famous victory at the imposing Luzhniki Stadium was frozen out by second-half goals from Yuri Zhirkov and the predatory Love, who netted CSKA's second in stoppage time. Villa had lost football's Cold War, which the fans might have accepted had the team gone on to clinch a Champions League spot. Instead, O'Neill's men won just two of their remaining dozen Premier League games, slipped to a finishing position of sixth, and were consigned to a qualifying tie in the new Europa League.

> **Round of 32, 2nd leg**
> **CSKA MOSKVA 2 ASTON VILLA 0**
> 26th February 2009, Luzhniki, Att: 25,650
> 1-0 ZHIRKOV (61) 2-0 SILVA DE SOUZA (90)
>
> **CSKA MOSKVA**
> Igor AKINFEEV (c), Deividas SEMBERAS, Sergey IGNASHEVICH, Alexey BEREZUTSKIY, Vagner SILVA DE SOUZA, Milos KRASIC, Yury ZHIRKOV, Vasiliy BEREZUTSKIY, Elvir RAHIMIC, Georgy SHCHENNIKOV, Alan DZAGOEV.
> **ASTON VILLA**
> Bradley GUZAN, Luke Paul YOUNG (c), Steven SIDWELL, Nathan DELFOUNESO, Curtis DAVIES (Isaiah OSBOURNE 84), Zatyiah KNIGHT, Moustapha SALIFOU (Marlon HAREWOOD HT), Nicky SHOREY, Craig GARDNER, Marc ALBRIGHTON, Barry BANNAN.

ICELANDIC HONEYMOON

Some supporters organise their holidays around Villa trips abroad, particularly when it comes to pre-season tours in attractive parts of the world. But Jon Gibbs and Camille Ginnelly could hardly believe their luck when their honeymoon coincided with the first leg UEFA Cup tie against Hafnarfjordur. The Villa-mad couple had already booked their romantic escape for Iceland when the draw was made, and were delighted that they would be able to attend the match in Reykjavik. They are pictured right in the stadium before the game.

"Once we knew Villa were playing there, we were on a mission to get tickets," said Jon. "I was apparently on Channel 5 before the game as one of the Villa fans asked to try to pronounce the Icelandic team's name – and after it we met Gareth Barry. All round, it was a honeymoon we will never forget, and Villa's win made it extra special."

A TOPICAL ISSUE

Here's a cracking pub quiz question: Which Villa programme contained an action photo from the game for which it was published? Sounds impossible, doesn't it? But it happened when the club faced Ajax in the group stages of the UEFA Cup. A souvenir programme was produced, featuring a stiff fold-out cover, and despite the £5 asking price, it completely sold out. Such was the demand that the club ordered a re-print but felt it only fair to distinguish between the two.

The original version had included a photo of Marlon Harewood scoring against Bulgarians Litex Lovech in the previous round, but it was replaced in the new version by a picture of Martin Laursen's opening goal against Ajax.

A similar souvenir was produced for the following group game against MSK Zilina, while the programme moved to another level (see photo right) for the round of 32 home leg against CSKA Moscow. The cover of this one had a detachable hologram which switched from Laursen celebrating his Ajax goal to David Platt doing likewise against Inter Milan in 1990.

Rapid exits

Villa had never been paired with Austrian opposition in European competition until 2009, and then it happened twice in quick succession. More appropriately, you might say it happened twice in rapid succession. They were drawn against Rapid Vienna two years running in the same qualifying round of the new Europa League. Not that anyone down Witton way will remember the two ties with any great affection. On the first occasion, most Villa supporters were still too busy cursing the previous season's missed opportunity of a Champions League place to be overly concerned about their team attempting to qualify for the group stages of the secondary tournament; 12 months later the club was in a state of turmoil over the shock resignation of Martin O'Neill.

Five days before the opening Barclays Premier League game at home to West Ham, the manager who had guided Villa to two Wembley appearances a few months earlier decided that, after four seasons at the helm, the Villa hot seat was no longer for him. Reserve coach Kevin MacDonald, a man highly respected by the players, took over in a caretaker capacity and did a fine job. When former Liverpool boss Gerard Houllier was appointed in September, Villa's impressive start had carried them to third in the table. Unfortunately, they had also made a rapid exit from Europe for the second year running.

Twelve months earlier, though, a squad who proved good enough to reach both the League Cup final and FA Cup semi-finals were beaten by the men from Vienna on the away-goals rule, losing 1-0 in the Austrian capital before winning the second leg 2-1 at Villa Park. O'Neill's side were effectively undone before the two-leg tie was a minute old. Just 17 seconds had elapsed in Vienna when Croatian striker Nikica Jelavic met a cross from the left with a powerful downward header that left goalkeeper Brad Guzan helpless.

One thing which became patently obvious at the Gerhard Hanappi Stadium was that Rapid's supporters are among the loudest and most vociferous Villa have encountered. Apart from one small pocket of travelling fans, the near-deafening volume was maintained from before the first whistle until

> **Play-off, 1st leg**
> **RAPID WIEN 1 ASTON VILLA 0**
> 20th August 2009, Gerhard Hanappi Stadion, Att: 17,500
> 1-0 JELAVIC (1)
>
> **RAPID WIEN**
> Helge PAYER, Jurgen PATOCKA, Milan JOVANOVIC, Markus HEIKKINEN, Steffen HOFMANN (c), Markus KATZER, Nikica JELAVIC, Christopher DRAZAN (Branco BOSKOVIC 83), Andreas DOBER, Mario KONRAD (Christopher TRIMMEL 62), Yasin PEHLIVAN.
> **ASTON VILLA**
> Bradley GUZAN, Steven SIDWELL, Ashley YOUNG, James MILNER, Curtis DAVIES (Shane Thomas LOWRY 81), Emile William HESKEY, Nigel REO-COKER (c), Nicky SHOREY, Habib BEYE, Carlos Javier CUELLAR JIMENEZ, Craig GARDNER (Gabriel AGBONLAHOR 55).

He's gonna score one or two – and John Carew did, indeed, hit the target in the 2009 home leg against Rapid Vienna. But this time his effort came to nothing as visiting defenders blocked his path

after the last – and it was a similar story when the teams reconvened for the second leg. The Villa Park attendance was a very modest 22,563 but the noise generated by the voices of Vienna made it feel almost like a capacity crowd. They had plenty to cheer about, too. As home players sat dejectedly in the dressing room, their opponents raced back on to the pitch to celebrate with their loyal followers long after the rest of the stadium had emptied.

For Villa, there was no consolation to be taken from the fact that they had followed up a magnificent Premier League success at Liverpool a few days earlier with another win. Victory at Anfield had earned three points; this one had achieved nothing. The disappointment of Ashley Young's 31st-minute penalty being saved by keeper Helge Payer was forgotten seven minutes later when Young was released by a fine Fabian Delph pass before being brought down in the area. James Milner was handed the responsibility for Villa's second penalty, prompting both delight and relief as he planted his kick beyond Payer's reach and into the left-hand corner.

Villa were ahead on aggregate when John Carew moved on to a Milner pass and cut inside Ragnvald Soma before drilling a left-foot shot inside the near post – and the tie was almost settled when Young's angled drive was parried by Payer parried before Milner hit the rebound into the side netting. At that point, we were starting to make plans for more excursions to the Continent, but even at 2-0 on the night, there was always a nagging fear that the Austrians needed only to pounce once. The nightmare scenario

Play-off, 2nd leg
ASTON VILLA 2 RAPID WIEN 1
27th August 2009, Villa Park, Att: 22,563
1-0 MILNER (38 pen) 2-0 CAREW (53) 2-1 JELAVIC (76)

ASTON VILLA
Bradley GUZAN, Ashley YOUNG, James MILNER, John Alieu CAREW, Curtis DAVIES (Shane Thomas LOWRY 83), Fabian DELPH (Marc ALBRIGHTON 86), Emile William HESKEY (Gabriel AGBONLAHOR 82), Stiliyan PETROV (c), Nicky SHOREY, Habib BEYE, Carlos Javier CUELLAR JIMENEZ.
RAPID WIEN
Helge PAYER, Jurgen PATOCKA, Markus HEIKKINEN, Steffen HOFMANN (c), Markus KATZER, Nikica JELAVIC (Branko BOSKOVIC 87), Christopher DRAZAN, Ragnvald SOMA, Andreas DOBER, Christopher TRIMMEL (Stefan MAIERHOFER 56), Yasin PEHLIVAN

turned into chilling reality in the 76th minute. Guzan saved from substitute Stefan Maierhofer with his legs but Jelavic was perfectly positioned to nudge home the rebound.

Who could have imagined, as Villa reluctantly came to terms with their exit from the new competition, that they would be lining up the same opponents exactly 12 months later? If the opposition and the dates were pretty much the same, though, the circumstances were vastly different. O'Neill's sudden departure on the Monday before the opening Premier League fixture against West Ham had sent shock waves through Villa Park, although the club were fortunate enough to have MacDonald on hand to take over in a caretaker capacity. The quietly-spoken Scot, who had nurtured several of the players in Villa's reserve side, could hardly have wished for a better response as every member of the team produced a positive performance to record a richly-deserved 3-0 victory over the Hammers.

The confidence-boosting start was maintained in Vienna the following Thursday, when MacDonald relied heavily on youngsters who had lifted the reserve league championship under his guidance the previous season. Four of them – Barry Bannan, Eric Lichaj Marc Albrighton and Jonathan Hogg – were handed their chance to impress from the outset, with Lichaj and Hogg making their senior debuts. It was a baptism of fire for the young duo in such a cauldron of noise, and

A beauty from Barry – Young midielder Barry Bannan wheels away after converting Marc Albrighton's cross to put Villa ahead at the Gerhard Hanappi stadium in 2010

raucous home supporters did their utmost to intimidate them. But Villa were far from overawed and in the 11th minute Bannan scored his first goal for the club to momentarily silence the deafening roar. It was a move straight from the academy pitches of Bodymoor Heath, Albrighton weaving his way down the right before sending the ball across the six-yard box, where the Scottish midfielder converted before home defenders could react.

Rapid drew level on 33 minutes when Atdhe Nuhiu got the faintest of touches to skipper Steffen Hofmann's inswinging cross,

> **Play-off, 1st leg**
> **RAPID WIEN 1 ASTON VILLA 1**
> 19th August 2010, Gerhard Hanappi Stadion, Att: 17,500
> 0-1 BANNAN (12) 1-1 NUHIU (32)
>
> **RAPID WIEN**
> Raimund HEDL, Mario SONNLEITNER, Markus HEIKKINEN, Hamdi SALHI (Rene GARTLER 73), Steffen HOFMANN (c), Markus KATZER, Atdhe NUHIU, Veli KAVLAK, Ragnvald SOMA, Tanju KAYHAN, Thomas HINUM (Christopher DRAZAN 86).
> **ASTON VILLA**
> Bradley GUZAN, Stephen WARNOCK, Stewart DOWNING, Marc ALBRIGHTON (Andreas WEIMANN 80, Isaiah OSBOURNE 86), Curtis DAVIES, Emile William HESKEY, Nigel REO-COKER (c), Habib BEYE, Eric LICHAJ, Barry BANNAN (Nathan DELFOUNESO 75), Jonathan HOGG.

but Villa suffered a more painful blow in the closing stages after Andreas Weimann (another of MacDonald's title-winning reserve team) had gone on as a 79th-minute substitute for Albrighton. Weimann's return to his home city was far from a triumphant one; five minutes later he was carried off after taking a nasty whack on his ankle and to add insult to injury he was subjected to a barrage of abuse by Rapid fans even as he lay on the ground in agony.

It was a cruel reaction to a young player who had been a regular on the terraces of the Gerhard Hanappi Stadium as a boy before accepting the opportunity to join Villa's academy. "I was angry at the time because I had once been one of those fans," said Weimann. "I used to go to every game and bounce up and down with all the other supporters. But I don't think it was personal – they would have done the same to any opposing player. I'd made my debut as a sub against West Ham at the weekend and that was on the Thursday, so I went from sky high to rock bottom in

▶ MATCH REPORT

ACTION**REPLAY** ▶▶▶▶

Kevin MacDonald found the perfect blend of youth and experience as Villa brought a draw and an all-important away goal back from Vienna.

One of the most thrilling aspects of the Villa caretaker manager's debut win over West Ham a few days earlier was the

A new-look back four, comprising Lichaj, Habib Beye, Davies and Stephen Warnock were collectively solid, while goalkeeper Brad Guzan made several terrific saves.

Moments before Bannan's goal, the American did well to thwart Atdhe Nuhiu from close range, while after the break he

How Villa's programme for the return against Rapid captured the joy on Barry Bannan's face as he opened the scoring in Vienna

High Heskey – Emile Heskey moves in for the rebound after Stiliyan Petrov's penalty was saved by Rapid keeper Raimund Held but his miscued shot goes over the bar. Heskey later put Villa 2-1 ahead but the night ended in disappointment. Right: Cool Curtis – Villa defender Curtis Davies holds off a challenge in the second leg at Villa Park

the space of five days." The injury put Weimann's career on hold for several months, just as he was promising to make a breakthrough and he didn't regain full fitness until January, when he joined Watford on loan for the remainder of the season.

Villa's more immediate concern was the return leg against Rapid and they approached it in a better position than 12 months earlier. This time they kicked off at Villa Park on level terms, with an away goal up their sleeves. Indeed, qualification looked highly likely when a stylish 22nd-minute move

Play-off, 2nd leg
ASTON VILLA 2 RAPID WIEN 3
26th August 2010, Villa Park, Att: 29,980
1-0 AGBONLAHOR (22) 1-1 NUHIU (52) 2-1 HESKEY (77)
2-2 SONNLEITNER (78) 2-3 GARTLER (81)

ASTON VILLA
Bradley GUZAN, Ashley YOUNG, Stephen IRELAND, Gabriel AGBONLAHOR (Marc ALBRIGHTON 40), Curtis DAVIES, Emile William HESKEY, Stiliyan PETROV (c), Nigel REO-COKER (Nathan DELFOUNESO 82), Habib BEYE, Carlos Javier CUELLAR JIMENEZ, James Michael COLLINS.
RAPID WIEN
Raimund HEDL, Mario SONNLEITNER, Markus HEIKKINEN, Steffen HOFMANN (c) (Jurgen PATOCKA 90), Markus KATZER, Atdhe NUHIU, Veli KAVLAK, Christoph SAURER (Christopher TRIMMEL 73), Ragnvald SOMA, Andreas DOBER, Yasin PEHLIVAN (Rene GARTLER 78)

involving skipper Stiliyan Petrov and Ashley Young paved the way for Gabby Agbonlahor to fire home from close range. That was how it stood at the interval, but it all went horribly wrong in the second half. Rapid, who had previously posed little threat, plundered three second-half goals to win 3-2 on the night and 4-3 on aggregate.

It is difficult to figure out exactly how it happened. Even after the visitors had drawn level early in the second half and Petrov had suffered the frustration of seeing his penalty saved by Rapid keeper Raimund Held, the impetus was back in Villa's favour when Emile Heskey restored the lead in the 76th minute by cleverly using his chest to divert Habib Beye's shot into the net from close range. But Rapid responded with two goals in the space of as many minutes to leave their supporters enjoying another late-night party in the corner of the Doug Ellis stand. As for Villa fans, the next European adventure can't come quickly enough.

HANAPPI THE ARCHITECT

Rapid's atmospheric stadium was named after one of their most famous players – and Gerhard Hanappi once scored at Villa Park. Nearly half a century before the teams met in the new Europa League, the men from Vienna visited Villa Park for a friendly in October 1959, when goals from forwards Peter McParland and Jimmy MacEwan earned Joe Mercer's men a 2-1 success in which Hanappi replied for the Austrians.

He was described in the programme that night as "the marvellous little man who captains the team." Capped 93 times by Austria, Hanappi became an architect after the end of his football career and designed the Rapid stadium. It was renamed in his honour following his death in 1980 and the match-night programme on sale for the 2010 visit came complete with a name check to him on its front cover.

Villa also faced Rapid in a home friendly in January 1981, winning 4-0 with two goals from Peter Withe plus one each from Ken McNaught and Eamonn Deacy.

TICKETS FOR MOZART

Lifelong Villa supporter Anne Edwards assumed the role of roving reporter for Villa's visit to Vienna in 2010, providing an hour-by-hour "diary" of her trip to the Austrian capital. Anne, a Villa fan since January 1957, made the journey with her friend Tina Clay, and they were offered tickets in the city centre – but not for the game.

"A glass of wine in the city centre and a first look at the beautiful buildings," she wrote in the Villa News & Record. "No indication that there is a football match or even that they have heard of football. We stroll around being accosted by various young men dressed as Mozart, selling concert tickets. They obviously do not believe that two women are only there to see the Villa."

An extract from Anne Edwards' entertaining diary from her first-leg trip

Villa's key Euro numbers

9   Gary Shaw and Peter Withe are the club's highest scorers in European competition with nine goals each. Villa's other Euro marksmen are:

5 – John Deehan, Ken McNaught, Tony Morley, Ian Taylor, Stan Collymore.

4 – Darius Vassell, Gareth Barry, Juan Pablo Angel, John Carew.

3 – Brian Little, Martin Laursen.

2 – Andy Gray, Dennis Mortimer, Terry Donovan, Mark Walters, Gordon Cowans, Colin Gibson, David Platt, Derek Mountfield, Dalian Atkinson, Savo Milosevic, Dwight Yorke, Dion Dublin, David Ginola, Lee Hendrie, Ashley Young, Gabby Agnonlahor, Nathan Delfouneso.

1 – Ray Graydon, Brendan Ormsby, Ian Olney, Kent Nielsen, Andy Townsend, Dean Saunders, Ray Houghton, Ugo Ehiogu, Tommy Johnson, Gary Charles, Julian Joachim, Luc Nilis, Moustapha Hadji, Michael Boulding, Paul Merson, Marcus Allback, Steve Staunton, Craig Gardner, Nigel Reo-Coker, Stiliyan Petrov, Marlon Harewood, James Milner, Barry Bannan, Emile Heskey.

2   Villa benefitted from just two own goals in a total of 89 European ties between 1975 and 2010. These were conceded by Athletic Bilbao goalkeeper Jose Angel Iribar in 1977 and Banik Ostrava's Ivo Stas in 1990. The Banik midfielder subsequently joined Villa but never played a competitive game for the club.

3   Three players have scored hat-tricks for Villa in European ties – Gary Shaw (v Dinamo Bucharest 1982), Peter Withe (v Vitoria Guimaraes, 1983) and Stan Collymore (v Stromsgodset, 1998).

4   Villa have converted four penalties in European ties, Gareth Barry netting two of them against Celta Vigo (2000) and Litex Lovech (2008). The others were scored by Stan Collymore (v Celta Vigo, 1998) and James Milner (v Rapid Vienna, 2009).

4-3   Only one of Villa's European ties has been decided by a shoot-out, Ron Atkinson's side beating Inter Milan 4-3 on penalties after the teams drew 1-1 on aggregate in a first-round tie September 1994. Conversions by Garry Parker, Steve Staunton, Andy Townsend and Phil King clinched a place in the second round. Two other ties were settled after extra-time, both in Villa's favour – the Super Cup triumph over Barcelona in 1983 and the first-round victory over Girondins de Bordeaux in 1997.

5   Five of Ken McNaught's 13 Villa goals were scored in European ties – all of them headers. The Scottish defender, on target twice against Gornik Zabrze in 1977, also scored against

Barcelona in the UEFA Cup (178), Dynamo Kiev in the European Cup (1982) and Barcelona again in the 1983 UEFA Super Cup.

Villa's biggest Euro wins were 5-0 against Valur of Iceland in the club's first European Cup-tie in September 1981 and Vitoria Guimaraes of Portugal in the UEFA Cup two years later.

7 Seven ties have been settled by the away goals rule, Villa winning two and losing five. They beat Dynamo Berlin in 1981 and Stade Rennais in 2001, but lost to Trabzonspor (1994), Helsingborgs (1996), Atletico Madrid (1998), Varteks (2001) and Rapid Vienna (2009).

8 Eight managers have overseen Villa in European ties – Ron Saunders, Tony Barton, Jozef Venglos, Ron Atkinson, Brian Little, John Gregory, Graham Taylor and Martin O'Neill. A ninth boss, Kevin MacDonald, was caretaker manager when Villa faced Rapid Vienna in the 2010 Europa League play-off.

9 Nine Villa players have been sent off during European ties:
John Gidman (1978 v Barcelona), Allan Evans (1983 v Barcelona), Mark Walters (1983 v Vitoria Guimaraes), Mark Delaney (2000 v Marila Pribram), Paul Merson (2000 v Marila Pribram), Alan Thompson (2001 v Celta Vigo), Ian Taylor (2001 v Celta Vigo), Jlloyd Samuel (2002 v Zurich), Steve Sidwell (2008 v Hamburger SV).

24 Apart from home games at Villa Park (and The Hawthorns), Villa have played European ties in 24 countries:
BELGIUM (Royal Antwerp 1975, Anderlecht 1982)
TURKEY (Fenerbahce 1977, Besiktas 1982, Trabzonspor 1994)
POLAND (Gornik Zabrze 1977)
SPAIN (Athletic Bilbao 1977, 1997, Barcelona 1978, 1983, Deportivo La Coruna 1993, Atletico Madrid 1998, Celta Vigo 1998, 2000)
ICELAND (Valur 1981, Hafnarfjordur 2008)
EAST GERMANY (Dynamo Berlin 1981)
UKRAINE (Dynamo Kiev 1982)
HOLLAND (Bayern Munich for the European Cup final in Rotterdam 1982)
ROMANIA (Dinamo Bucharest 1982, Steaua Bucharest 1997)
ITALY (Juventus 1983, Inter Milan 1990, 1994)
PORTUGAL (Vitoria Guimaraes 1983)
RUSSIA (Moscow Spartak 1983, CSKA Moscow 2009)
CZECHOSLOVAKIA (Banik Ostrava 1990)
SLOVAKIA (Slovan Bratislava 1993)
SWEDEN (Helsingborgs 1996)
FRANCE (Girondins de Bordeaux 1997, Stade Rennais 2001, Lille 2002)

NORWAY (Stromsgodset 1998)
CZECH REPUBLIC (Marila Pribram 2000, Slavia Prague 2008)
CROATIA (Slaven Belupo 2001, Varteks 2001)
SWITZERLAND (Basel 2001, Zurich 2002)
DENMARK (Odense 2008)
BULGARIA (Litex Lovech 2008)
GERMANY (Hamburg 2008)
AUSTRIA (Rapid Vienna 2009, 2010)

29 Gordon Cowans and Dennis Mortimer have made the most appearances for Villa in European competition with 29 each.

40 Villa have won 40 of their 89 European games, drawing 21 and losing 28.

50 The highest number shirt worn by a Villa player in any European competition. Young Middlesbrough-born midfielder Jonathan Hogg wore No 50 in the first leg of the Europa League play-off against Rapid Vienna in August 2010.

125 The number of Villa goals in European ties between 1975 and 2010.

167 The official "gate" for the first round European Cup home clash with Besiktas (pictured) in September 1982, which was played behind closed doors following crowd disturbances at the previous season's semi-final away to Anderlecht.

2750 Villa's players each received a bonus of £2,750 for winning the European Cup. Bayern Munich's players were reported to be on £10,000 a man to lift the trophy.

49619 The highest attendance for a European tie at Villa Park was 49,619 for the first leg of the UEFA Cup quarter-final against Barcelona in 1978.

UP THE VILLA!

Many thanks to everyone who has helped to fund this project by pre-ordering a copy of Euros & Villans. Your support is greatly appreciated.

Colin Abbott
Geoff Adams
Danial Adilypour
Rob Alcock
Mark Alford
Samantha Allan
Adrian Allen
James Allen
Roger Allen
John Ambler (In memory)
Mark James Andradade
Duncan Andrews
Stefano Armellini
Steven Ashman
Michele Astbury
Mick Atkinson
Nick Atkinson
Brian Atwick
Steve Ashford
Ryan Astley
Rhys Astley
Rob Aston
Michael Ault

Simon & James Back
Dean Baker
Ken, Russ & Greg Baldwin
Andrew Balmforth
Eric Banner
Simon Banner
Dan Bardell
David Bardell
Steve Barney
Ann-Marie Bass
Steve Bateman
Adam Bath
Francoise & Jean-Michel Baudet
Jake Bedford
Michael Bedford
Ian Beesley
Louis Edward Beesley
Arthur Bent
John Betts
Paul Betts
BezVilla

Lee Bickerton
Bob Biddulph
Derek Bignell
Graham Bird
David Birt
Norma Bishop
Gavin Blackwell
Ronnie Bowden
Nigel Boyle
Glenn William Boyman
Ron Boyman (In memory)
Matt Braddock
David Bradley
Neil Brailsford
Dan Brawn
Kathrin Brehm
Bobby Bridgeman
Dave Bridgewater
Pam Bridgewater
Paul Brown
Kate & Phil Brown (married at Villa Park, 24/8/18)
Dave Buet
Marg Buet
Paul Buet
Michael Bundgaard
Roger Bunn
Clive Burford
John Busst
Stephen Byrne
Dave Bytheway

Joe Caffrey
Nigel Call
Pauline Calvert
John Chadwick
John A Chamberlain
Bethany Chester
Peter George Clark
Dozz Coates
Phil Coldicott
Tom Cole
Harvey-Lee Collins
Efan Collins
Lee Collins
Nathan Collins

Andy Congrave

Gerry Coniff

Dan Conor

Gary Cooke

Phil Cookes

Robert Cooley

Aidan Cooper

Nathan Cooper

Neil Cooper

 Neil Copper

Richard Coward

Andy Cowdrill

Kelvin Cox

Aaron Crackett

Darren Crombie

Tracy Crombie

Hazel Curtis

Paul Darlington

Georgina Dawson

George Daley

Ian Day

Ray Day

Peter Day

Rhys Day

Chris Deakin

Simon Daykin

Chris, George & Harry Deakin

Ferdi Delies

Leigh & Jack Douglas

David Dovey

Ron Dovey

Noel Doyle

Shirley Dreelan

Philip Drew

Patrick Drummey

Gemma Duah

Stephen Duffy

Ian Duggan

Anne Edwards

Gareth Edwards

Paul Alan Edwards

Paul Edwards

Simon Edwards

Vaughan Ellis

Rob Emslie

Clive Evans

Stephen John Evans

David Everitt

George Everitt

Samuel Everitt

Brian Farrelly

Jon Farrelly

Paul Farrington

Jonathan Fear

Bob Fearn

Keith Feaver

Terri Fellows

Chris Fetters

Lucy Finney

Ian Flanner

John Flanner

Paul Flanner

Richard & Sue Ford

David & William Foster

John Foster

Kevin Fox

Allan Melvyn Freeman

Richard Freeth

Rita Freeth

Justin Garratt

John Gateley

Martin Gilson

Cornelius Glover

Roger Goldman

Mark Goodwin

Jordan Goodridge

Mike Goostry

Robert Gough

Steve Gough

Andrew Gould

Ian Graham

Philip Gray

Malcolm Greatrex

Brian Greenfield

Chris Grey

Troy Griffin

Carol Griffiths

Mark Gwilliam

Pearl Hadley

Richard Hales

William L Hales

Nick Harper

Luke J Harris

Paige Harris

Peter Harrold

Andrea Hartman

Andrea Harvey

Heather Harvey
Paul Harvey
W A Harvey
Susan Haskins
Paul Hassam
Ros Haswell
Philip Haywood
Rongtian He
Emily Heath
Richard Heath
David Heaton
Chris Hill
Keith Hill
William Hinks
David Hitchman
John Hitchman
Odd Erling Hoberg
David Hodges
Dek Hogan
John Holder
Joanne Hollis
Christian Holt
Frank Holt
Matthew Holt
Michael Holt
Noah Holt
Rebecca Holt
Mark Homer
Matt Hook
Nick Hook
John Hopkins
Archie Horton
Nigel Horton
Adel Hudson
Mark & Louis Hudson
Ste Hughes
Will Hughes
Darren Hunt
John Hussey
Rob Hussey
Bob Hutchison
Nicky Huxtable
Jason, Lisa & Emma Hynes
L M Hynes

Stuart Iles

Leon James
James Jeavons
Cyril Jones (In memory)
Neil & Daniel Jones

Paul Jones
Stephen Jones
Steve Jones
Ian Johnson
Rob Johnson
Steve Johnson
Edward Judd

Lucy Keeling
John Kelly
Andy Kelly
Evan Kelly
Mat Kendrick
Mark King
Jon & Pauline Knibb
Simon Knight
Steve Knott
Ken Knowles
Liam Nordbo Knudsen
Simon Kuker
Geoff Kyte
K.B. English Emporium

Pete Lansbury
Pete Lavender
Michael Leahy
James Lee
Kevan Lee
Mark Leonard
John Lewis
Peter Leydon
Debbie Liles
Emily Liles
Matt Lintern
Trevor Lintern
Darren W Lippett
Andrew Litchfield
Marie Lynch

Chloe Macrow
Nigel Macrow
Matt Maher
Rachel Malloch
Peeter Malmius
Jeffery Mann
William Marron
Lee Marsham
James Martin
Brod Mason
Nigel Masters
Paul Matthews

Sheila Maybury
Rob McCann
Brendan McCarthy
Noel McCarthy
Tom McCormack
Allan McCullagh
Andrew, Ivan & Arlo McDouall
Nina McDougall
John McElhoney
Mark McGuiness
Matjaz Mikuletic
Keith Miller
Keith Minshull
John Mitchell
Darren Monaghan
Gary Montgomery
Bob, Helen & Karen Moore
Connor Moore
Vivien Moorhouse
Sarah Moran
Jay Morgan
Mike Morley
Keith Morris
Tyler Morris
Gerry Mulholland
David Mulvey
John Murphy
Tim Murphy

Chris Nason
Alan Newton
Craig Newton
Dave Nixon
Jonathan Northall

Gwynn John O'Brien
John O'Brien
Martin O'Connell
Matthew O'Connell
Mark O'Grady
Gerry O'Halloran
Luke Organ
Mikkel Becker Ottesen
Tom Otrebski

Gianluca Pagliuca
Darren Palin
Michael Parker
Nigel Parsons
Martyn & Teresa Pass
Rik Patel

John Patterson
Frank Pattison
Kevin Pearce
Mark Pearce
John Penlington
Simon Penn
Tony "Badges" Penn
Steven Perks
Danny Perrett
Alan Perrins
James Perrins
Jim Perrins
John Perry
David Pettitt
Olivia Pettitt
Gregory Phillip
Greg Phillips
Ian Phillips
Richard Pilkington
Michael Plant
Tom Podmore
Chris Poole
Kieran Portman
Mark Poultney
John Villa Power
Daniel Kenneth Adam Price
Ivor & Gladys Price (In memory)
Dave Prince
Premier Entertainments

Ray Ralton
Simon Rawlins
Stuart Reilly
Ian Rennie
Steven Richards
James Riley
Jodie Roberts
Martin Roberts
Peter Rodgers
John Rollason
John Rooker
Peter J Ross
Christine Rossiter
Stephen Rudge
Christian Russ
Derek Russell
Diane Russell
Simon Russell
Lewis Rymond

Sandeep Singh Sagoo

Karen Salsbury
Mark Samuels
Barry & Mark Santy
Andrea Sbalchiero
Bob Scott
Brian C Seadon
Andy Seferta
Laura Sensier-Willdigg
Alexandra Sewell
Nigel Shaw
Dan Shepherd
Eddie Sheppard
George Shore
Maisie Shore
Olivia Shore
Reuben Shore
Tom Shore
Gregory Shutt
Craig Singleton
Chris Simkin
Alan Smith
Jeremy Smith
John Bryan Smith
Joshua Smith
Kevin Smith
Les Smith
Marcus Smith
Susan Smith
Liam Smyth
Stephen Smyth
George Sneddon-Coombes
Nigel Spink
Michael Stanford
Neil Stevens
Peter Stokes
Matthew Stride
Steven Stride
James Stuart
Sutton Coldfield Villans
Paul Sweetman

Mark Tamburro
Tony Tamburro
Andrew Taylor
Peter Tennant
James Terry
David Thomas
Paul Thomas
Nigel Thompson
Chris Thornicroft
Sue & Mick Tilt

John Timperley
Aiden & Kian Timperley
John Towey
Eliot Tremayne
Chris Trickett
Dene Trouth
Lynne Tucker
Trinity Turford
Dave Turner

Andy 'Turnstile' Ullah
Malcolm Upford
Gregory Upton

Thierry Vautrat

Lynn Wain
Andy Wainwright
Hayden Wakeling
Neil Walker
Simon Walsh
Scott Walters
Terry Walters
Louise Ward
John Ward
John Ward-gwilliam
Steve Watson
Carol Watts
Jack Watts (In memory)
Stephen Webster
Ryan Whiley
Alan White
Michael White
Andrew Whitehouse
Martyn Whybrow
Simon Wiggin
Robin Wilkes
Gareth Wilkinson
David Williams
Donna M Williams
Gary Williams
Paul Williams
Bill Willis (In memory)
Chris Numan Willis
Sarah Willis
Lynne Wilson
Keith Wiseman
Darren Woolley
Helen Woolridge
Stephen Wright